CROSS-BORDER CRIME
IN A CHANGING EUROPE

CROSS-BORDER CRIME IN A CHANGING EUROPE

PETRUS C. VAN DUYNE
VINZENCO RUGGIERO
MIROSLAV SCHEINOST
WIM VALKENBURG

Nova Science Publishers, Inc.

Huntington, New York

Senior Editors: Susan Boriotti and Donna Dennis
Coordinating Editor: Tatiana Shohov
Office Manager: Annette Hellinger
Graphics: Wanda Serrano and Dorothy Marczak
Book Production: Matthew Kozlowski, Jonathan Rose and Jennifer Vogt
Circulation: Cathy DeGregory and Ave Maria Gonzalez
Communications and Acquisition: Serge P. Shohov

Library of Congress Cataloging-in-Publication Data
Available Upon Request

ISBN 1-56072-966-X.

Copyright © 2001 by Nova Science Publishers, Inc.
227 Main Street, Suite 100
Huntington, New York 11743
Tele. 631-424-6682 Fax 631-425-5933
e-mail: Novascience@earthlink.net
Web Site: http://www.nexusworld.com/nova

Printed in the United States of America

CONTENTS

LIST OF CONTRIBUTORS

S. Adamoli
Senior Researcher at Transcrime, Trento University, Italy

C. Daams
Researcher at the Law Faculty of Basel University, Switzerland

P.C. van Duyne
Professor of Empirical Penal Science, Tilburg University, Netherlands

M. Joutsen
Head of the Heuni-Research Institute, Hensinki, Finland

M. Junninen
This report is based on the Master's thesis (sociology) of Mika Junninen: Ammattimaiset
    rikoksentekijät Virossa 1991-1998, University of Helsinki, Institute of Sociology

K. Krajewski
Adjunct Professor of Criminology at the Jagiellonian University of Cracow, Poland

M. Levi
Professor of Criminology at Cardiff University, Wales

A. di Nocila
Researcher at Transcrime, Research Group on Transnational Crime, University of Trento

I. Osyka
Researcher of the Department of Criminalistics of the University of Internal Affairs
    which is a part of the Ministry of Interior of Ukraine; Senior Lieutenant of Militia.

viii   Petrus C. Van Duyne, Vinzenco Ruggiero, Miroslav Scheinost, Wim Valkenburg

M. Scheinost
Deputy Director of the Institute of Criminology and Social Prevention in Prague

B. de Ruyver
Professor of Criminology and Researcher at the University of Gent, Belgium

N. Passas
Professor of Criminal Justice at Temple University, Philadelphia US

M. Pheijffer
Registered Accountant at the Dutch Fiscal Intelligence and Investigation Service and
    Lecturer at Leyden University

*B. Quirk*e
Senior Lecturer in Accounting & Finance in the Business School of Liverpool John
    Moores University

V. Ruggiero
Professor of Criminal Law

W. Valkenburg
Senior Lecturer Criminal Law at Tilburg University

Chapter 1

CROSS-BORDER CRIME: A RELATIVE CONCEPT AND BROAD PHENOMENON

Petrus C. van Duyne

Professor of Empirical Penal Science,
Tilburg University, Netherlands

INTRODUCTION

The present interest in the phenomenon of cross-border crime in Europe should not obscure the fact that it concerns a very relative geographic concept indeed. After all, it all depends on *national territories*. Before the unification of Germany and Italy under Bismarck and Cavour around 1870, there was a real cross-border crime problem in these countries, while before the fall of the Iron curtain, it was considered counter-revolutionary to speak of cross-border crime between for example Latvia and Russia. In the European Union 'as far as the Schengen Countries are concerned' one may wonder whether the concept of cross-border crime is not becoming a bit out of date: the free flow of goods, capital and people can always be prefixed with the adjective 'criminal', though law enforcement actions are still a matter of national sovereignty. One may even consider the cross-border criminal flow of goods, capital and people a normal correlate of the legitimate trade, while the cross-border law enforcement cooperation appears to be problematic.

Despite these reflections it cannot be denied that in the broader European space the phenomenon of cross-border crime has become a reality, particularly after the fall of the Iron curtain in 1989 and the abolishment of the inner border controls between most member states in the European Union a few years later. How does the European criminal landscape look like? Has it developed the grim menace as depicted by the threat assessment industry and hastily (sometimes even greedily) endorsed by many law enforcement agencies and policy makers? Particularly the association of cross-border crime with *organised crime* evoked all sorts of nightmares, like 'organised crime on the march', the 'Pact Mafiosi' of Claire Sterling (1995) or the 'Criminal Holding' of Roth and Frey (1993).[1] It is tempting to look back at the beginning of this millennium, using some of the evidence collected by the experts in this volume as well as elsewhere. Predictably we will again face the familiar problems of definition and empirical evidence. But nevertheless, let us survey some of the highlights.

CRIME TRADE AND CRIME-ENTREPRENEURS

Methodologically, but also pragmatically, one may doubt whether there is much point in rehearsing the debate on the definition or the essence of organised crime. All definitions that have been suggested thus far have failed on one important point: they cannot be operationalised. They remain *open* concepts, unable to delineate the borders of the phenomenon and therefore cannot be considered a definition in the analytical sense of the word at all (Van Duyne, 1996). If the concept has something to do with systematically earning illegal income by more than two persons, the definition should draw a borderline not only with *un*organised crime, but also with its 'white' or legitimate counterpart being the other side of the coin. However, there is some irony in the fact that those who think they can define organised crime have never bothered to define licit 'organised industry' or 'organised trade'. The correct objection that the concept of organised trade encompasses a too diverse range of activities and enterprises to be meaningful, is rarely applied to the supposed organised crime phenomenon which encompasses a similar diversity. Maybe we can cut a long discussion short by leaving the organised crime concept where it belongs, namely in the emotional arena of politics and the entertaining media, and return to what can be observed empirically: the human conduct of combinations of entrepreneurs earning money by systematic law breaking, frequently cooperating in networks of like minded, some of whom even happen to establish real organisations.[2] From this empirical perspective I doubt whether we need the additional construct of organised crime at all. If despite these critical comments these two words happen to pop up from time to time in this contribution, they are not intended as an empirical denotation, but as a rough shorthand to demarcate the discourse.

When we look at the crime developments in this decade we can observe an interesting pattern of criminal market behaviour of an unbridled buccaneer criminal capitalism. This has been very elegantly summarized by Matti Joutsen in his contribution to this volume. Looking at the available data, we are first of all struck by the quick rise of a broad smugglers' economy spread over the whole of the European continent and beyond. As a matter of fact, this development may be considered the natural economic

---

[1] The subtitle adds a somewhat more threatening overtone to the book:'The United Europe in the grip of the organised crime'.

[2] There is an abundant amount of literature on the definition of organised crime, (See Maltz, 1990), apparently more than research reports on the empirical manifestations of it. Unfortunately the usual social science standard of *concept validity* appears to play no role in the definition efforts, in which a curious mixture of criminal *acts*, the nature of the *persons* involved and some value judgement about the badness of all of it can be observed (See Fijnaut c.s., 1998).

and social outcome of new opportunities, given the big price differences for many (illegal) commodities between the economic regions in Europe, the looser customs controls between the previous Warsaw-block and Western Europe, the abolishment of border controls between the so-called Schengen states of the EU and also the need of many people in Central and Eastern Europe to make up their sometimes dramatic fall in income. Depending on the locations of demand and supply the eastern half of Europe had as much to fear from the western half as the other way round. For example, when in the beginning of this decennium it had become clear that western (stolen) cars were in high demand in the regions east of the Oder-Neisse, not only did thieves started to export their loot to the new commercial outlets, but also many 'decent' family men realised that selling their cars on the eastern black market and reporting it as being stolen, would yield a handsome fraudulent return. Joutsen mentions a later stabilisation of this trend and an increase in motor vehicle theft in most of the new states in the Baltic, Belarus and some of the successor states of Yugoslavia.

Meanwhile a reverse flow of contraband found its way to eager purchasers in Western Europe and the American hemisphere: the cultural heritage of the slavonic countries has been bled white, because of the unscrupulous export of objects of art, often consisting of stolen icons (Handelman, 1994). To this criminal export may be added the financial bloodletting caused by high level economic crime and the unrelenting export of flight capital from the CIS countries in the first place (see Osyka, this volume and Sinuraja, 1995), which presupposed at least some helpful interaction with or complaisance of western financial institutes. Criminals in the eastern regions and western criminals can be observed operating in close as well as uneasy co-ordination, which sometimes degenerates into a survival of the meanest.

> In two cases that I studied it proved difficult to disentangle the criminal victim and the criminal profiteer. In one fraud case concerning EU fraud with milk powder to be re-exported as transit good from Lithuania to a third country, the Dutch crime-entrepreneurs took the initiative. When one of the Dutch failed to pay his debt to the Lithuanians, they muscled into the Dutch crime network forcing them to play according to their rules in a multi million scam (Van Duyne, 1995). Another international Dutch financial swindler remained much more elusive. He is alleged to have provided services to Russian corrupt officials in getting a $ 13 million state investment in Siberia out of the country. However, it remains uncertain whether the Siberian officials succeeded in getting any return from this unsavoury character.

Instead of looking at the dichotomy of east versus west and sketch doomsday scenarios of the 'organised crime on its march', it may be more appropriate to look at the dynamics of the extended economic (criminal) space and to consider the criminal commodities and services to be handled as the core business of the crime-entrepreneurs. This core business is the basis of their organisations, not the other way round. Given the price differences, the various locations of supply and demand and sometimes technical requirements, most of the core business is bound to be multi-country from the outset, as has always been the case with the drug trade (McCoy, 19XX). It goes without saying that we are not dealing with a dehumanised criminal economy: the human element does not merely add some local colour as a kind of local by-product, but creates a behavioural mould of its own, sometimes furthering as well as hampering the potentials of the economic environment. For example, crime-enterprises developing in regions with a strong patriarchal extended family culture are more likely to develop hierarchical family organisations than crime-enterprises in countries in which the family (one third divorced) has shrunk to two parents and one or two children. Crime-enterprises are rarely innovative bodies; they are rather little more than (distorted) copies of their cultural surroundings.

SOME CROSS-BORDER CRIME-MARKETS

Any commodity subjected to price increasing regulations or prohibition can become attractive for entrepreneurial criminals as long there is demand. The ways entrepreneurs organise their crime-trade depends (among other factors) on whether the goods are prohibited or licit, but the way of handling the commodity or the management is criminal. The handling of prohibited goods must entirely take place in the underground economy. With licit commodities trading takes place in the upperworld, but the criminal profit arises in dodging the administrative requirements or deceiving one's trading partner. Both kinds of criminal activities should not be lumped together, given the different skills and social relations that are required to become a successful crime-entrepreneur. I will briefly sketch the contributions in these areas of cross-border crime-trade below.

Prohibited Goods

In the market of prohibited goods most attention is devoted to various sorts of drugs, which since the beginning of this century have been declared illegal or 'controlled substances' by various US dominated international bodies. Leaving aside that the criminalised drug problem is largely a US export product,[3] we face an insatiable demand for substances that influence our state of mind. Given the forbidden fruit effect of the prohibited substances it hardly requires much deep thought to find out that this is the market of adventurous entrepreneurs, whose 'adventure' consists of the risks of law enforcement, which is compensated by high profit margins. It is interesting to observe that owing to social pressure and/or 'quoting processes' the politically correct phrases to describe such criminal market developments appears to be the organised crime framework.

In his contribution to this volume Krajewski transcends this political correctness by lively sketching the development of the entrepreneurial Polish drug scene, ranging from amateur entrepreneurs to more sophisticated crime-entrepreneur exploiting the potential

---

[3] To this should be added that the drug trade itself is a western colonial heritage. For a good account of the history of the US-driven drug policy see Musto (1973), Himmelstein (1983), Wigotsky (1986) and McCoy (1991).

of the Polish indigenous production facilities of amphetamine as well as the weak spots in the border controls. When we compare the entrepreneurial crime scene of Poland with the countries west of the Oder-Neisse border, we may observe more similarities than differences. One of the differences concerns the Polish production facilities of amphetamine. Better-educated chemists, some supplementing their low licit salary with underground trade and the availability of precursors contributed to the manufacture of a high quality product that out-competed the traditional Dutch suppliers of the Scandinavian market. However, the higher level of productive professionalism does not necessarily entail an increase in organisational 'sophistication', if that means larger and more structured crime-enterprises. As a matter of fact the scarce findings released by the Polish police match the crime pattern thus far found in Western Europe: small crime-enterprises, consisting in its core of three to five members prevail. Of course, crime-enterprises are in need of more 'remote' (outer circle) executives and aids they can dispose of (and which are disposable). Together the enterprises form networks, but usually not tight knit organisations (Weschke, 1986; Van Duyne, 1993; Kleemans c.s., 1998). Why should they? Good crime organisers are risk averse (Dorn, c.s., 1998), while extending crime organisations is risk enhancing due to the increased danger of information leaks, inherent in involving more people (Van Duyne, 1998).

Together with other law enforcement reports of this decade the overview of Krajewski also sketches the changed criminal geography of the European continent, which rather reflects the adaptive capacity of crime-entrepreneurs and the geographic diversification of the supply than some sinister plot. The general increased commercial and personal mobility in the belt of the Central European states, the high prices and purchasing capacity in Western Europe, the increased supply of virtually all kinds of drugs (many originating from the central Asian republics) and the hazards of the traditional Balkan Route contributed to a shift to the Black Sea countries, the Czech and Slovakian Republics and Poland. Police reports mention the wholesale delivery to depots and the subsequent repackaging of larger cargos of heroin into smaller parcels marked by symbols for individual purchasers in the Netherlands and Germany, carried out in small vans or private cars.

Given the volatile nature of the market of prohibited goods, this account is only a temporary one: new drug fashions in the consumption countries, poverty and war in the Balkan and the Caucasian and Central Asian regions, new profit opportunities in other markets, contribute to new patterns of criminal (and law enforcement) employment.

Human Misery and Trafficking

There is sinister form of 'human resource management': humans trafficking. This has a long history, also in Europe. The autobiography of the German J.G. Seume mentions his abduction in Kassel, his 22 day transport and his work in an old coppermine. He was lucky, because 4300 fellows from the same regions have been sold for 7.4.4. each, for a more dangerous job in her majesty's army (Presser, 1965). As one may notice, these are old pounds and the purchaser and sellers are of old times: Britains buying German young men and boys from their princes to fight the rebellious Americans during their war of independence. Given the death rate in the 18th century armies few survived their purchase. Most survivors of this human traffic have become loyal and industrious US citizens. Today the trading partners and historic conditions have changed, but humans are still trafficking their fellow (wo)man or taking advantage of their sorrow plight by selling transport to pretended green meadows elsewhere.

In the last fifteen years the impact on the industrialised countries of this exploitation of human desperation has become acute again. The papers of Di Nicola, Scheinost and De Ruyver provide an overview of 'human trafficking', a too broad denotation ranging from the delivery of women for sexual exploitation to providing transport and (counterfeited) papers to enable their transfer or to help other economic refugies. The authors express their horror and the attribution of this trade to 'organised crime' is easily made, though that label does not make the crime more heinous. Yet, looking at the diversity of this phenomenon as sketched by De Ruyver c.s., we should not neglect the distinctions between voluntary and involuntary victims (including those who wanted to migrate for a better life to become victim after all), revealing the deceptively imprecise meaning of the concept of 'trafficking'.

Much 'trafficking' consists of no more than counterfeiting travel documents and guiding the willing 'victim' to the country of his/her choice: De Ruyver coins this 'frontier running', which can be carried out by professionals but also by 'self-help groups'. Sometimes a strong male with sufficient self-confidence to challenge the economic hardship of pioneering in the country of destination goes first. When he succeeds and has saved some money, the 'organisation' of the passage of the remaining relatives will be planned. This has been observed with the illegal migration of various Chinese groups to the US (Zhang and Gaylord, 1996) and Indians (children) to Canada.[4] However, the pressure (or supply) of migration may suddenly surpass the travel facilities dramatically, mainly because of man-made disasters, like (civil) wars and political suppression. Whom to turn to? Emergency situations such as between the Balkan and Italy may easily be exploited by local (crime)-entrepreneurs who possess the means of transport, which they already use for other criminal businesses like smuggling cigarettes and drugs. The subsequent disasters are well known and not only to be observed in the Adriatic Sea: around Gibraltar dead refugees are daily washed ashore.

Apart from these waves of exploited human misery, an equally serious problem consists of the organised labour exploitation, which approaches more the meaning of 'human trafficking'. Though much of the focus is on sexual exploitation of women and (male) youngsters, the authors correctly also point at the Belgian concern for the exploitation of illegal immigrants in industry and agriculture, leaving the workers at the whim of the employer, having no rights whatsoever. Whatever the motivation to find once's luck abroad, in sexual or industrial employment, many find themselves either

---

[4] In a case of transferring children from India (1997) to Canada the Dutch police and prosecution at first proclaimed to have detected an extended 'organised child trafficking ring'. Later it turned out that the parents took great care for their safe passage and reception by friends and relatives in America (US and Canada). Granted, the documents were counterfeited by a professional, which rather shows the parents were not careless.

deceived (no folk dancing, but prostitution) and/or treated like merchandise being sold from employer to employer. Sometimes the real trafficking begins in the country of destination or in transit countries like the Czech Republic where a certain percentage of the migrants get stuck.

It is not without reason that trafficking in women and youngsters has attracted increased (though still too fragmented) attention. The vulnerability and the impact of victimization is considered to be profound and traumatic, while the background figures are projected as 'organised crime', illustrating that this attribute is readily used to increase the 'heinousness level' of a phenomenon. Indeed, there is evidence showing the presence of some better integrated crime-enterprises with a division of tasks (recruiters, supplying regularly new women; transporters or guides), and established outlets in the sex industry as far as the organisers do not control brothels or 'window prostitution' themselves. However, most trafficking is being carried out by network of men and women in the delivering region as well as the country of destination: small well organised trafficking rings with some division of labour. For example: a man, being a brothel owner operates with his wife or girlfriend, who travels to the Czech Republic or Poland where she knows 'recruiters' who can supply with 'new faces'. This picture of organised trafficking for sexual purposes corresponds roughly with the earlier description one may find in Sieber and Bögel (1993).

So far we have been looking at two crime-markets which are supposed to be the domain of the 'organised crime': drugs and human trafficking (or shall I say: the criminal human mobility market?), which are described in terms of criminal entrepreneurial behaviour and the related social and economic patterns. Applying the methodological principle of parsimoniousness we do not need the emotive concept of organised crime to provide an accurate and concise presentation.

Economic Crime and Corruption

At the beginning of this introduction I referred to the bias of thinking that the criminal wind is blowing from the Ural while neglecting the mutual victimisation of east and west. Junninen and Aromaa's paper provide good examples of shrewd Finnish businessmen taking criminal advantage of the good relations between the Finland and Estonia and the huge price difference between the two countries of coveted commodities particularly alcohol. Apart from depicting the 'classical' smuggling, which includes moderate quantities of dope (small compared to the quantities intercepted at he main ports of Western Europe) and the regular flow of tax free alcohol to boost the gloomy Finnish midwinter temper, the authors provide a good insight into the way advanced businessmen may take advantage of the credibility of entrepreneurs in a transit economy. You may say the wily Finnish bird catches the naive Estonian worm. Ironically, the author quotes Finnish businessmen saying that they learned the dirty tricks from Western European businessmen in the first place. Is the evil coming from the West after all?

When we take a further look at the contributions of Quirke, Levi and Osyka and the other publications in the area of economic crime, one may notice that the manifestations are different, reflecting the differences in economic opportunities, but that some common traits are clearly recognizable. The European Union is not a closed bastion, the 'fortress Europe', but rather a juridical swamp of fifteen jurisdictions, some of which are rotten through of corruption. The reader will remember that the multiple indicted (but acquitted) figurehead of Italian corruption, Andriotti, was fêted as a kind of national hero by the Italian Parliament and all prominent figures in Italy (including the pope) at his eighties birthday; that both the European Commission as well as Parliament have shown at least complacence regarding nepotism, pocketeering and corruption; that the multiple indicted mayor of Marbella has taken over the smuggle enclave of Ceuta by pure bribery or the obscure finances of the 'solid' previous Bundeskanzler Kohl. I also described earlier how a regular flow of fraudulent transit goods have been covered by false Spanish customs stamps (Van Duyne, 1996) merely illustrating a profitable corrupt interaction between crime-entrepreneurs and the authorities.[5] Political swamp inhabitants use to eschew light from outside. Understandably, the fraud fighting unit of the Commission, the UCLAF, having a hard time remedying these ills, shunned every fresh or independent light that might be thrawn at these problems.[6] Nevertheless research in cross-border economic crime has brought substantial fraud schemes to the surface: the mega-bonanza of organised VAT fraud scams (Van Duyne, 1999; Arts, 1999), which has spread from the BENELUX countries over all the member states of the EU.[7]

Though the basic traits may not be very different, the manifestations may be worsened by the shape of the state in which they occur. The chapter about the Ukrainian economic crime as well as the literature on the situation in the Russian Federation provide some insight into the aggravating factors, particularly the state of rampant corruption in all layers of administration and business. This element appears as a common denominator, which as remarked above, is certainly not restricted to the new states in transition, but also applies to many Western jurisdictions which are not supposed to be 'in transition'. What do they have in common? Maybe the absence of the notion of 'common wealth', the community understanding that the people should collectively compose the state instead of considering the state as a strange or even hostile body, which is only useful when one can take advantage of its facilities: jobs, subsidies, power positions or (as a member of Parliament) immunity.

Looking at the problem of organised economic crime, related to corruption and the underground economy in which crime-organisations undeniably wield their power, the similarity between for example Italy and the successor states of the previous Soviet Union are striking: the lack of public spirit which has been replaced by clientilism; the venality of law enforcement and the widespread disrespect of the law; the breakdown of

---

[5] All rogatory commissions failed to penetrate in inch into the local fog of law enforcement (or protection). For an overview on organised crime in Spain (mentioning corruption only as the eighth factor) Resa-Nestares (1999).

[6] The UCLAF successfully frustrated an initiative of Parliament to develop an independent research body, simply by refusing to release the budget on flimsy excuses, taking months to reply to simple correspondence and stalling so long that the enterprise petered out.

[7] When the European Commission was warned that the new VAT-system introduced in 1993 would open the gates wide open to the already established VAT fraudsters, senior civil servants showed no interest (Van Duyne, 1993b).

the tax system; the protection industry; the interaction between politics and crime-organisations; oligarchical economic relationships. Given the huge differences in historical backgrounds, these similarities are remarkable indeed and warrant a deeper thought and research than these few introductory lines can provide (Rawlinson, 1996).[8]

As far as economic crime in the previous Soviet states is concerned one may say that there is a kind of continuum. As the Soviet state was the owner of all production factors, entrepreneurial citizens could not but resort to theft if they wanted to set up a small business in the shadow economy (Sinuraja, 1995). Who cared for such pilfering? The Soviet state itself pilfered and defrauded its economic figures wholesale, starting right from the time of its founding father. Virtually all statistics were a fraud, because one had to comply with the unrealistic five years plans: then options were defraud and remain silent or complain and lose one's job (or get a compulsory job in Siberia). The socialist plan economy has been swept away and replaced by a crude form of buccaneer market economy, however the public spirit, or rather the lack thereof, remains the same. Small wonder that the economic opportunities have been exploited fully. Given the poor protection of the law, one of the economic opportunities of those who have muscles and guns is protecting (whether or not voluntary) those who produce and those who steal alike, giving a criminal *raison d'être* to so many protection/extortion crime-enterprises. Here one can again descry a common pattern with the Italian mafia though with different cultural backgrounds.

It would of course be wrong to lump every criminal phenomenon together. The western economic structures, including its legislation and public as well as private law enforcement do not particularly favour the development of entrenched organised economic or businesses crime victimizing private industry. The reason is simple: the victim alert rate is high, which makes it difficult to develop a position of economic power. This does not exclude an extensive underground 'fraud' market at the expense of citizens as well as the financial institutes, as described by Levi in his contribution on credit card fraud. Here we witness another interaction between the underworld and upperworld with the key elements *time* and *technique*. It is interesting to observe, that this is not a fully-fledged arms race. Most criminals are not that bright as the police suppose they are (or only slightly brighter than the police) and many still stick to simple traditional forms of credit and cheque fraud (using stolen cards), while sophisticated techniques are available for modest prices. The literature provides some indications of sophisticated counterfeiting enterprises, supposedly originating from Far East based Chinese gangs, which may be under less pressure from their (corrupt) law enforcement agencies. Those who 'take the heat' are the uneducated couriers cashing the cheques and facing potential detection and arrest. Otherwise, the credit and cheque market looks, like most underground crime markets, pretty low organised, which does not exclude substantial losses suffered by the bank.

---

[8] For an excellent study on the mafia see Gambetta (1993). For an account of Russian organised crime see volume 2 of the 1996 journal: *Transnational Organized Crime*.

Money-Laundering

There are a lot of proverbs concerning money and crime. 'Crime does not pay' and 'riches alone make no man happy'. Unfortunately, such moralistic proverbs have too many exceptions. Usually only stupid crime does not pay, while having no money is closely associated with distress and misery. Still, 'money is the root of all evil', and in recent times a common opinion has developed, according to which money derived from the evil of crime will lead to more evil if not to The Evil himself. It goes without saying that so much evil requires adequate tools to combat it. These tools are described by Adamoli and Daams.

Adamoli describes the recent concerns about increased money-laundering opportunities in the transit economies, which corresponds to the disturbing situation in Ukraine elaborated by Osyka. Recent revelations as well as the actions of the Swiss bank authorities and the US and UK secret services to investigate the whereabouts of the riches of some of Russia's tycoons and the IMF credits, underlines the concern about questionable cross-border money flows. Add to this the many rumours and (expensive commercial) 'threat assessments' in the beginning nineties that the Russian organised crime was 'on its march' towards the green meadows west of the Elbe and it is clear that the call for more far reaching anti money-laundering tools is uncritically accepted indeed.

A similar concern can be discerned in relation to the phenomenon of 'underground banking', which in its origin is neither criminal nor banking. Passas describes in his contribution the backgrounds and varieties of this form of money-management. He also makes clear how many mythical notions surround this concept. Nevertheless, the fear for this phenomenon remains, leading to reports with as much ignorance as concern.

Unfortunately there remains a huge gap between the deep colored intensity of the worries of so many high level experts and the paleness of the underlying empirical evidence as well as the experts' lack of curiosity for facts and figures. To put it simple: after so many years of widely propagated anti money-laundering policy we still have no overview, no valid statistics, sophisticated databases, no trained staff or subsidised research institutes to carry out basic research in this field. Brief: there are no (independent) performance indicators and those formulated by knowledgeable scholars, remain unheeded (Levi, 1997). All we know consists of isolated critical evaluation reports like those of Levi and Osofsky (1995) and a view bits and glimpses from 'the field' providing a collage of the most spicy cases from law enforcement officers. This collage is economically hardly impressive. Despite this sorrow state of affairs we continue pasting more and more frightening cases together, because our lack of overview make us hungry for more of such juicy details about the 'laundrymen' (Powis, 1992; Robinson, 1994).

There are some ironic aspects in anti-laundering policy, which does not imply that the legislation is wrong or inadequate. Combatting laundering implies using sophisticated information tools. Handling these tools should create a twofold information base: first at *micro* level against individual villains; secondly this micro information data base should be fit for *macro* strategic analysis which yields some performance measures about the effects of the anti-laundering policy and the developments on the various crime markets itself. As remarked above, it is sad as well as telling, that provisions for this strategic performance information has not been built into the information system from the start, while from the apparent lack of interest one may deduce it may not be not forthcoming in the near future either[9].

Given this lack of insight into the performance of a very expensive instrument, we will have to look for other, more indirect parameters to measure the impact of the anti laundering tools. These parameters may be found in the cost and price structure of the crime markets. It would be wrong to think that the lack of hard facts imply that the anti-laundering measures are ineffective. On the contrary, they have many effects indeed: apart from having a moral impact on the financial institutions, they should make crime-business more expensive. Like the handling of any 'hot stuff', the management of hot money is expensive, increasing the demand for new well paid financial secrecy experts. Will crime-entrepreneurs pass these expenses to their customers who may be less willing to pay the inflated prices, reducing the volume of trade? That is a very interesting economic question, which, after being raised by Levi (1997), has not been addressed so far. Though more specific research is needed, the present scattered evidence contradicts this hypothesis. As far as the drug market is concerned, the new policy has not made a single dent in the ongoing business: in the past fifteen years the prices of cocaine and heroin have gradually gone down in virtually all consumers countries (Farrell c.s., 1996). The number of interceptions and convicts have gone up, all to no avail. There is still ample supply of contraband as well as of lower level couriers recruited by organisers of whom there is not the slightest hint that some may have quit their business for not making any profit 'because of the FATF'.[10] I would like to invite the juridical authors to peep over the fence of the law books at the real empirical life out there.

WHAT TO DO?

Describing all this international mischief is an interesting exercise in itself, but for some collective implicit understanding no one is allowed to do so for its own sake without providing practical tools to do something about it. Woe betide the researcher if he breaks this silent agreement. So we find most papers concluding with recommendations how to reduce this criminal state of the art. The paper of the Dutch fiscal police by Marcel Pheijffer is primarily devoted to improvements of law enforcement measures. Understandably the paper approaches the criminal landscape from the financial perspective. However, though financial investigation should be the logical consequence of the anti money-laundering policy, it is still very much in its infancy. It appears easier to make recommendations and draft new regulations like the anti money-

---

[9] This lack of interest is waning, though. At the time of writing the multidisciplinary group of high level civil servants is in the process of stimulating the member states to remedy this shortcoming.

[10] There is some irony in the message of the British customs, that some old time dope smugglers are alleged to have left the drug market, not for lack of profit, but for *safer* profits on the alcohol and tobacco market, after the latest increase of the excises: lower law enforcement risks and still handsome profits. Do policy makers ever learn?

laundering laws, than learning to unravel the financial ramifications of crime-enterprises. Lack of attention and interest in this field, together with poor training and insufficient skills (in the police forces as well as the public prosecution service) instead of the organised crime threat, may lead to the predictable negative spiral of: new legislation-->disappointing results-->additional legislation-->still disappointing results etc. nibbling away our civil rights, because these 'might protect the (organised) criminal'.

Financial investigation is not a magic bullet to success, but a necessary element in a more comprehensive law enforcement policy. This applies particularly to the cross-border crime phenomenon we are dealing with, because it is about a profit making crime-trade and international crime-markets. In the paper of Pheijffer examples are given of investigating drugs by following the money-flows for buying transport as well as financial crimes in the stock market. Financial investigation may equally be applied in cases of human trafficking or used in such a way that the market structure for organised business crime is fragmentated. In the case of organised VAT fraud the Dutch fiscal police succeeded in impeding organisers by systematically weeding out their bust firms, headed by strawmen, instead of carrying out a major investigation against the principals, which would last for years on end. Did this financial approach work? For the Netherlands it worked out highly preventive: the organisational profit structure within the Netherlands crumbled. The side effect was an 'exportation' of the scams to the member states with a lower victim alert rate and less cooperation between the various agencies.

Inter-agency cooperation remains a problem in Europe, though the situation has improved more than some complainers would like us to belief. Nevertheless, much remains still to be wanted, certainly concerning a *multi-disciplinary* approach, as advocated by De Ruyver concerning human trafficking. This plea for interdisciplinarity applies to other criminal phenomena as well, to which I would like to add that it can only bear fruit if supported by the authorities in more jurisdictions. Unfortunately there are still few European countries in which law enforcement agencies would endorse this approach beyond the level of lip service. Though gradual improvements are being made, the police has no great reputation for cooperation with other experts, like fiscal inspectors or officers from other agencies, let alone sharing knowledge with knowledgeable researchers, even if all the legal obstacles because of privacy problems have been solved.

At this point we face the problem of *knowledge management.* This has a juridical as well as an empirical aspect. Juridical knowledge management is greatly hampered because of the maladapted different legal systems, each with their own culture and history. Valkenburg's contribution provides a view on this fragmented landscape and on the need to develop a European corpus iuris. If policy makers are concerned about the weaknesses in law enforcement they may well realise how much efforts and resources are spent on learning one's way in this European maze, better suited in safeguarding jurists' jobs than preventing crime.

As far as the empirical aspect of the knowledge management is concerned, one can say that the police are to a large degree our social-criminological ears and eyes: they determine to a large extent what policy makers and members of parliaments will know and believe. However, in many European countries the police 'books of knowledge' are either closed or -if finally inspected- appear to be so disorderly, that if a modest candy store would maintain a similar administration it would not survive a fortnight. On this sensitive point of knowledge management improvements are required to make an efficient use of the scarce resources in combatting cross-border crime in Europe. It goes without saying that such an improvement cannot be restricted to a few countries: knowledge should always be shared.

To develop an information and knowledge based interdisciplinary law enforcement policy, police, policy makers, special agencies and academic experts could very well develop an fruitful interaction, assuming they are willing to a mutual open minded approach. This volume aims to provide a stimulus in this direction.

LITERATURE

Arts, R., Hollevaten, Kinken het hardst. Een onderzoek haar de huidige situatie met bettrekking tot de BTW-carrouselfraude. Tilburg University, 1999.

Dorn, N., L. Oette and S. White, Drugs importation and the bifurcation of risk. *The British Journal of Criminology*, 1998, *nr. 4*. 537-561

Duyne, P.C., van, Organized crime and business crime-enterprises in the Netherlands. *Crime, Law and Social Change*, 1993, nr. *19*, 103-142

Duyne, P.C. van, Implications of cross-border crime risks in an open Europe. *Crime, Law and Social Change*, 1993b, nr. *20*, 99-111

Duyne, P.C. van, *Het spook en de dreiging van de georganiseerde misdaad*. Den Haag, SDU-uitgeverij, 1995

Duyne, P.C. van, Definitie en kompaswerking. In: F. Bovenkerk (ed.), *De georganiseerde criminaliteit in Nederland. Het criminologisch onderzoek voor de enquêtecommissie opsporingsmethoden in discussie*. Arnhem, Gouda-Quint, 1996

Duyne, P.C. van, The phantom and threat of organized crime. *Crime, Law and Social Change*, 1996, nr. 4, 241-377

Duyne, P.C. van, Die Organisation der grenzüberschreitenden Kriminalität in Europa. In G. Wolf (ed.), *Kriminalität im Grenzgebiet*. Berlin, Springer, 1998

Farrell, G., M. Kashfia and M. Tullis, Cocaine and heroin in Europe 1983-1993. A cross-national comparison of trafficking and prices. *British Journal of Criminology*, 1996, nr. *2*, 255-281

Fijnaut, C., F. Bovenkerk, G. Bruinsma, and H.G. van de Bunt, *Organized Crime in the Netherlands*, Den Haag, Kluwer Law International, 1998

Gambetta, D., *The Sicilian Mafia. The business of private protection*. Harvard University Press, 1993

Handelman, S., *Comrade Criminal. The theft of the second Russian Revolution*. London, Michael Joseph, 1994

Himmelstein, *The strange career of marijuana; politics and ideology of drug control in America*, Westport, Greenwood, 1983

Kleemans, E.R., E.A.I.M. van den Berg and H.G. van de Bunt, *Georganiseerde criminaliteit in Nederland*. Den Haag, WODC, 1998

Levi, M., Evaluating the 'New Policy': attacking the money trail of organised crime. *Australian and New Zealand Journal of Criminology*, 1997, *vol. 30*, 1-25

Levi, M. and L. Osofsky, *Investigating, seizing, and confiscating the proceeds of crime*. London, Police Research Group Paper 61, Home Office, 1995

Maltz, M., Defining organized crime. In: *Measuring the effectiviness of organized crime control efforts*. Chicago OICJ.

McCoy, A.W., *The politics of heroin. CIA global complicity in the global drug trade*. New York, Lawrence Hill Books, 1991

Musto, D.F., *The American disease. Origins of narcotic control*. New Haven, Yale University Press, 1973

Powis, R.E., *The Money Launderers*. Probus, Chicago, 1992

Presser, J., *Amerika. Van kolonie tot wereldmacht*. Amsterdam, Elsevier, 1965

Rawlinson, P., Russian organized crime: a brief history. *Transnational Organized Crime*, 1996, *nr. 2/3*, 28-52

Resa-Nestaras, C., Transnational organised crime in Spain: structural factors explaining its penetration. In: E.C. Viano (ed.), *Global Organized Crime and International Security*. Aldershot, Ashgate, 1999

Robinson, J., *The Laundrymen*. London, Simon & Schuster, 1994

Roth, J. and M. Frey, *Die Verbrecherholding. Das vereinte Europa im Griff der Mafia*. München, Piper, 1993

Sieber, U. and M. Bögel, *Logistik der organisierten Kriminalität*. Wiesbaden, BKA-Forschungsreihe, 1993

Sinuraja, T., Internationalization of organized economic crime: the Russian Federation case. *European Journal on Criminal Policy and Research*, 1995, *nr. 3.4*, 26-33

Sterling, C., *Crime without frontiers. The worldwide expansion of organised crrime and the Pax Mafioso*. London, Hamish Hamilton, 1995

Wisotsky, S., *Breaking the impasse in the war on drugs*. New York, Greenwood Press, 1986

Zhang, S.X. and M.S. Gaylord, Bound for the golden mountain: the social organisation of Chinese alien smugling. *Crime, Law and Social Change*, 1996, *nr. 1*, 1-16

Chapter 2

CROSS-BORDER CRIME PATTERNS BETWEEN EASTERN EUROPE AND THE EUROPEAN UNION

M. Joutsen
Head of the Heuni-Research Institute, Hensinki, Finland

INTRODUCTION

Before the fall of the Berlin Wall, East-West crime in Europe was very much a curiosity. The meagre flow of tourists and businessmen crossing from Western Europe over to the Central and Eastern European countries engendered small-time smuggling and foreign exchange offences, feeding the underground economy that existed in the socialist countries. In turn, the equally meagre flow of persons crossing from East to West, often as members of official delegations, brought with it some small-time smuggling, for example of alcohol and icons.

There were two major exceptions to this testimony to the role of the 'Iron Curtain' in controlling the ebb and flow of crime. One was drug trafficking from the Golden Crescent through the Balkans into Western Europe, trafficking which had continued for decades. The second exception was the alleged role of some countries in fostering terrorism. For example the United States has asserted not only that Bulgaria harboured heroin laboratories and helped narcotics traffickers move drugs and cash across its borders (Royce 1998, *passim*), but that it also supported international terrorism (see. e.g., Lupsha 1988, p. 179 and Donev 1992, p. 56). This suspicion was strengthened by the allegedly a Bulgarian connection in the 1981 attempted assassination of Pope John Paul II.

Perestroika radically altered the patterns of movement of offenders and offences in Europe.

- The opportunity for cross-border crime along all the state lines (also between Eastern European states) grew almost exponentially along with the weakening of border controls, privatization in the East, the role of the EU as the horn of plenty, and a number of other social, economic and cultural push and pull factors.

- East-West crime expanded. Regardless of how we measure the amount of crime (the number of offences or offenders detected, the sums of money involved, the damage done to society, and so on), it appears to be a growth industry.

- East-West crime diversified. Drug trafficking and petty smuggling have been supplemented by the smuggling of aliens and of firearms, by trafficking in stolen goods ranging from new BMWs to Nokia and Ericsson mobile telephones, by trademark piracy and economic crime, and by money laundering.

- East-West crime became organized. East-West crime is no longer the province solely of individual enterprises; it has attracted organized crime groups from around the world.

In the following, the focus will be on what patterns can be detected in East-West crime. The stage will be set by looking at some of the factors in Central and Eastern Europe that have contributed to the developments. This should not be understood to imply that East-West crime is unidirectional, with a spectre of an 'Eastern Mafia' preying on innocent Western Europe. Western Europe has had no lack of crime, organized or more traditional. The home-grown organized crime groups in the European Union, together with Chinese, Japanese, Colombian, Maghreb, Pakistani, Turkish and other foreign organized crime groups that have already established themselves in Western Europe, have apparently not been slow in taking advantage of the new routes and markets that have opened up to and through Central and Eastern Europe (see, for example, Adamoli et al 1998).

The reason for the focus in this paper on the East is that the existence of organized crime in Central and Eastern Europe had not received much attention until the fall of the Soviet empire. Suddenly, the 'Eastern Mafia' has become the popular bugbear, used to inflame public opinion in many Western European countries against 'Easties'. Disentangling myth from reality requires a look at the background and the available indicators of actual criminal activity.

THE TRANSITION IN CENTRAL AND EASTERN EUROPE

The fundamental transformation in all of Central and Eastern Europe over the past ten years has changed many aspects of every-day life. It has also increased the potential for crime in general, and of organized crime in particular.

The shift from a planned economy to a market economy and the rush towards adoption of a capitalist ethos have brought with them, for the first time in this area of the world, a surge in unemployment and (officially recognized) rapid inflation, a surge which lasted several years.

The changes have also affected social welfare, health and education. In many countries, the safety net provided by the cradle-to-grave welfare system has been radically cut back. The problems appear to be particularly acute in the Russian Federation, where statistics suggest that only one out of every seven children can be said to be in good health, and, to a large degree because of increased use of alcohol, the average male life-span is now shorter than what it was at the beginning of the century, in pre-Revolutionary Russia.

The discrediting of the previous political system and the immense problems encountered in day-to-day survival have had their effect on crime. With the significant weakening of formal and informal social control in Central and Eastern Europe, the rates of reported and, apparently, hidden crime have increased considerably (see, in particular, Zvekic 1998). This has come as a shock to many, since these countries have long been vaunted as success stories in the prevention and control of crime.

The rapid period of transition is now coming to a close. Most importantly, the increase in both reported crime and unreported crime (as shown, for example, by repeated victimization surveys) slowed, and rates tended to stabilize in 1992 and 1993 (Zvekic 1998). It is presumably not a coincidence that at about the same time, the economy and the political and social situation stabilized in many of these countries.

Nonetheless, the increase in crime has been well publicized by the media, and crime remains a serious concern for the public and for policy-makers. While the majority of the population has joined the "new poor," a counterpoint is provided by the successful entrepreneurs who have taken advantage of the new market economy to buy and sell wherever there is an opportunity. Those with the right contacts and capital at the beginning of the 1990s could buy up huge stocks of privatization coupons, raw materials or products in hot demand and sell them for an enormous profit.

Entrepreneurs, however, come in many shapes and sizes. The push of poverty, the pull of hitherto unheard-of riches, the enormous uncertainty over what is possible and what is not under the new precepts of capitalism, and the collapse of formal and informal social control have led to a considerable expansion of organized crime.

THE EMERGENCE OF ORGANISED CRIME IN CENTRAL AND EASTERN EUROPE

Organized crime is not new to Central and Eastern Europe. According to largely anecdotal evidence, economic crime and corruption was built in to certain facets of the Soviet model.

Organized crime had a fertile soil in which to grow. What is now recognized as organized crime took root in corruption and the 'shadow economy'. The official economy rarely operated effectively, and was notoriously poor in providing 'what the customer wanted', consumer goods. A barter economy developed, where each consumer relied on a network of friends and relatives to secure necessities. In such an atmosphere, it was difficult to distinguish between gifts, favours and bribes. A shop clerk would be bribed to set aside a few oranges from the next shipment, or a hospital clerk would be bribed to take in a patient requiring treatment, past the long waiting line.

This barter economy was fed by the shadow economy, which sought to supply whatever the rigid and moralistic legal market could not produce and distribute in sufficient quantities and/or of adequate quality -- which often seemed to be just about anything and everything. This led, among others, to theft by employees, theft of state property, and foreign exchange violations. It also led, by definition, to profiteering and speculation; essentially, to unauthorized free enterprise.

The shadow economy consisted of two sectors. The goods traded on the black market were and to some extent still are entirely illegal; examples are smuggled and stolen goods, foreign currency, pornography and drugs. The gray market provided goods and services in competition with the State-controlled market, but at free-market prices. The gray market often served as a channel for goods embezzled from the State, and/or it provided services on 'company' time. For example, many State factories had siphoned off part of their raw materials to be used in the 'illegal' production of high-quality goods, and then shared the profits among the employees involved.

The State was unable to stamp this out, primarily due to the lack of resources and the unwillingness of the public to cooperate with the authorities on this issue. The State was also, to a large extent, unwilling to intervene, since the shadow economy worked after a fashion, thus cutting down on public discontent. Moreover, the State did not intervene in many cases because often, the responsible officials were raking off bribes.

The opening of the markets ten years ago raised the stakes. The new international connections brought in a thriving trade in contraband (a mishmash of icons, natural resources, firearms, illegal aliens and others going out of the country, and for example stolen cars coming in), and economic crimes. The stockpiling of money inevitably led to increased money laundering.

These crimes continue to be committed by enterprising individuals acting on their own. However, they have also become a growth area for organized crime, which is using its organization and resources to produce greater profits.

THE SCOPE OF EAST-WEST CRIME

1. Drug Trafficking

Drug trafficking is perhaps the archetypical cross-border crime today, in Europe as well as world-wide. The United Nations International Drug Control Programme estimates the global turnover to be between USD 300 billion to 500 billion. The major source areas of drugs continue to be Colombia, the Golden Triangle and the Golden Crescent. The Central and Eastern European countries appear above all to be transit countries, although there now appears to be a considerable production of drugs in this area (including such synthetic drugs as amphetamines, methamphetamine, methcathinone, MDMA and LSD; see, for example, Plywaczewski 1998, p. 6), as well as a growing problem with consumption. The attractiveness of the Central and Eastern European countries for drug traffickers is increased by the difficulties that in particular the newly independent countries have in staffing and equipping their Customs service and law enforcement agencies.

Globally, illicit drug production is expanding, although the production of some drugs, such as coca and cannabis, is stagnating or even falling (Juppin de Fondaumière 1997, p. 4). Furthermore, there appears to be a shift in where drugs are produced, with for example the Central Asian republics of the CIS becoming relatively recent or potential major producers of both opiates and cannabis (ibid., p. 5). This will presumably increase the potential for a flow of these drugs through the Central and Eastern European countries into Western Europe. The Russian Federation is apparently already a well-established transit country for opium, heroin and marijuana from Central Asia and the Golden Crescent, in addition to for cocaine from Colombia (Williams 1997, p. 19).

The traffickers represent a number of nationalities. Italian groups have long experience in drug trafficking, not only in Italy but also in, for example, France and Germany. Other European groups include groups in Belgium, England, France, the Netherlands and Spain. They compete or cooperate with, for example, Chinese, Colombian, Maghreb, Nigerian, Pakistani, Turkish and Vietnamese groups (Adamoli et al 1998, pp. 37-39). Today, the offenders are increasingly coming for example from the Czech Republic, Poland, Romania, the Russian Federation and former Yugoslavia (ibid.). This increase in traffickers from former Yugoslavia may well be a general phenomenon. The importance of the Balkan route -- long an important conduit -- was apparently not interrupted by the extended civil war in the former Yugoslavia. On the contrary, it would appear that the break-up of Yugoslavia and the civil war led to a diversification and expansion of drug trafficking through the region, with an impact as far away as the Baltic. (According to reports, many of the militias that were engaged in the war in former Yugoslavia either actively engaged in, or supported, drug trafficking since this provided a source of revenue for purchasing ordnance.) The growing supply of drugs in Europe is reflected in the number and size of seizures, the number of cases of hepatitis or drug overdoses dealt with in the hospitals, the decreasing street price of drugs, and the results of various surveys of drug use.

2. The Smuggling of Alcohol and Tobacco

The significance of drug trafficking tends to overshadow the smuggling of other goods. The efforts of some European Union countries (such as the Nordic countries) to decrease the consumption of alcohol and tobacco by increasing their price have almost inevitably led to an increase in smuggling. Moreover, the traffic goes both ways: there appears to be a growing market for Western (primarily American) cigarettes in Central and Eastern Europe. The primary area for smuggling appears to be in the Mediterranean, in particular between Albania and Italy, although some large seizures have been made in the Baltic.[1] Because of the controls on the sales of tobacco and alcohol, wholesale and retail distribution of illicit alcohol and tobacco may be difficult. The counterfeiting of revenue stamps, however, can allow activity to continue for a while without being detected.

The (potential) market for illicit alcohol includes not only private individuals but also (illegal) brothels, illegal gambling halls and illegal restaurants -- establishments which tend to be rather short-lived. Another market consists of buyers for legitimate retail outlets who are willing to take the risk of paying less for illicit products.

The retail trade in cigarettes involves many more outlets than does the distribution of alcohol, and so there is a somewhat larger potential for black-market cigarettes to enter the legal market.

3. Trafficking in Stolen Property

In 1995, the latest year for which data are available, approximately 2 million motor vehicles were stolen in Europe alone (Liukkonen 1997, p. 5). Traditionally, most thefts of motor vehicles have been connected with joy-riding; young persons steal a car, ride around until the car runs out of petrol (or crashes), and then abandon it. A significant number of stolen cars are also used in connection with burglaries or robberies.

Recently, however, the number of stolen motor vehicles that could not be traced has increased. In 1995, this was true of over one half of the vehicles stolen in Belarus, Croatia, Estonia, Greece, Kyrgystan, Latvia, Lithuania, Luxembourg, Moldova and Slovenia (ibid., pp. 7-8). (The corresponding rates for selected other countries are Belgium, 42%; Germany, 24%; Sweden, 29%; and Finland, 5%.) There are indications that a large proportion of these untraced motor vehicles have been driven across the border, and that much of the trafficking is organized.

The trend in the rate of car thefts has varied. The rate increased during the beginning of the 1990s, when the direction of the traffic was from West to East, but the rate has stabilized since then (ibid., p. 10). The situational crime prevention theory may help to explain shifts in patterns in the trafficking of stolen vehicles (see, e.g., Cohen and Felson 1979 and Felson 1997). The opening of the borders, the wide availability of high-status cars in Western Europe, the unmet demand for such cars in Central and Eastern Europe, the increasing purchasing power of many individuals in the ex-socialist countries, and the problems that law enforcement has in tracing stolen cars that disappear across borders explain much of the growth of this type of crime during the late 1980s and early 1990s. Now, as a result of the increase in the number and quality of vehicles throughout Central and Eastern Europe, also these countries are beginning to be a source for stolen motor vehicles - as shown by the fact that the highest rate of theft in 1995 was in Latvia, where over 6% of all registered motor vehicles were stolen in 1995.

---

[1] Finnish customs seized 7 million cigarettes during 1996. Most of this was in one shipment of 5,5 million cigarettes that had come from Lithuania, on through Estonia, and was on its way through Sweden to Germany -- a nice example of international trade around the Baltic.

The value of stolen motor vehicles on the black market may be decreasing, but other goods are taking their place. Mobile telephones, lap-top computers and similar status items have entered the mass-market stage. They have a substantial resale value and are easy to transport. Not surprisingly, they are finding their way onto the black market.

4. Trafficking in Dangerous Substances

References to trafficking in radioactive or other dangerous substances come from Germany, Latvia (Usca 1998, p. 8), Poland (Plywaczewski 1998, p. 6), Sweden (Daniels-son 1993, p. 61) and, above all, the Russian Federation (Lee, in Williams 1997). The sources appaear to be poorly guarded reactors or military installations in the former USSR, primarily in the Russian Federation (Lee, op.cit.).

The dangerous substances can be divided into three categories:

1. weapons-grade material (uranium-235, plutonium, lithium; such substances as hafnium, beryllium and zirconium can be used either in the construction of nuclear weapons or in civilian industry);
2. other radioactive or dangerous substances (e.g. cesium-137, strontium-90 and cobalt-60); and
3. radioactive scrap metal.

Trafficking in radioactive materials has received considerable attention in the media. It appears to fit in with the worst-case scenario of Cold War die-hards, who continue to see the Russian Federation as a nuclear threat, and are prepared to claim that the KGB is deliberately marketing nuclear material or even nuclear weapons abroad for their own nefarious purposes. So far, there has not been public confirmation of the collusion of any governmental authorities, or even of ex-governmental authorities, in the trafficking. Instead, it can be conjectured that the offenders are primarily free-lance amateurs who place both themselves and their environment at great risks in handling such contraband. Lee (in Williams 1997, p. 111) notes that organized crime groups in the Russian Federation are simply not interested in this type of trafficking, largely because of the difficulties in identifying 'legitimate' buyers (as opposed to undercover law enforcement agents).[2]

Some indications of the scope of the trafficking can be seen from the seizures made, primarily in Germany: between October 1992 and December 1994, the authorities reported six seizures, including shipments of 1,5, 2,73 and 3,05 kg of highly enriched U-235 (Lee 1997, p. 110). The intended use is uncertain, although some suggestions have been made that the uranium was intended for the Near East. During more recent years, however, very few seizures have been reported, notwithstanding such recent Hollywood productions as the movie, 'Peacemaker'.

---

[2] The thrust of Lee's argument, however, is that there is a considerable risk that weapons-grade nuclear substances will be diverted to Iran, Iraq, North Korea or terrorist groups in the Middle East.

5. Trafficking in Firearms

A large proportion of the global supply of firearms is produced in Europe. Some 125 of the 300 companies identified by the United Nations as manufacturers of small arms, equipment and accessories are located in two dozen European countries (Rana 1995, Annexes II and III). The close supervision of the manufacture and trade in firearms in Western Europe has been believed to restrict the availability of illicit arms. In Central and Eastern Europe, the situation has been quite different. The lax supervision within (former) Soviet army installations in Central and Eastern Europe, the large-scale transfers of men and matériel back to the Russian Federation at the end of the 1980s and the early 1990s, the large-scale demobilization of soldiers in the (former) USSR, and the weakening of government control over the firearms industry have greatly expanded the number of illicit weapons available and have reduced the amount of risk involved.

Many of these weapons have stayed in Central and Eastern Europe; one sign of this has been the fact that almost throughout the region there has been a rapid increase in the number of homicides and other violent offences committed with firearms and explosives. Many more weapons, however, are shipped to Western Europe or elsewhere (see, for example, Sterling 1995, esp. pp. 264 ff., "The Illegal Arms Trade 1993", and "Russia's Yard Sale" 1994). At the same time, with the restructuring of the markets, many Eastern European and Commonwealth of Independent State manufacturers of military hardware have been forced to choose between bankruptcy and the promotion of arms exports (Rana 1995, p. 13; Klare 1995b, p. 36; Gonchar and Lock 1995, p. 117 and passim).

One feature of the flow of illegal firearms in Europe is that the prices are well below production costs, suggesting that the most likely source of supplies is "leakage" from existing stocks controlled by the military (Lock 1995, pp. 1-2 and 4). This leakage can take the form of thefts and robberies from poorly guarded armouries (especially in connection with the large-scale transfers of troops and equipment that have occurred throughout Central and Eastern Europe over the past years), and illegal sales by members of the military (see, especially, Gonchar and Lock 1995, pp. 118-122).

On the *demand* side, globally speaking there are three main types of potential buyers for illicit weapons: "ordinary" criminals, including those engaged in organized crime; terrorists; and military procurers, especially for armies subjected to a blockade and thus unable to use legal channels. (In addition, private citizens concerned about their safety but unable to obtain a licence may buy an illegal firearm.) Klare (1995a, p. 4 and 1995b, p. 35) argues that the end of the Cold War has apparently led to a transformation of the international arms market. Earlier, the market had been dominated by purchases by client States dependent on the United States and the USSR of major weapons systems as protection against potential external enemies. Now, these same ex-client States are buying - more small arms and counterinsurgency gear for internal defence. At the same time, various ethnic and insurgent forces are picking up small arms and ammunition -- often from black market sources.

The break-up of the USSR and Yugoslavia has created a number of new states with independent armies, all of which must be supplied with small arms. Moreover, a number of these new states see the threat of border conflicts with some of their neighbours. This has been the self-evident case in former Yugoslavia, but it is also true of, for example, the Russian Federation on one hand and Ukraine, Moldova and the Central Asian republics on the other.

Throughout large parts of Europe, therefore, the supply of and the demand for illicit firearms appears to be growing. The weakening of government control in many countries and the porousness of many borders immeasurably hampers any attempts at control.

6. Trafficking in Illegal Immigrants

The reputation of some European Union countries for providing well-paid employment or generous welfare benefits -- although perhaps somewhat tarnished with widespread employment and with the cut-backs during the 1990s in benefits -- continues to lure people from developing countries and countries in transition. The profits from this trafficking in Europe have recently been estimated at USD 3 to 4 billion each year (Economist 1999).

In Europe, a great number of aliens are transported by professional traffickers from Morocco to Spain, from Tunisia to Italy, and through Russia, the Baltic countries and other Central and Eastern European countries to Western Europe and beyond. A 1994 United Nations report stated that '[t]hose in transit include 60,000 Chinese in Moscow [and] 80,000 or more Asians, Africans and people from the Middle East in Romania' (UN 1994, p. 17). The report goes on to claim that some 100,000 - 200,000 Chinese are smuggled into Europe each year (p. 18). Chinese Triad organizations engaged in the smuggling of aliens have been detected in, for example, Austria, Spain and the United Kingdom (Adamoli et al 1998, pp. 42-43).

However, the aliens are not only from outside Europe. The break-up of Yugoslavia reportedly led in Germany to 'an influx of 650,000 foreigners seeking asylum from Bulgaria, Romania, the Balkans and other areas . . .' (CJ International, 1993).

The European Union has devoted considerable attention to stopping the traffic in illegal migrants, not the least because this has led to a growth in racist and xenophobic violence in a number of countries, and because the persons being smuggled are often victimized by the traffickers. Another reason is that some illegal immigrants abuse the right of asylum. There are indeed a great number of applicants. During 1998 alone, some 350,000 asylum applications were filed in the European Union, Norway and Switzerland (Economist 1999); it is, of course, difficult to assess what proportion may be ungrounded.

As a result of tighter controls in the transit countries and countries of destination, it had seemed as if the scope of the traffic in Europe had been decreasing over the past few years. More recently, however, considerable concern has been expressed about the increased flow of illegal immigrants into the European Union in particular from and through Albania; many have been claiming (rightly or wrongly) to be refugees from Kosovo, and thus deserving of being granted refugee status. The media has already featured many reports on how organized groups are taking advantage of the refugees packed into camps in Albania and Macedonia, to extort fees for smuggling these refugees into European Union countries.

One special form of the smuggling of migrants is trafficking in women and children, which is largely carried out in order to feed the demand for prostitution. In Germany and the Netherlands, where prostitution is legal, the market is said to be influenced primarily by Albanian, Turkish and former Yugoslavian groups (Lilic 1998, pp. 4-5), although also Russian and Ukrainian connections have been suspected. Prostitution is also a widespread problem almost everywhere else in Europe, from the Mediterranean up to the Nordic countries. The prostitutes -- who come not only from throughout Central and Eastern Europe, but also for example from the Far East -- are often recruited with promises of work as *au pairs,* secretaries or entertainers, or are otherwise given highly misleading information as to what to expect. Also in this respect organized crime groups have taken advatage of Kosovar refugees in Albania and Macedonia.

7. Other Illegal Trafficking

A thriving illegal international trade has developed in oil products, non-ferrous metals and rare metals. An example is provided by the recent case involving a company called Tess Petroleum, which imported oil products from Russia, through Kaliningrad and Lithuania into Latvia; the loss to the Latvian State was one million US dollars (Usca 1998, p. 10). Dolgova (1998, p. 21), in turn, suggests that some 50 % of the USD 15-20 billion in gas and oil exported from the Russian Federation annually is smuggled.

A second category of goods being smuggled to the West is cultural artifacts, in particular icons. Already in 1991, it was estimated that as much as 80% of the some 30 million icons that had been assumed to have been in the USSR ten years earlier had been stolen and taken out of the country (Johnson 1993, s. 46). Less attention has been paid to this problem more recently; two quite probable reasons are that what can be stolen easily has already disappeared, and the remaining cultural treasures are protected much more carefully.

8. Economic Crime, Trademark Piracy and Money Laundering

In an integrating Western Europe, economic crime and money laundering appears to have expanded. For the European Union, of course, a major concern is fraud directed against the European Union itself, for example in the form of value-added taxation fraud involving commodities such as mineral oil, cigarettes, alcohol, home electronics and livestock. Such activity appears to be widespread in, for example, Belgium, France, Greece, the Netherlands, and above all Italy (Adamoli et al 1998, p. 43). An emerging concern is the counterfeiting of the new euro, the currency that eleven European Union countries have begun taking into common use since the beginning of this year.

In the Central and Eastern European countries, the key factors behind the growth of economic crime have been the dissolution in 1990 of the Comecon trading bloc, the disrupture of inter-republic industrial and economic ties, the creation of separate currencies, and above all the privatization process. In the former USSR, the economic restructuring could be said to have begun with the 1987 Law on State Enterprises, and continued with the 1988 Law on Cooperatives, steps taken without creating the proper legal environment for regulation of these new forms of economic activity. Dolgova (1998, pp. 18-19) estimates that in Moscow alone, 'breaches of privatisation legislation have resulted in damage to the State amounting to some USD 100 billion'.

The restructuring of the markets in Central and Eastern Europe without proper control has led to the use of a huge variety of methods in committing economic crime, such as loans by banks to non-existent firms or to firms which immediately declare bankruptcy, dummy transactions with shell companies (especially in the CIS), unregulated exporting of currency, the "milking" of privatized companies, purchases of securities by dummy corporations, illegal transactions, insurance fraud, tax evasion and bankruptcy fraud.

Throughout Central and Eastern Europe, trademark piracy has been much in evidence, despite attempts by respective Governments now and then to crack down. In the Russian Federation, for example, by far the majority of computer programs are illegal copies. Pirated videos have been widely available, in some cases only days after the original release of the movies in Western countries.

In Western Europe, money laundering is often associated with the tax havens of Luxembourg, Malta and the Channel Islands. However, it appears to be strongly present also elsewhere. Media reports have suggested that some US 50 billion are laundered each year in Germany alone, making it one of the world centres for this activity. Much of the money comes from the Cali cartel and Italian organized crime (Savona and DeFeo 1994, p. 67). Increasing sums are also coming into other EU member States (ibid., pp. 64-77).

The growth of joint ventures between Western companies and Central and Eastern European countries have considerably facilitated money laundering (Rawlinson 1997, pp. 46-47). Moreover, because of the possibilities that control over banks provides for money laundering (and also for defrauding the public and the State), they have become targets of organized crime take-over bids in some Central and Eastern European countries. Williams (1997, p. 17) cites an estimate by the MVD All-Russia Scientific Research Institute in August 1995 that criminal groups controlled over 400 banks and some 50 currency exchanges in the Russian Federation. It is presumably no coincidence that many Eastern European banks have established branches abroad; for example over 40 Russian banks have opened branches on the island of Cyprus alone. Control of banks by organized crime may help to explain a very recent phenomenon: today, more and more "illegal" money is coming into the Russian Federation to be laundered, instead of being taken out of the country.

9. Corruption, Racketeering and the Use of Violence

Because of the secretive nature of corruption and racketeering, it is difficult to assess their extent. International comparisons are largely limited to subjective assessments. HEUNI has recently published a report on crime in Europe which has sought to compare, among other crimes, the levels of corruption in the different countries (Kangaspunta,

Joutsen and Ollus 1998). The results suggest that the prevalence of corruption is strongly related to the state of the economy. Economies in transition and, more generally, weaker economies tend to experience higher levels of manifest corruption of public officials. The level of corruption appears to be lower in the countries where economic restructuring is relatively advanced, e.g. in Estonia and Hungary. In fact the level of corruption in these countries is lower than in some Western countries.

Perhaps the most widely cited comparison is that prepared by Transparency International. The Transparency International ranking for 1998 included 85 countries. These are based on the subjective perception that businessmen have of the amount of corruption in certain countries. Since the polls are repeated and the results show a considerable degree of consistency, they can be regarded as providing at least an international benchmark.

All in all, Western European countries do well, and Central and Eastern European countries do poorly in this comparison. Fifteen of the 25 countries with the least amount of perceived corruption are from Western Europe (with Denmark, Finland and Sweden in the top three positions). The Western European countries with the lowest rankings are Greece, at 36, and Italy, at 39. The 'best' Central and Eastern European countries are Estonia (26th), Hungary (33rd), the Czech Republic (37th) and Poland (39th, the same as Italy), while Ukraine (69th), Latvia (71st) and the Russian Federation (76th) are near the bottom of the list of 85 countries.

This assessment that corruption is a particular problem in the Russian Federation is in line with other data. The most recent sweep of the international crime victimization survey included a question on corruption. According to the results, 1,0% of the respondents in industrialized countries, and 12,8% of the respondents in countries in transition, had been asked for, or had been expected to give, a bribe to a government official during the preceding year. The highest rate was in Georgia (29,9%) and the second highest was in Kyrgyzstan (21,3), but the third highest was in the Russian Federation (18,7%, or almost one out of every five respondents) (Zvekic 1998, p. 49).

Also racketeering appears to be relatively widespread in the Russian Federation. (It appears to be less widespread in other Central and Eastern European countries.) According to one estimate, 70-80 % of companies and commercial banks in the Russian Federation pay a 'roof' ('krysha', protection) or bribes. Studies of problems faced by Finnish companies in the Baltic region (Lehti and Aromaa 1996) showed that there was only a thin line between security services and racketeering in St. Petersburg. Experiences with racketeering were much rarer in Latvia and Estonia. Of the 85 companies studied in St. Petersburg, 42 % were victims of a protection racket and another 16 % of other extortion; the corresponding figures for Latvia were 11 and 20 %, and for Estonia only 3 and 5 % (ibid., p. 20).

Violence and the threat of violence is a part of racketeering. Such violence can consist of arson, injury to personnel, and even murder. Contract killings have also been used in connection with battles between organized crime groups over territory. Tass has estimated that there were 500 contract killings in the Russian Federation in 1995 (cited in Williams 1997, p. 18), and there were an estimated 74 contract killings during 1996 in Moscow alone (Dolgova 1998, pp. 10-11). Presumably in connection with the attempts of organized crime to take over financial institutions, a considerable number of Russian bank managers have been murdered since 1993; there were 30 such assassination attempts during 1994 and the first half of 1995 (Williams 1997, p. 15).

HOW BIG A THREAT IS EAST-WEST CRIME?

Does organized crime on such a large scale constitute a threat? Borrowing on Williams (1997), we can identify two quite different ways of looking at East-West crime, and in particular at the growth of organized crime in Central and Eastern Europe. Williams calls these the "worst case" and the 'best case' scenario.

According to the worst case scenario, organized crime in Europe is developing into a tight, well-planned, well-structured and smoothly operating network, which will continue to fuel East-West crime.

- First of all, the key organized crime figures are said to be either long-term, well-established Godfathers, or (in the East) ex-KGB agents, who have brought in the skills of their trade.
- Second, the past ten years have been said to have led to a shaking-out of the weaker competitors, with those left standing in the ring agreeing on how to divide the illegal market.
- Third, the new breed of organized crime figures in Central and Eastern Europe are said to be exceedingly violent, ruthless and skilled, with training either in the military or in prison (and often both).
- Fourth, organized crime has been said to have spread so much that it has taken over large shares of the legal economy, especially in several Central and Eastern European countries, and is seeking to take over control of the bureaucracy, the criminal justice system and politicians.
- Fifth, the criminal justice system in Central and Eastern Europe - what little is said to remain uncorrupted or uncowed - has been so weakened that it is unable to respond effectively to the endemic corruption and organized crime.
- Finally, organized crime groups have been said to have forged international contacts with other crime groups, inside and outside of Europe, including with the Latin American cartels, the Yakuza and the triads. Together they are poised to strengthen their global activities. In this view, East-West crime will expand beyond Europe to become a global power factor.

The best case scenario is more optimistic. Although the situation at present may indeed look bad, organized crime has some positive social functions, and it is largely a transitional phenomenon.

- First, organized crime figures are said to provide goods and services that the public demands, and that the State has been unable to deliver.

- Second, according to this view organized crime figures in Central and Eastern Europe are not that different from the 'robber barons'in the United States at the turn of the century. They provide goods and services in an environment where legislation and the economic situation is changing so rapidly that the distinction between legal and illegal is not at all clear.
- Along the same lines, during this transition period organized crime figures are said in effect to be budding capitalists, testing the possibilities that the system offers to make money. Once the transition period in Central and Eastern Europe is over, they will presumably become well-respected members of their community, and will seek to remain respected by cutting their ties with violent and illegal activities.
- Finally, the proponents of the best case scenario emphasize that the transition period is coming to an end. Once the rules of the game have been established and the capacity of the criminal justice system to provide an effective response has been restored, the combination of legal competition, public disapproval, and swift and harsh criminal justice will sweep the organized crime elements out.

CONCLUSIONS

Which is closer to the mark, the worst case scenario or the best case scenario?

The proponents of the worst case scenario are apparently wrong in painting organized crime in Europe as a smoothly-operating, hideously effective monolith. The in-fighting among the organized crime groups remains intense. Presumably very few of the players are the skilled KGB operatives feared by this line of thought. Certainly the groups have at least their fair share of bumbling, strutting wanna-bes and losers.

Also, the criminal justice system has been able to recover its hold, as shown by the stabilization of crime. Each country has taken a number of steps to strengthen the prevention and control of crime. The action plan adopted by the European Union during the spring of 1997 will help in improving national and international coordination of the response to organized crime. The pre-accession pacts being formed with the eleven candidate countries to the European Union will ensure that the elements of this action plan are adopted more widely.

Moreover, the hold that organized crime has on the economy, on the bureaucracy and on politics varies considerably from city to city and country to country. There are several countries and large regions in Central and Eastern Europe which apparently have been at least as successful as many of their Western European neighbours in responding to organized crime.

Also the proponents of the best case scenario, however, are probably wrong when they say, essentially, that 'closing your eyes and wishing will make it go away'. For example in Albania, Bulgaria, Romania and much of the Russian Federation organized crime has become endemic and has gained a powerful hold on the legitimate economy.

There is a clear potential for growth in organized crime in Europe, and in East-West crime more generally. The criminal justice system in most countries in the region is only slowly recovering from a crisis in morale, resources and direction, a crisis that has sapped its possibility to respond effectively.

One of the fears in Western Europe is that organized crime will begin to cross the borders from the East. This has certainly been happening with drug trafficking, and on a lesser scale with organized theft, the exploitation of illegal immigration and prostitution, and the illegal sale of firearms. Suitable international contacts are being forged. So far, growth may have been inhibited by the fact that sufficient opportunities have been available in the domestic market. Furthermore, operating in the West has drawbacks and dangers: it is more expensive, there may be competition from local organized crime, and the police may be more efficient.

The danger posed by organized crime nonetheless remains, both to the countries themselves and internationally. This has already been recognized, as shown by the strengthening of the legislative framework, the reorganization of the criminal justice system, the growing network of bilateral and multilateral agreements, and the strengthening of informal international contacts among the police. Many Western European countries are providing technical assistance to Central and Eastern Europe in the form of training, consultation and the exchange of information.

The problem is that, in the control of organized crime, both the West and the East have a long way to go.

LITERATURE

Sabrina, A., A. Di Nicola, E.U. Savona and P. Zoffi, *Organised Crime around the World*, Helsinki, HEUNI publication no. 31, 1998

CJ International, May-June 1993, vol. 9, no. 3, 14

Cohen, L. and M. Felson, Social change and crime rate trends: A routine activity approach, *American Sociological Review,* 1979, *vol. 44*, 588-608

Danielsson, A., Brottsutvecklingen i det forna Sovjet (Trends in Crime in the Former Soviet), in *Brottsutvecklingen - ett hot mot demokratin?* (Crime Trends - A Threat to Democracy?), Stockholm, 51-65, 1993

Dolgova, A., Organized Crime in Russia, *Nouvelles etudes pénales*, 1998, *no. 16*, 175-191

Donev, E., in: Dekleva, Boyan (ed.) *Organized Crime - Problems, Prevention and Control. Materials of a Conference*, Sofia (untitled summary), 1992, 56

Dunn, G., Major Mafia Gangs in Russia, in: Williams (1997), 63-87 *The Economist*, London, 20 February 1999, pp. 29-30

Felson, Marcus, A "Routine Activity" Analysis of Recent Crime Reductions, *The Criminologist*, 1997, *vol. 22, no. 6*, 1 and 3

Gonchar, Ksenia and Peter Lock. Small Arms and Light Weapons: Russia and the Former Soviet Union, in: J. Boutwell, M.T. Klare and L.W. Reed (eds), *Lethal Commerce. The Global Trade in Small Arms and Light Weapon*s, Cambridge, Massachusetts, American Academy of Arts and Sciences, 1995, 116-123

The Illegal Arms Trade, *Intersec*, June 1993, *vol. 3, no. 2*, 64-65

Jonson, L., Brottsligheten - ett hot mot det ryska samhället (Crime - a threat to Russian society?), in: *Brottsutvecklingen - ett hot mot demokratin?* (Crime trends - a threat to democracy?), Stockholm, 39-49, 1993

Juppin de Fondaumiĕre, B., Keynote speech. *Drugs and Security: Risks and Challenges.* Paper presented at the Organisation for Security and Co-operation in Europe Seminar on Specific Risks and Challenges Within the Framework of the Common and Comprehensive Security Model for Europe for the Twenty-First Century, Vienna, 6 May 1997

Kangaspunta, K., M. Joutsen and N. Ollus (eds.), *Crime and Criminal Justice in Europe and North America 1990-1994.* Helsinki, HEUNI publication no. 32, 1998

Klare, M., *Light Weapons Arm Trafficking and the World Security Environment of the 1990s*, paper presented at the Proliferation of Light Weapons in the Post-Cold War World: A Global Problem" conference organized by UNIDIR with the cooperation of the Presse- und Informationsamt der Bundesregierung, Berlin 4-5 May 1995 (1995a)

Klare, M., The Global Trade in Light Weapons and the International System in the Post-Cold War Era, in Jeffrey Boutwell, Michael T. Klare and Laura W. Reed (eds), *Lethal Commerce. The Global Trade in Small Arms and Light Weapons,* Cambridge, Massachusetts, American Academy of Arts and Sciences, 31-43, 1995b

Lee, R., *Recent Trends in Nuclear Smuggling*, in Williams 1997 (op.cit.), pp. 109-121

Lehti, M. and K. Aromaa, *Suomalaisten yritysten turvallisuus Latviassa* (The security of Finnish companies in Latvia), Helsinki, National Research Institute of Legal Policy Research Communication 27, 1996

Lilie, H., Organized Crime in the Baltic Area. National Report / Germany, *Nouvelles etudes pénales*, 1998, *no. 16*, 107-119

Liukkonen, M., *Motor Vehicle Theft in Europe*, Helsinki, HEUNI Papers no. 9, 1997

Lock, P., *The Flow of Illegal Weapons in Europe*, paper presented at the Proliferation of Light Weapons in the Post-Cold War World: A Global Problem" conference organized by UNIDIR with the cooperation of the Presse- und Informationsamt der Bundesregierung, Berlin 4-5 May 1995

Lupsha, Peter A., The Role of Drugs and Drug Trafficking in the Invisible Wars, in Richard H. Ward and Harold E. Smith (eds.), *International Terrorism: Operational Issues*, Chicago 1988, pp. 177-190

Plywaczewski, E. and S. Waltos, Organized Crime in Poland, *Nouvelles etudes pénales*, 1998, *no. 16*, 153-174

Qvigstad, L., Organized Crime in the Baltic Area. National Report / Norway, *Nouvelles etudes pénales*, 1998, *no. 16*, 147-152

Raig, U., Situation in Estonia Regarding Organized Crime, *Nouvelles etudes pénales*, 1998, *no. 16*, 71-76

Rana, S., *Small Arms and Intra-State Conflicts*, paper presented at the Proliferation of Light Weapons in the Post-Cold War World: A Global Problem" conference organized by UNIDIR with the cooperation of the Presse- und Informationsamt der Bundesregierung, Berlin 4-5 May 1995, originally published as Research Paper No. 34 of the United Nations Institute for Disarmament Research, Geneva

Rawlinson, P., *Russian Organized Crime: A Brief History*, in Williams 1997 (op.cit.), 28-52

Royce, K., Drug Supply - Money Laundering Linked to Bulgaria, *International Drug Report*, New York, International Narcotic Enforcement Officers Association, May 1989, 2 and 12

Russia's Yard Sale, *Time*, 18 April 1994

Savona, E. U. and M. A. DeFeo, *Money Trails: International Money Laundering Trends and Prevention/Control Policies*. HEUNI, published in: International Conference on Preventing and Controlling Money Laundering and the Use of the Proceeds of Crime: A Global Approach, Fondazione Centre Internazionale su Diritto, Società e Economia, Courmayeur, Italy, 1994

Smith, Hedrick, *The New Russians*, New York, 1991

Sterling, C., *Crime Without Frontiers. The Worldwide Expansion of Organised Crime and the Pax Mafioso*, London, 1995

UN, *Problems and Dangers Posed by Organized Transnational Crime in the Various Regions of the World*, E/CONF.88/2, 18 August 1994

Usca, Dagmara, Trends in the Development of Organized Crime in Latvia, *Nouvelles etudes pénales*, 1998, *no. 16*, 119-133

Voronin, Y.A., *The Emerging Criminal State: Economic and Political Aspects of Organized Crime in Russia*, in Williams 1997 (op.cit.), 53-62

Williams, Ph. (ed.), *Russian Organized Crime: The New Threat?*, London, Frank Cass, 1007

Zvekic, U., *Criminal Victimisation in Countries in Transition*, Rome, UNICRI publication no. 61, 1998

Transnational Organised Crime and Cross-Border Trafficking in Human Beings in the Czech Republic

Dr. Miroslav Scheinost
Deputy Director of the Institute of Criminology and
Social Prevention in Prague.

The Roots

Under the conditions of the previous regime, before 1989, the problem of organised crime in the Czech Republic (or in the Czechoslovak Socialist Republic) was not very prominent. The former economic and political power model and the relative isolation from the free world did not further the emergence of any large scale 'classical' forms of organised crime. Usual organised crime activities, like racketeering, drug trafficking, trafficking in human beings and arms, thefts of expensive cars, porno-business, were too risky due to the totalitarian police regime, while the market for trading illegal goods and services was too limited to generate large illegal revenues. Therefore we cannot speak of the 'classical' organised crime and about extensive criminal organisations of a Mafia-type before 1989, either domestic or international.

Despite this police regime, some domestic forms of crime, particularly economic crime (illegal exchange of currency, import of some scarce commodities etc.) were to certain extend tolerated by the regime, although they had some characteristics of organised crime as described in the West. The offences were carried out by usually small crime-groups, characterised by a division of labour, some having corrupt contacts with officials.[1] The means of corruption consisted of providing some scarce goods or services including 'special' ones like prostitution.[2]

It means that though officially denied even in the former CSSR there were some tokens of small scale organised criminal activities, including corrupt contacts with law enforcement officers, state and communist party officials, but they existed relatively isolated without international connections. They were based on a social and economic structure that differed substantially from the open capitalist societies.

Emerged in the so-called shadow economy in the former CSSR, forms of local organised crime reflected its structure and scale. Compared to the shadow economy in the former USSR, it did not match its importance in economic and political terms. Under the conditions of a state managed 'deficit economy', the shadow economy took the form of a system of mutual exchanges of advantages and scarce goods and services, which were available only to some privileged professions ('networks of mutual favours'). These exchange relationships involved usually the abuse of state property for personal purposes. This phenomenon was very common and widespread, but it still concerned mainly minor offences, though some succeeded in amassing a substantial, undeclared wealth.

It should be reminded, that the Czech society was going through deep historical experience, connected to a radical conversion of officially presented value systems and behaviour patterns during the lifetime of the last three generations, which affected the identity and certitude of the people. Under the rule of the communist regime the power of the state was in principle superior to the law. The individual has been reduced to an object, manipulated by the state power. This resulted in an engrained distrust and decreased feeling of belonging to or a responsibility to a community. The informal social control nearly disappeared or it was limited to the trusted circle of the own family. The society became more and more atomised, sceptical and dissimulating. The tendency to take advantage and prejudice the own vicinity and of course the authorities became one of the important outlets of 'purposeful' behaviour. Moreover, the communist regime in the former CSSR nationalised nearly all the property exceeding the personal needs of people. Property had no longer concrete owners: it was designated as 'all-people-property' and therefore it became in fact anonymous. Gradually the relationship of people to this anonymous property became divorced from the daily morality. Abusing or even pilfering this property became accepted as something not uncommon or reprehensible (Osmančík, 1996).

---

[1] For example illegal changers of foreign currency (veksláci), overtly operating mainly on the streets in full sight of the police.

[2] Prostitution has not been criminalised in the Penal Code, but it was prosecuted as so-called 'parasitism'. Nevertheless, the activities of networks, composed of prostitutes, taxi drivers, receptionists in hotels etc. were tolerated and prostitutes, working in hotels were used by the secret police as informers.

AFTER THE CHANGE

After 1989 our society has undergone the deep conversion. This conversion was ' conditio sine qua non' to overcome the period of stagnation and isolation and to open up the space to establish the democratic society. Nevertheless, the development brought some risky factors that must be taken into account.

The fundamental economic transformation was connected with an enormous shift of property, with the broad privatisation process of the previous state property and with a rapid establishing of a liberal market under a situation of critical shortage of capital. The economy broadened significantly. The motto of this process was that it is more required to keep up its speed than to slow down it by excessive control and the application of strict legal provisions. It meant that the opportunities for various illegal activities increased, which was not only due to the economic transformation process itself and the unpreparedness of the legislation and supervising authorities, but also due to the insufficient control and the underestimation of an adequate legal framework for this process.

The open economy and a free and open society requires open borders, which implies that the restrictions concerning the movement of people, goods and capital had to be abolished. It is obvious that the CSFR and later the Czech Republic is geographically favourably situated between the states of European Union and the states of former socialist block. Czech territory is well accessible from the countries of former Soviet Union and from the Balkan. Consequently this means broad opportunities for transit, for the mobility of goods, capital and people in the legal but as well as the illegal economy, which implies an abuse of the Czech facilities as a starting point for the 'penetration' from East to the countries of EU and visa versa (for example the sale of stolen cars). At the same time the Czech Republic, as well as the whole European continent, has been affected by a wave of migration, including the illegal one. The Czech Republic is mainly a transit country. However, the number of migrants crossing our territory have reached tens of thousands per year, contributing to an increase of the foreigners who remain behind in this country.

The Czech law enforcement authorities, i.e. police, courts, state attorney offices, customs service went through a fundamental reform, affecting the organisational structure as well as the staff. It resulted not only in an exodus of officials compromised by the collaboration with the communist regime (and sometimes not compromised but simply wanted to be better paid), temporarily weakening the effectiveness of the police and the justice system, which was not redeemed by the recruitment of many new people, sometimes without experience and required qualifications. The justice and police bodies has been understaffed and unprepared to face the growth of crime or to solve the more sophisticated problems resulting from the changes in the economy, from the privatisation process and other social-economic forces. In addition the justice and police are still suffering from the mistrust of people (Scheinost, Cejp, Musil, Brabcová, Budka, 1997).

The Czech legislation went through a similar fundamental rebuilding and the means of effectively combatting new forms of crime have only been recently developed. For example, the provision concerning the so-called criminal conspiracy was introduced into the Penal Code in 1995. In the same year the possibility to obtain information concerning the bank secrecy for the purpose of police investigation and prosecution was enlarged under certain conditions. At the same time the witness protection was modified too. The amendment of the Police Law enabling to use undercover agents has also been enacted in 1995. The anti-money laundering act has come into force only a year later (Karabec, 1998).

From the previous description it may be concluded that after 1989 Czech society had come at risk for being highly attractive for the penetration by cross-border crime and foreign organised groups, along with the potential rise of domestic forms of organised crime on the background of increasing crime rate in general.

THE EXPANSION OF CRIME IN GENERAL

The increase of the crime rate was huge: the number of registered crimes tripled in 1993 compared with 1989 (1989: 120,768 registered crimes, 1993: 398,505), followed by a slight decrease and relative stabilisation. In the last two years the crime rate rose again. Not only the numbers but also the structure of crime has changed. The growth of property crimes has been the most remarkable. Their proportion in the total of all registered crimes increased from 49% in 1989 to 82% in 1993 and 74% in 1998, which was the most significant factor contributing to the growth of the general crime rate. As far as economic crime is concerned, it cannot be compared with the situation before 1989, because of the fundamental change of the economic landscape and legislation. Nevertheless, from the beginning of 1990s till 1995 its proportion did not exceed 5%, but in 1997 it rose to 7,5% and 8,5% in 1998. Much more significant is the amount of damage caused by economic crime. Since 1995 the economic crime accounted for 60% of the total loss caused by criminality (in 1998 it was 62,7%). Expressed in Czech crowns it means 14 billions Czech crowns in 1995 and almost 21 billions in 1998. Compared with 1990 the loss caused by economic crime expressed in Czech crowns have risen fourteen times, corrected for inflation. The relative number of violent crimes decreased, but its absolute numbers increased twice in comparison with 1989 and 1998. A growing brutality could be observed. The most serious offence, i.e. murder, shows a rising tendency: 126 murders and attempted murders have been registered in 1989, contrasting with more than 200 from 1990 till 1997, being surpassed in 1998 with 300 cases. A remarkable increase could be observed also in the number of drug related offences. In 1993, only 261 drug related offences were registered and 251 offenders were prosecuted. In 1998 5234 such offences were registered and 1355 offenders were prosecuted with a growing participation of juveniles and women.

The outcomes of victim research provide an illustration for the crime statistics. The international comparative victim research, carried out in the Czech Republic in 1992 and 1996, shows that the personal experience with eleven selected kinds of crime had increased. While in 1991 every fourth citizen became a victim of at least one of the selected crimes, in 1995 it was every third citizen. With this rate of victimisation the Czech society has not been slow in reaching the level of the industrialised western countries and in some aspects (or kinds of crime) even surpassed the European average (Válková, 1999). The impact of crime has become a part of personal experience of a substantial part of population, indeed. It could result in the radicalisation of the public opinion in the sense of a growing fear of crime and a development of more severe punitive attitudes or -on the contrary- the acceptation of crime as a 'normal' part of public life. Both tendencies could be observed in the Czech society.

A remarkable and serious phenomenon is that the proportion of habitual offenders (recidivists) of the total prosecuted offenders has decreased from 41% in 1991, 33% in 1993, to 29% in 1995, after which it stabilised at this level. The number of all prosecuted offenders increased from 1989 till 1998 with 58,000, while the number of recidivists increased with only 8,500. This means that an increasing number of people with no previous criminal record begins to engage in crime. Though these first offenders cover all age groups, there is a predominance of younger people. People with higher professional qualification and organisational ability are represented as well. In connection with other criminogenic factors this may provide the breeding ground for a potential collaboration with (foreign) criminal organisations and for the emergence of sophisticated domestic organised forms of criminal activities.

The resulting crime rate in the CR. is not extraordinary compared with the one in the developed western countries. However, the question remains why this increase took place so rapidly and why so many people started breaking the law.

To answer this question we have to take into account the profound changes in social consciousness. The social structure in the Czech republic has altered, together with the development of new values and social status symbols. The prevalent liberal attitude that has determined the major social climate, created another pattern of desirable social behaviour based on values like the individual liberty, success in business, a high material standard of living, the principle of competition and the criterion of high performance. Some social groups have been characterised by high aspirations and by the effort to accomplish a rapid vertical mobility accompanied by impatience and by a relatively strong orientation to consumerism. However, not all of them have been capable of fulfilling their ambitions while remaining within the law. Some people who have been flung into 'open space' of individual liberty and free market with the new vision of personal success often did so with weakened moral standards due to the situation under the previous regime. Other social groups have been marginalised in the turmoil of the social changes and subsequently felt frustrated because of the inability to reach the coveted standard of living and a higher social status.

The social consciousness after 1989 was characterised by a high level of positive expectation. Based on the research carried out in 1991 45% of people expected the rapid improvement of the social and economic situation in the near future. It was found in 1994 that 33% of population expected the improvement of their level of live within one year, 64% of people within five years (Mladá fronta Dnes, 1994). If this high level of positive expectations came in conflict with the reality (and it came) it may cause an increased risk of deviant or even pathological forms of solution. Taking into account the previously

mentioned criminogenic factors the trends in the development of crime may be
interpreted along three possible lines:

1. Crime as the product of the process of social disintegration resulting from the
    transformation of the Czech society. This disintegration manifests itself in a form
    of disorganisation of social institutions and social relations as well as in a form of
    disorientation, leading to a change and relativisation of social values and
    patterns, which could be the explanation of some part of the criminality of
    youngsters and first-time offenders.
2. Crime as a rational choice of an adaptation strategy. This means the intentional
    and willfully law breaking. This conduct derives from a rational evaluation of
    potential gains and risks with regard to the opportunities offered by the social
    situation (see the Merton's concept of deviant behaviour as an innovative reaction
    of adaptation strategy). This may be an adequate explanation for the criminality
    of some new offenders or rather 'crime-entrepreneurs'.
3. Crime as a routine activity connected with the daily way of life. It reflects the
    classical social background of crime, the crime that originates from a criminal
    subculture. The criminogenity of this milieu has been strengthened by the growth
    of various social problems accompanying the transformation of the post 1989
    Czech society (criminality of Romanies, migrants, homeless people etc.
    Lubelcová, 1998).

The proportion of foreigners in the number of registered and cleared up crimes is not
very high, but the number of *prosecuted* foreigners has been steadily increasing. If the
citizens of the Slovak Republic are omitted the proportion of foreigners of the prosecuted
offenders has increased from 2.3% in 1994 to 3.7% in 1998. Even if the Slovak citizens
are included, the portion of foreigners in the number of prosecuted offenders would still
be significantly lower than in some neighbouring countries such as Austria and Germany.
Nevertheless we can ignore neither the continuing increase of the number and of the
proportion of foreigners (except Slovaks) of the total number of offenders, nor their share
in some kinds of crime. For example, in 1997, the involvement of foreigners in robberies
was 15.4 %, in murders 10.1 %, in rapes 11.2 %, in pandering 11.3 %, in frauds 15.5 %,
in pickpocketing 21.5 %.

The main part of the criminal activities of foreigners was committed in 1998 by
citizens of the following states: Slovak Republic (38.4% of all prosecuted foreigners,
especially crimes against property), Ukraine (18.5%, but 24.5% of them were engaged in
the violent crimes), Vietnam (9.4%, especially economic crime), Poland (5.4%), Bulgaria
(4.0%), Germany (3.3 %), Yugoslavia (2.5 %), Romania (2.2 %), Russia (2.2 %). The
citizens from the European countries constituted in this year 85 % of all prosecuted
foreign offenders, the citizens from Asian countries 12.2 %, of Africa 1 %, of North
America only 0.8 %. Crimes committed by foreigners have been concentrated mainly in
the Prague region, North Moravia and in the frontier districts.

Regarding the foreign citizens convicted for crimes committed in an organised group
during the last years (with the exception of Slovak citizens), most of them are citizens of

the former Yugoslavia, former USSR, Vietnam and Colombia. The reasons for conviction were predominantly drug trafficking, blackmailing and robbery.

The source of the above mentioned figures is the statistics of the Police of the Czech Republic. This statistics does not include the special data on (cross-border) organised crime. But on the basis of qualitative analysis of police information and of the criminological research on organised crime, which began in 1993, we may formulate some characteristics of the cross-border organised crime in the Czech republic.

THE DEVELOPMENT OF ORGANISED CRIME GROUPS

Even if the influences of foreign crime groups would be disregarded, there was still sufficient potential for the emergence of domestic organised crime groups. Under the previous regime there existed some criminal groups with a certain level of organisation; there were also people who got rich in so-called shadow economy; there were people who covered and profited from such criminal activities and all of them suddenly got a chance to take advantage of the changing social conditions to carry on their activities in the new favourable situation, adopting quickly developing new opportunities.

The results of the 1997 expert inquiry among policemen, judges and state attorneys dealing with organised crime and the analysis of a few criminal cases and available information, lends evidence to the conclusion of the existence of Czech organised crime in the sense that there are a few groups composed of Czech citizens which manifest some of the distinguishing features of organised crime: groups at a certain level of organisation, structured and hierarchical which develop the systematic planned criminal activity in order to gain the maximal profit. The size of these groups is not very large and their criminal activities are rather specialised than versatile. Three types may be distinguished. Criminal groups of the first type develop their activities predominantly in drug trafficking, thefts and the smuggling of stolen cars. Criminal groups of the second type are involved in activities which are classified as *economic* and *financial* crime.[3] The third most widespread activity of Czech organised criminal groups has been organised prostitution, pornography and women trafficking and the organisation of illegal migration.

According to experts the members of Czech organised groups have two types of social or criminal backgrounds: there are members with *no* previous criminal records ('respectable' citizens), and members who were engaged in the so-called shadow economy already before 1989. In both groups young men prevail. These findings correspond to the data on the criminal situation in general (Scheinost, 1998).

Notwithstanding these findings, available evidence indicates that the major part of the criminal organisations operating in the Czech Republic are still of foreign origin. Some of the activities of foreign groups have been furthered by the existing backgrounds of their compatriots living in the Czech Republic. Its history goes back to the era before

---

[3] The qualification these economic but criminal activities as organised crime is still disputed, particular by the perpetrators themselves who would rather consider it 'sophisticated business practice'.

1989, when about 100,000 foreigners -workers, students, businessmen- stayed as legal residents in the CSFR. Their number decreased to about 35,000 in 1990 and then gradually increased again. Till the end of 1997 the number of foreigners who have obtained a permanent or long-term residence permit (i.e. beyond 180 days) in the CR. was about 210,000. Apart from the citizens of the Slovak Republic, the citizens of Ukraine, Poland and Vietnam are strongly represented in this group. In addition to this contingent of foreigners it should be reminded that every day about 1.3 million foreigners (including tourists) stay in the Czech Republic, i.e. more than 10% of the number of the Czech citizens. However, the number of foreigners that legally arrive in the Czech Republic significantly exceeds the number of those who leave the country. This difference also exceeds the number of residence permits. Most of those foreigners probably leave the Czech Republic illegally, but we may assume that a part of them stay behind illegally and represent a potential criminogenic risk. The increase of the number of people from abroad in the CR. was of course also influenced by the enormous migration wave using the Czech territory as a transit to the Europe Union or beyond.

The illegal migrants originated mainly from the Balkan countries and to a smaller extent from Asian and African countries. The special problem is represented by the Ukrainians entering the Czech Republic in search for employment, very often as illegal workers. Only a minor part of the migrants is interested in staying as refugees using the humanitarian care or asylum. Most of them want to leave the Czech territory as quickly as possible and to continue to the West. But certain number of them remain behind, constituting the ethnic background that may serve as a basis for foreign organised criminals. Criminal organisations of the same ethnic origin may search for and find helpers, aids, but very often also the first victims among their compatriots.

Cross-border organised crime is undoubtedly present in the Czech Republic and criminal organisations operating along multiple national links, with the leading unit or organisers outside the Czech Republic, have been identified and analysed.

Due to the fundamental change after 1989, the Czech Republic became much more attractive for the penetration of various forms and various groups of organised crime from abroad. During a relatively short time span the Czech Republic became an important link in the international network of drug trafficking, illegal migration, import and export of stolen cars and probably of money laundering as well. In addition, big criminal organisations from abroad probably try to use the Czech Republic as a basis for a further expansion of their activities. Therefore they refrain from carrying out overt criminal activities in this country, but they try to establish a kind of bridgehead using the legitimate means of investment, establishing companies and firms, purchase of the real estate etc. At the same time a few smaller organised groups coming from abroad began to develop their criminal activities in various crime markets like drugs and racketeering.

In the Czech Republic, we can observe activities of criminal groups from the former USSR (the Ukraine, Russia, the Caucasus area), of Chinese groups (differentiated according to the place of origin and dialect) and of Balkan groups (mainly from the former Yugoslavia, especially Albanians from the Kosovo region, and Bulgarian groups). To a lesser extent, the activities of Italian, Nigerian and Colombian crime groups have been recorded. A certain portion of the organised crime is committed by groups of

Vietnamese, Arabs, and marginally also, by people of some other nationalities like Poles and Romanians.

The activities of crime groups from the former USSR can be observed at two levels. At a higher level the activities are carried out by members representing the connecting links of large criminal organisations. They are not themselves involved in any 'visible' criminal activity, but they have an interest in establishing contacts, legitimate companies, in investment and financial operations. At a lower level, we can observe the activities of smaller crime groups specialised in particular criminal activities including (violent) crimes: racketeering, organising prostitution and women trafficking, trafficking in arms, thefts, smuggling of cars and organising illegal labour rackets.

The Chinese activities are mainly focussed on the organisation of illegal migration of their compatriots, to establish possibilities for money laundering (network of restaurants, shops, trade companies) and trade contacts. The 'visible' criminal activities (racketeering, loan sharking, prostitution and relatively frequent violent conflicts) usually take place inside the Chinese community with a clear effort to avoid conflicts with the outside environment.

Groups of Albanians from the Kosovo region are mainly active in drug trafficking (heroin), in organising illegal migration, car thefts and smuggling, and in blackmailing and racketeering. Their organisations operate in various countries with links in multiple countries and 'supreme' leading units outside the Czech territory.

The activities of Vietnamese take place all over the Czech Republic and consist mainly in smuggling commodities and breaking trade mark regulations, usually brand piracy. The number of acts of violence within the Vietnamese community has been increasing. The effort to achieve an economic expansion is evident and confirmed, for example, by the investment in the Czech Republic, by establishing firms and companies concealing the Vietnamese capital.

The Italian activities whose linkage to the Italian organised crime (Camorra) is supposed to be limited to building up contacts and trade network consisting of legal companies.

Arabs have been mainly active in the Czech Republic in drug trafficking. However, even in those activities, the citizens from the former Yugoslavia have taken over the leading role and have reduced the Arabs to serve mainly as local dealers.

Nigerians emerged as relatively new participants on the drug market and their activities reveal a smartly operating organisation. At present they probably use the Czech Republic as a transit country. However, Nigerian criminal activities can also be observed in the economic field, particularly financial frauds.

Regarding Colombian drug cartels (especially the Cali cartel) the Czech Republic probably serves as a transit zone, where they try to establish a trade territorial connections. Recently, Bulgarian citizens have become involved in drug trafficking. Previously, Bulgarian crime groups in the Czech Republic had specialised in car thefts and smuggling (Macháček, Rumpl, 1997).

Organised crime in the territory of the Czech Republic manifests itself by a number of criminal activities, whose extent and frequency have been changing in time. The most frequent criminal activities of the organised groups (assessed by the police experts) are traditionally thefts and smuggling of cars, organised prostitution and 'white-slave' trafficking. A significant increase has been recorded in the field of production, smuggling and distribution of drugs. The crime connected with drugs appeared in 1995 at the top of the activities of the organised crime in the CR. and this trend was confirmed in 1996 as well as in 1998. In the recent period also the importance of tax, credit, insurance and bill of exchange frauds have increased (Cejp, 1998).

According to the available information from the Czech milieu, the core of all groups maintain their ethnic integrity. Usually ethnic mixing takes place at the lowest level of the organisation or group only, i.e. at the level of executive functions.

Some ethnic groups are more open to co-operation with other ethnic groups in their criminal activities, like people from the former Yugoslavia. Others, clinging to their cultural, historical and linguistic differences, strictly maintain their ethnic exclusiveness, like the Chinese and partly Vietnamese groups, that typically seek to attain a maximal isolation from the Czech environment.

In the groups of foreign origin, Czechs provide the 'upperworld' services for leaders of the groups, acting as advisers, lawyers, persons mediating contacts, straw men for companies and, most often, performing executive tasks as ordinary members of the criminal groups (couriers, smugglers, etc.). Czechs, however, are also sometimes in the position of customers, who buy the commodities and services supplied illegally by foreign groups (Scheinost, 1996).

CROSS-BORDER ORGANISED CRIME TRADE

Cross-border organised crime trade activities have been very versatile. They involve trafficking in illegal commodities as drugs, in legitimate (taxed) goods and custom frauds, as well as trafficking in human beings. The trafficking in heroin provides a good example of the Czech situation. The Czech Republic is situated on the northern branch of the so-called Balkan route. This branch branches off in the Czech region into three destinations: Scandinavia, Great Britain and Germany. The ring leaders of the organisations involved in heroin trafficking is composed of Turks, but in the Czech Republic we encounter only the executives at middle level, who are Kosovo-Albanians. They manage the transport of heroin across the Czech territory and handle the distribution in this country (the distribution is sometimes also carried out by Arabs). The Czechs serve as dealers or couriers, but they show a tendency to rise to higher positions in the hierarchy. In addition there are also relatively independent Czech groups, which purchase heroin from Albanian suppliers and transport it to the West or distribute it on their own account. Other Czech groups are involved in the production of the special Czech synthetic drug 'pervitin'.

Regarding the trafficking in legitimate goods we may presume the extensive involvement of Czech groups. The trafficking in object of arts (mostly stolen from Czech churches, museums and art galleries), the illegal import of alcohol (declared as another commodity in order to pay a lower tax rate and custom duties), frauds connected with import and export of so-called light mineral oil, abusing the differential custom and tax rates for light oil and for naphtha, are examples of cross-border activities of Czech groups in this field.

Illegal trafficking in human beings is one of the most important activities of the transnational organised crime in the Czech Republic. The research on the phenomenon of illegal migration showed that the number of illegal migrants are around tens of thousands per year. These figures include only the numbers of persons, who were detected and apprehended while crossing the borders. There is evidence that organised crime groups profit from this illegal migration by providing well paid services: forged passports and other travel documents, transport, accommodation, smuggling migrants across the border, etc.

The main part of the detected migrants consists of citizens from the Balkan countries. During the last four years the portion of apprehended migrants from other European countries significantly decreased in comparison with 1994, whereas the portion of people from Asia rapidly increased (*see the table*).

Table 1

	1994 %	1995 %	1996 %	1997 %	I-VI/1999 %
European countries	84.1	62.4	66.9	64.0	57.7
Asian countries	11.4	33.2	26.2	30.2	40.0
African countries	3.8	2.9	4.7	3.8	
other countries	0.7	1.5	2.2	2.0	2.3

Migrants from Balkan countries usually arrive to the Czech Republic by buses and trains via Hungary and Slovakia, but the illegal pedestrian traffic across the Czech-Slovakian border has increased gradually. The migration route from Asia leads across the area of the former USSR. Asian migrants arrive through the territory of Russia and Ukraine to the Czech Republic by plane or train (more rarely by other means of traffic), most often via Slovakia. This route is also used by some migrants from Africa, after they arrive in the former USSR.

The majority of migrants attempt to cross the Czech Republic to enter the Federal Republic of Germany (64.7 % of all apprehended migrants in 1997 were detected while crossing the borders from the Czech Republic to the Germany).

Only a few citizens from the former USSR (mostly from Ukraine) and a part of the migrants from China try to settle for some time as illegal workers in the Czech Republic. The greater majority of migrants remains in the Czech Republic until they are able to cross the western border (75 % of the migrants attached in 1997 crossed the borders within five days of their arrival to the Czech Republic).

Even though the volume of illegal migration in 1994 and 1995 decreased (in absolute numbers), compared to 1993, the proportion of migrant smuggling (i.e. organised form of illegal migration) has increased. Since 1996 the number of illegal migrants has been growing again.

The service of the smugglers or a smugglers organisation has mainly been used by the citizens of the former Yugoslavia states, Romania and those from Asia and Africa. In general, it is quite an exception when migrants from distant countries try to cross borders without smuggler's service. In addition the Asian migrants most often use forges or tampered documents.

Stricter measures (visas, organisational measures, reinforcement of frontier police, etc.) result in an improvement of the migration organisation. Uncontrolled, individual migration and individual smugglers has been replaced by organisations by now. These organisations are highly developed and their activities has been spreading world wide.

Ring leaders of the international organisations tend to operate outside the Czech Republic, but lower level executive staff operates on the Czech territory, usually seeking a legal cover for their activities and either knows the Czech milieu or uses Czech contact persons. The Chinese tend to use Vietnamese in order to mediate the necessary contacts.

In these organisation or more precise in their units operating in Czech Republic Czechs citizens use to occupy executive positions as smugglers: drivers, persons providing transport and accommodation. In most cases they are low educated youngsters. Only a smaller part of the Czech aids come from the criminal milieu or have previously committed some crimes. This applies mainly to the above mentioned contact persons, who have the task to establish contacts with the 'organisers' belonging to other nationalities in the Czech milieu, including the recruitment of persons for the executive functions. The findings show that these contact persons are often middle aged.

Among the smugglers, a minority of people of other nationalities can observed too. The number of Slovaks increased, particularly involved in smuggling of people across the Czech - Slovak border. There are also Vietnamese smugglers (mostly used for smuggling Chinese people). The portion of Yugoslavian nationalities among smugglers decreased. Smugglers of non-Czech nationality are more specialised in the directions and routes of smuggling as well as in smuggling of people of a particular nationality (like the Vietnamese smuggling Chinese). The sums of money paid by migrants to the organisers range from hundreds to thousands US dollars or German marks, according to the type and complexity of the service.

Based on the research we may outline the probable structure of such an transnational smuggler organisation operating in the CR.:

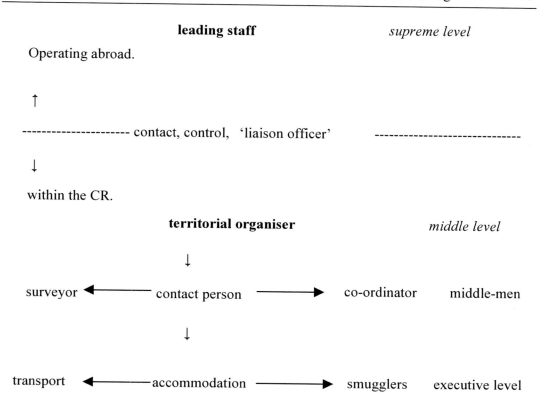

The functions of surveyor and co-ordinator are probably present within larger organisations and may be combined with some other function. In the Chinese organisations there are Vietnamese at the executive level; only the function of accommodation provider is exclusively fulfilled by Chinese members.

It is likely that such a linear structure has mainly developed witin organisations smuggling people from Asia. It is not quite clear whether the Balkan organisations have the similar linear structure or whether they have formed various local cells cooperating at an equal level. According to experts violence is considered the usual method to maintain the internal discipline or to solve conflicts arising from competition.

The forgery of documents and the attempts of corruption are often significant features of the activity of smuggler organisations. There is no evidence that human smugglers are involved in other kinds of organised cross-border crime (for example smuggling of drugs or illegal arms trafficking). Despite this specialisation one should not underestimate the possibility to use the established structures and the profits from the organised illegal migration for the other, possibly more dangerous objectives.

The occurrence of the organised illegal migration in the Czech Republic is expected to persist, its extent depending on the international situation, as well as on a increasing importance of the Czech Republic as the migration terminus. A development towards a more sophisticated organisation is also expected, together with potential connections with other forms of organised crime. It is likely that the control will remain in the hands of international organisations in which Czechs will less often occupy higher positions.

These organisations will dominate the market and the individual organisers and groups will participate only on a minor scale (Scheinost, 1995).

Trafficking of women is also considered to be the widespread form of cross-border organised crime in this country. The increase of prostitution is considered to be one of the most important social problems for the Czech society. Prostitution itself has not been criminalised and a large part of the women involved in prostitution pursue still this activity without compulsion. However, as a result of the high profits a number of women who have been forced into prostitution, at least at the beginning of their prostitute career (by pimps, organisers or initially by their own social situation), has grown. Women involved in prostitution are abused to earn money for their 'protectors', pimps. This kind of prostitution is qualified and prosecuted by our Penal Code as *procuring*.

Organised procuring is usually committed by a groups of persons operatinging with a certain division of tasks: the tipper who looks for women and girls; the caller or 'recruiting officer' who contacts and recruits them often under false pretentions, the transporter (often a taxi driver); the procurer-pimp; the middleman who mediates the contact between customer and prostitute, etc. Czech street and road prostitution is largely controled by Romanies, some of whom have contacts abroad including the cross-border exchange of prostitutes. 'Indoor' prostitution is concentrated in night clubs and similar entertainment establishments, mainly managed by Czech owners, but sometimes with the participation of foreign capital. coming often from abroad, like the former Soviet Union or Germany. These night clubs employ usually Czech women, but there are also girls from Belarus, Ukraine and in one odd case Philippines. They are imported by organised foreign groups and delivered to the Czech brothel keepers. This is not a 'free service': usually the victims must also pay a part of their income to the purveyor as well to the owner of the nightclub.

The Czech Penal Code considers 'white slavery' (cross-border traffic of women for prostitution) a special form of procuring. The contemporary boom of this form of organised crime is caused by the substantial demand for 'cheap sex' in the developed countries and by the demand for the 'new faces' in the sex industry, i.e. for girls from Middle and Eastern Europe, apart from South America and Asia.

The Czech Republic has become the crossing point of the international white-slave trafficking between East and West. Some experts estimate, that since the beginning of the 1990s tens of thousands of women destined for prostitution in Western Europe passed the Czech territory. The Czech Republic does not only serve as the transit country for trafficking women from Russia, Belarus, Ukraine and Asia, but also as the source for exporting Czech girls and women. Well-organised and ramified groups from the former Soviet Union, China, former Yugoslavia, Poland as well as native offenders and people from Germany, Italy, Belgium, the Netherlands etc. are involved in this traffic.

Prostitutes who become victims of this traffic can be divided into two groups: the first group consists of women prostituting themselves voluntarily, consenting to being sent abroad. The second consists of women and girls who have been coerced into prostitution by physical or psychological violence. Most of them have been promised to work abroad as waitress, dancers, hostess, models etc. Some of them have even been kidnapped from their place of residence and transported to the place of destination.

Groups involved in the white-slave trafficking exporting Czech women abroad consist of about 5 to 10 members with similar division of tasks as mentioned above, enlarged with a seller having contacts abroad. This seller takes over the girls from procurers and 'recruiting officers' and delivers them to the purchaser - mostly a foreigner - who sends them to the place of destination. These groups may also employ persons providing the forged travel documents, the guards who look after the girls during transport, etc. (Trávníčková, 1995, Milička, 1997).

CONCLUSIONS

Before 1989 there were forms of crime bearing some features of organised crime but they took the shape corresponding with the previous political, economic and social system. Groups were mostly of domestic origin and their activities had rarely a cross-border character.

After the fall of the communist regime, the isolation was lifted and the borders opened simultaneously with the establishing of open market economy. The opened space was used for involving the Czech Republic into the international networks of cross-border crime and for developing sophisticated forms of organised criminal activities. Nevertheless the situation in the Czech Republic has developed to such a critical nature as for example in Russia or Ukraine, where Louisa I.Shelley speaks about 'political-criminal nexus' (Shelley, 1999), but it is obvious that the international cross-border crime uses this country not only as a logistic opportunity or as a transit country but also as the location for direct criminal activities. There are not only the groups and organisations from abroad that develop their cross-border criminal activities, but there are also the groups of domestic Czech origin involved in the international networks and crime markets. The speed of the process of formation and penetration of those groups and organisations was stipulated by the specific factors resulting on the one hand from the rapid transformation of our society and on the other hand from the lowering of social consciousness caused by the character of the previous regime. Recently we face the same problems with regard to the phenomenon of cross-border crime as the developed western countries.

LITERATURE

Cejp, M., *Expertízy k problematice organizovaného zločinu* (The expertise on the problem of organised crime), Prague, IKSP, 1998

Karabec, Z., *Účinnost legislativních změn ve vztahu k organizovanému zločinu* (The effectiveness of legislation changes in relation to organised crime), Prague, IKSP, 1998

Lubelcová, G., *Kriminalita v kontexte sociálnej transformácie na Slovensku* (Criminality in the context of social transformation in Slovakia), in: Radičová,I., Vieme čo odmietame a vieme čo chceme?, Bratislava, SPACE, 1998, pp. 131-134

Macháček, Z., Rumpl, T., Zahraniční skupiny organizovaného zločinu a jejich aktivity na českém území (Foreign organised crime groups and their activites on the territory of the Czech Republic), in: Nožina, M.(ed.), *Mezinárodní organizovaný zločin v ČR*, Prague, Ústav mezinárodních vztahů, 1997

Milička, J., Obchod s lidmi (Trafficking in people). In: M. Nožina, (ed.), *Mezinárodníorganizovaný zločin v ČR* (Transnational organised crime in the CR). Prague, Ústav mezinárodních vztahů, 1997

Mladá fronta Dnes (journal), 23.2.1994

Osmančík, O., paper presented on the conference 'Penal Justice and Crime Control in the CR', Prague 13.-14.5.1996

Scheinost, M., *Nelegální migrace a převaděčství jako jedna z aktivit organizovaného zločinu* (Illegal migration and smuggling as one of the activities of organised crime), Prague, IKSP, 1995

Scheinost, M., *Trestná činnost cizích státních příslušníků v ČR a etnický faktor v organizované kriminalitě* (The criminal activity of foreigners in the CR and ethnic factor in organised crime). Prague, IKSP, 1996

Scheinost, M., Cejp, M., Musil, J., Budka, I., Brabcová, I., *Výzkum struktury, forem a možností postihu organizovaného zločinu v České republice* (Research on the structure, forms and recourse of organised crime in the CR), Prague, IKSP, 1997

Scheinost, M., *Organizovaná trestná činnost občanů ČR* (Organised criminal activity of Czech citizens), Prague, IKSP, 1998

Shelley, L.I., The Political-Criminal Nexus: Russian-Ukrainian Case Studies, *Trends in Organised Crime*, 1999, Vol. 4, *nr.3*, 81-107

Trávníčková, I., *Prostituce jako jedna z možých aktivit organizovaného zločinu* (Prostitution as one of the possible activities of organised crime), Prague, IKSP, 1995

Válková, J., Jak je u nás bezpčěně? Hlavní výsledky výzkumu obětí trestných činů v ČR. In: *K problematice obětí trestných činů a výsledkům výzkumu obětí v České republice* (What is the safety ? The main results of the research of victims of crime in the CR), Prague, IKSP, 1999

THE NEED FOR A MULTIDISCIPLINARY AND PROACTIVE APPROACH TO HUMAN TRAFFICKING. REFLECTIONS FROM TWO PILOTS

B. de Ruyver, K. van Impe and J. Meese
Professor in Criminology and Researchers
at the University of Gent, Belgium

INTRODUCTION

During the last decades the phenomenon of trafficking in human beings has taken a universal dimension. This is due to political and socio-economic developments. For example, there are the drastic (r)evolutions in Eastern European countries, there is the persistent political commotion in Africa, South Asia and a number of countries in Central and Latin America and some Central- and South American States, as well as the escalation of economic problems in Southeast Asia. Individuals as well as criminal organisations use the weak spots in legislation to realise their ambitions. These weak spots are to be situated in the field of diverging regulations between different states, but also in the context of national legislation in the countries of origin and destination.

World-wide, the desire to migrate is continuously increasing, but the legal means to do so are, certainly in the United States and Europe, smaller then ever. Consequently, black markets and criminal organisations meet this demand by offering an illegal supply of migration possibilities. Consequently, the migration issue in general is often associated with illegality and criminality, while criminal organisations find a new area of business As the phenomenon of trafficking in human beings manifested itself during the last decade, policy makers were put under pressure to come up with proper responses. Public concern about the problematic character and the dangerous consequences of human trade led to various initiatives, on both the national and international level.

Three of the four on research projects on human trafficking received funding under the STOP-programme. The first project studied the phenomenon of trafficking in human beings from Poland and Hungary to Belgium and other EU Member States. The second project examined the feasibility and the opportunity of the international gathering and administration of data concerning missing and sexually exploited minors. The third STOP-project aimed at evaluating the phenomenon of transmigration via Poland with a view to controlling human trafficking.

A fourth project was funded by the Belgian State Secretariat for Development Co-operation. It was a two-year bilateral project, promoting a multidisciplinary approach to deal with human trafficking between Belgium and the Philippines.

A common conclusion emerging from these studies is that restrictive measures alone cannot stop human trafficking, as there are powerful push factors in countries of origin as well as pull factors in receiving countries. In order to be effective, a strategy to combat human trafficking needs to be sufficiently comprehensive to address both sets of factors. The research findings have clearly shown that there is no easy or uni-dimensional solution to human trafficking, as the phenomenon originates from a complex set of factors, often in combination with one another.

An effective strategy must address various aspects and must combine and balance punitive and preventive measures, law enforcement and protection of basic human rights, stricter border control and the remotion of the causes of illegal migration. Measures taken by the countries of origin, transit and destination must be part of an integrated approach. There is a real danger that, in order to curb human trafficking as quickly as possible, the receiving countries would attach a disproportionate importance to a set of narrow and ad hoc measures, focussing on short-term cures through border controls and punitive action. It would be unfortunate if preventive action to remove the causes is neglected or receives only scant attention (Ghosh, 1998).

Hereafter, before discussing the need for a multidisciplinary and pro-active approach towards human trafficking, the phenomenon will be analysed and some research findings discussed.

THE ANALYSIS OF THE PHENOMENON

If we consider the case of Poland the causes of trafficking in human beings can be tentatively identified as follows.

First, the social-economic situation should be examined. The economic revolution that followed the radical political and social changes in several Central European countries since 1989 had a tremendous impact. Although Poland managed to control inflation, the country faced a huge level of unemployment. Mainly young people, aged between 15 and 25, and especially large sections of the female population shared this fate. Besides, the very weak social safety net with extremely low social security benefits, the high burden of tax, the lack of social retraining and reintegration and the need for proper education funds encouraged more and more (young) people to emigrate to the West (Hummel, 1993; Franssen, 1994). Apart from these economic motives, however, it is essential to recognise that for most migrants the desire to improve the quality of their life or enhance their personal status have provided the incentive for migration (Kupryashinka, 1996).

Second, human trade became possible because of the increased freedom of movement (Bruinsma and Meershoek, 1999). Therefore, the existence of a fourth wave[1] of female victims of trafficking in human beings to Europe can be noticed, coming from Central and Eastern Europe (Hungary, Poland, Czech Republic, Russia and Romania) since 1994. The first wave was made up of Asian women (mainly from Thailand and the Philippines, since 1992), the second came from South America (Dominican Republic and Colombia, and to a lesser extent also Venezuela, Brazil and Ecuador since 1993) and the third wave came from Africa (Ghana and Nigeria, since 1993).

The existence of criminal organisations in the countries of origin also facilitates human trade. The fact that smuggling and trafficking in human beings is associated with huge profits and that the burden of proof in cases of smuggling and trafficking makes the work of the judicial authorities very difficult without the victim's co-operation, make this business attractive to criminal networks. In other words, the overall risk of trafficking in human beings is very low compared to other forms of trafficking, like trafficking in drugs. In addition, the profits are large.

The business of trafficking in human beings is increasingly controlled by Eastern European criminal organisations, operating both in the country where recruiting takes place as well as in the destination country. The organisations are characterised by a high degree of specialisation, extreme violence and involvement in other lucrative criminal activities such as vehicle theft and trafficking in arms and drugs.[2] The reason why the smuggling of migrants takes place from or via, Poland, is that certain criminals and their organisations in this country have established more effective networks, consisting of recruiters, traffickers and exploiters.[3]

Another important factor encouraging Polish women to migrate is their search for independence and emancipation. After the Communist regime was overthrown, the new establishment propagated the conservative family model. This evolution together with violence and alcohol abuse in many families, reinforced the intentions of many young women to look for a better future, and employment in the rich West. Women are therefore not only attracted by the myth of welfare and prosperity, but also by the

---

[1] See the IOM report Trafficking and Prostitution: the growing exploitation of migrant women from Central and Eastern Europe, May 1995, p. 8 and ff.

[2] See: Migrant Trafficking. Overwiew. Migration and Organized Crime, in *Trends in Organized Crime*, Transaction Periodicals Consortium Rutgers University, New Brunswick, New Jersey, with the Regional Strategy Information Center, Winter 1996, Vol. 2, no. 2, p. 58-90

[3] See: *Mensenhandel vanuit Centraal- en Oost-Europa*, afdeling Advies en Informatie, IRT-NON, Internationaal Politie-instituut Twente, Universiteit Twente, De Admiraal, Enschede, 1997, p. 43. Schiffer (1995) uses a very similar classification into three types (Schiffer, K.; *Migrationsprostitution und Frauenhandel. Strukturwandel der europäischen Sexindustrie*, Mr. A. de Graaf Stichting, January, 1995, 42-44). IOM has also worked out a system of classification, and distinguishes occasional traffickers, small well-organised trafficking rings and organised, international trafficking networks (IOM, *Trafficking of women to Countries of the European Union: Characteristics, Trends and Policy Issues*, Conference on trafficking in Women for Sexual Exploitation, Vienna, June, 1996, 10-11). See also Sieber (1998, p. 97-98); Flormann (1995) and Sieber and Bögel (1993)

prospects of (financial) independence and a stable family life based on the 'partnership model' where men and women as equals (Oleszczuk and Buchowska, 1996).

Finally, there is increasing competition in the sex industry. Some studies have estimated that more than 40 % of the women working in Warsaw as prostitutes are originally from the former Soviet Union (Gramenga, 1997). Their number is continuously growing, and the police report that Russian women successfully undermine the position of Polish prostitutes. For these Polish women, who are already working in the sex industry, migration to Germany, the Netherlands, Belgium or another Western European country, making use of traffickers if necessary, seems a plausible solution.

Therefore there are two groups of women coming to the West to work in the sex industry. On the one hand there are those who leave their country of origin knowing that they will end up in prostitution. In other words, these are prostitutes who are hoping to earn more money from doing the same work abroad. The large numbers of sex clubs, massage parlours and escort agencies mushrooming throughout Central and Eastern Europe are the ideal place from which to recruit Polish, Hungarian, Russian, Czech, Romanian and other women. Women in this category are therefore clearly aware of the job that will be awaiting them in the West. As far as these women are concerned, it is only possible to speak of trafficking in human beings if a conflict situation arises in the destination country: for example if they have to prostitute themselves under coercion, are resident in the country illegally and cannot voluntarily leave the sex industry or have to hand over large parts of their earnings.

There is a second group of people who are lured to the West under false pretences, using deceptive artifices, or who are simply deceived. For example, these people respond to the huge numbers of 'job offers' in Polish newspaper advertisements. They sign fictitious contracts of employment for a job in the West as cleaners, household helper, nurses, teachers etc. Others are persuaded by friends and acquaintances. Recruiters seem to be trustworthy, as they help to sort out the formalities, lend money for the trip and often drive customers to the destination country. In other words, recruiters take advantage of the desire and expectations of customers and victimise them by tying them in a web of dependency and obligation. Victims are employed in prostitution, in the construction sector, in cleaning companies, sewing workshops, where they are held and exploited by means of blackmail and violence.

In the case of the Philippines, human trafficking has to be seen as a component within the continuum of the migration cycle.

The phenomenon of trafficking in Filipino women has to be analysed within the context of the massive migration of Filipino workers since the 1970s. The largest wave of migration started in 1974 with the introduction of the Labour Code and the overseas employment program of the Philippines that came with it.[4] Since then and throughout the

---

[4] See Handbook on Labour Representation, Philippine Overseas Employment Administration 1995, 48 p, with annexes (Republic Act No. 8042.; Guidelines on the Training, Testing, Certification and Employment of Performing Artists. Department Order No. 3, Department of Labour and Employment, 1994; X., Foreign Service Circular No. 221-86, Ministry of Foreign Affairs; Laurel, S.H., Rules and Regulations Governing Overseas Employment, as amended 1991, Department of Labour and Employment; Administrative Rules

1980s, government policy-makers regarded overseas employment as a strategy to boost the sinking economy and partly solve the problem of unemployment, (Ofreneo and Ofreneo, 1998). Overseas employment became an integral and indispensable feature of the global Philippine economy. By the 1980s, the labour migration flow became increasingly feminised with the demand for nurses, domestic helpers, and other types of carers in East Asian countries, the Middle East, and Europe (Go, 1998). During the 1990s, however, government policy officially shifted from exporting the country's labour surplus to managing the tide of labour migration. In reality, the Philippine government currently promotes western lifestyle[5], propagated by media and the stories told by returning migrants. At the micro social level, Filipino women are accustomed to sacrifice herself to help and support the family. This[6] exposes them to many negative -- often exploitative -- experiences abroad, such as accepting dehumanising work or a marriage proposal from a stranger in order to earn money for the family back home.[7] Nevertheless, in this process, they acquire status and power within her family and in the community. The interaction between economic status (low family income), gender-role socialisation, and the family dynamics (problems/tensions) reinforced by pressures from significant others[8] make Filipino women vulnerable to trafficking.

Several factors are responsible for the attractiveness of Belgium, like other EU countries, as a country of destination. These forces include the high demand for cheap

---

and Regulations. Omnibus Rules and Regulations Implementing the Migrant and Workers and Overseas Filipinos Act 1995, Department of Foreign Affairs/Department of Labour and Employment).

[5] The economic situation in the countries of origin (not infrequently developing countries) is and remains the main cause of human trafficking. The fight against this phenomenon therefore requires a fundamental change in North-South/East-West relations and, besides fair international trade relations, solutions to the problem of debt repayment. Poverty is thus unarguable a very important push factor. However, it should be noted that the desire to raise the current standard of living is not infrequently the principal motivation. In other words, individual, well-considered motives, related to the desire to optimise the quality of life or to enhance personal status (and no so much the search for essential means of existence), underlie most migratory movements (Vasquez c.s. 1995).

[6] The problem of human trafficking has to be correlated to a significant cultural differentiation. Women play a highly subordinate role in the Philippines, Thailand and the other Mekong countries, especially in rural areas. Gender roles and socialisation in Philippines society are based on values formed by patriarchy that explains the dominant role of men.

[7] The profession of prostitute is for many families at the border of the poverty line often a respectable and necessary choice. In this way, village girls have from time immemorial played the traditional role of financial mainstay of the family by forwarding their income earned (abroad). Prostitution is accepted in the region (Thailand, Myanmar, Cambodia, the Philippines) even when children are involved. Although, this mentality seems to have changed substantially over the last few years which is reflected by recent changes of law. X., *Trafficking in Children B International Labor Office/IPEC Responses in South EastAsia*, 1998, 8 p; X. *Questionnaire on Projects/Activities on Trafficking in Women and Children in ESCAP Region*, 1998, 8 p.; X., *Child Labor: Trends and Challenges in Asia*, 1997, 25 p.; DERKS, A., *Trafficking of Cambodian Women and Children to Thailand*, IOM, Geneva, 1997, 54 p.; X., *IOM=s Regional Strategy and Plan of Action to Combat Trafficking in Women and Children*, IOM, February 1997, 14 p.; X., Combating Trafficking in Children for Labor Exploitation in the Mekong Sub-Region. A Proposed framework or ILO/IPEC Action and Proceedings of a Mekong Sub Regional Consultation, ILO/IPEC, South-East Asia, October 1998, Bangkok, 87 p.; http://intlrel.soc.hawaii.edu/ps321/chapter5.htlm.

[8] A considerable number of women are still recruited by agents/agencies/impresa-rios but those recruited by friends and family are rapidly increasing. This is a definite shift from formal recruitment practices in the 1970s and 1980s and might mean that cross-border migration is becoming more difficult to monitor and control. Getting information from personal sources seems to be more powerful in influencing the women to migrate, rather than being 'informed' by advertisements and agencies.

labour for carrying out the so-called three D-jobs (dirty, demanding and dangerous). However, the migration flow between Belgium and the Philippines is also informed by the convergence of a specific demand and supply, particularly in the area of domestic work. The chances for a low-skilled Filipino woman finding a job in Belgium are enhanced by the presence of a large diplomatic community (embassies, EC, NATO) which can afford to hire domestic servants. The Filippinos, on the other hand, are known for their efficiency, for speaking Englisch and for being obedient workers. Aside from domestic work, a number of Filipino women also end up as prostitutes in Belgium or neighbouring countries.[9] The fact that there is demand in the West, linked to the reality that foreign victims are easier to manipulate or exploit -- because they usually do not speak the language, are unfamiliar with the customs and the laws in the West, cannot fall back on friends or acquaintances and are often mistrustful of the police system - turns human trafficking into a highly lucrative business.

TACKLING THE PROBLEM

A Multidisciplinary Approach

As mentioned in the introduction, action towards a phenomenon like human trafficking cannot be limited to the expansion of a mere repressive legislative arsenal. A mainly criminal restraint of the phenomenon may cause undesired effect: there is a real danger that a repressive approach will promote rather than halt traffic in human beings. It is believed that by punishing the criminals the problem will be solved, but in reality this one-sided approach often causes several side-effects such as an increased dependence of the victims on the criminal environment, double victimisation and a shift of prostitution towards more hidden forms of sex exploitation. Moreover, the success of a criminal trial is highly dependent on the testimony of victims, who may suffer severe consequences from their decision to provide evidence against those exploiting them.

These elements strengthen the conviction that the best way to tackle the problem is to include a variety of measures and leave repressive measures as a last resort.

- Firstly, measures should be devised in the field of administrative law.
- Secondly, more attention should be paid to the problems that arise in the field of social policy. Only in as far as preventive action fails to tackle human trafficking, criminal legislation should be brought to the task.

---

[9] As a result of booming sex tourism, certain Philippine provinces witnessed a considerable development of the sex industry. Initially, the prostitutes were recruited locally, but from the 1990s onwards the traffickers' focus of attention shifted to the surrounding countries: women from Laos, Cambodja, but mainly from Myanmar entered the Philippine prostitution market. Besides, sex tourism was often led to trafficking in women to countries outside the Mekong region. Germany, Taiwan, but mainly Japan, are currently the most attractive countries, especially for Thai and Philippines women. This trade usually takes place in stages, characterised by exploitation in each intermediate country.

It is essential to elaborate this approach on the international, and in particular the European level. To prevent traffickers taking advantage of loopholes and differences in different national legislations, consistent European administrative, social and criminal measures are needed.

Administrative Law

The channels of migration, by which (potential) victims are being traded, are often legal, though they are used in an illegal fashion.[10] Abuse is found in the ways in which work permits are obtained, but also in the way in wich visas are requested. For example, visa applicants may claim family reunion and the phenomenon of marriage purposes of (usually with mail-order brides). They may seek authorisation for temporary residence of au-pair girls. Abuse is also rife among applicants to special identity cards for technical staff or staff of embassies and international organisations. The use of false documents is also widespread while abuse of refugee-status, adoption, of student-status, of the regulations for minors and employment-status are frequent.

The migration pressure will not be eliminated by closing all doors and windows, but the replacement of the (de facto) quasi migration freeze with open borders is equally indefensible. That is why we proposed in the context of the Belgo-Philippine research project that the European Union Member States should consider the introduction of quotas for migrants. By giving a fixed number of migrants access to their territory every year, and by giving them access to the labour market, trafficking in human beings and the marginal situation of 'illegal aliens' could be controlled.

In exchange, the countries of origin should commit themselves to an effective fight against illegal human trafficking networks. In order to manage the migration problem, the governments of the countries of origin should therefore primarily focus on channelling the migration flows within a legal framework. This presupposes that the number of - mala fide - recruitment channels (travel agencies, employment offices, marriage agencies) should be curtailed, or generally that a more transparent migration policy should be pursued.

Within the European Union, the diplomatic and consular missions have also a crucial role to play. First of all, they should be better equipped to obtain an overall view of the phenomenon. This requires further computerisation of their services, development of 'additional' consultation structures and a more efficient use of visa registers and diplomatic annual reports. In addition a de facto uniform and detailed policy should be pursued with regard to the treatment of visa applications in the diplomatic missions of the different Schengen Member States, in order to prevent 'embassy shopping'.

---

[10] See Report on the conference on Trafficking in Women, Vienna, 10-11 June 1996, Workshop on Migration Policy, European Commission, Doc. CAB./183/96-EN, p. 47-49; See in this respect: Lap-Chew and Wijers (1996)

Social Policy

Most countries still have gaps and difficulties in their social legislation making it almost impossible for the victims to claim their rights and compensations.

For instance, female forced to work illegally in clothing workshops, are regarded as moonlighters. As a rule, the employer does not pay social contributions, while wages are lower than stipulated by law. An employer who is caught has to pay such contributions. In addition, the employee can submit a claim to demand payment of arrears wages in. However, employees taking such a step are faced with a heavy burden of proof. The starting date of employment, the number of hours worked (generally higher than statutorily established) are often hard to prove.

An additional problem arises if the victim is working in the sex industry. Although prostitution is tolerated, Belgian labour law acts as if prostitutes did not exist. For a victim of trafficking in human beings, who ends up in the sex industry, it will be impossible to claim what she/he can normally receive on the basis of an employment contract since an agreement that infringes public order and morality has no legal value. A slight amendment to the (Belgian) Law on Labour Agreements would avoid this, making it possible for any employer to come forward.

The Criminal Law

Trafficking in human beings by definition is a crime that, is of an international nature. The fight against this crime necessitates not only co-ordinated action on a national level but also on an international level. The international nature of trafficking, however, is the reason why the various countries involved in fighting it are faced with different practices, different approaches and different legislations. In other words, states increasingly feel the need for an efficient set of rules that can be applied internationally.

However, aiming for international legal measures is not completely satisfactory. More than four international Conventions were drawn in the period 1900 to 1950 dealing with trafficking in persons and prostitution. These Conventions were replaced by the Convention for the Suppression of the Traffic in Persons and the Exploitation of Prostitution on 21 March 1950.

Through these Conventions the signatories of the Agreement of 1950 have introduced stricter rules, ranging from fighting only forced trafficking in human beings to curbing trafficking in human beings and sexual exploitation, in both cases even with the consent of 'the victim' (Hamerlynck, 1992; Kootstra c.s., 1996). The Convention of 1950 in doing so confuses the offence 'trafficking in human beings' with the incrimination of 'smuggling in people'.

When people, undoubtedly most often to make a profit, 'help' others to gain unlawful entry to or a residence in a certain State, this is usually a matter of smuggling people. Trafficking in human beings, on the other hand, should be associated with an aspect of coercion.

The UN Treaty of 1950, moreover, only mentions recruiting, taking away and forcing people into prostitution. In this way, the other aspects of trafficking in human beings, aimed at economic exploitation, are overlooked.

Furthermore, the current developments show that several States are discussing or implementing regulation, if not decriminalization of prostitution. Should not the abolitionist tone of the Treaty of 1950 make way for a more regulatory approach? Should one not consider decriminalization of certain types of exploitation such as prostitution when this take place does not under coercion or, deception?

It is obvious that there is a need to adapt the UN Convention to the current times, by making the Treaty more up-to-date. In this context it's worth mentioning that on 18 May 1999 the Ad Hoc Committee on the Elaboration of a Convention against Transnational Organised Crime adopted the Revised draft Protocol to Prevent, Suppress and Punish Trafficking in Persons, especially Women and Children, Supplementing the United Nations Convention against Transnational Organised Crime. The purpose of this (draft) Protocol is to promote and facilitate co-operation among member states to prevent, investigate and punish international trafficking in persons for the purpose of forced labour or sexual exploitation. To that end, member states shall adopt effective measures to prevent trafficking in human beings, ensure that victims of receive appropriate assistance and protection, promote the co-operation between States, provide in appropriate cases for the safe and voluntary return of victims to their countries of origin, and inform and educate the public.

It is certain that in the absence of a approximation of the legal definition of the crime of trafficking in human beings throughout the EU, it is extremely difficult to carry out a valid analysis of the phenomenon or to develop a uniform prevention and repression policy. This confirms the need for a minimum legal standard on a European level. As far as this is concerned it should be pointed out that article 31, under c) and article 34, under 2,b) of the consolidated version of the Treaty on European Union give the Council the opportunity to ensure by common action the compatibility of the applicable rules and to adopt framework decisions for the purpose of the approximation of the laws and regulations of the Member States.

Before the entry into force of the Amsterdam Treaty, the Treaty on European Union[11] gave the Council, in Article K3, paragraph 2b), the authority to decide on a joint action[12] at the initiative of a Member State. This form of intergovernmental co-operation was

---

[11] Treaty on European Union, signed in Maastricht on 7 February 1992, *Official Journal EC*, No. C/191, of 29 July 1992.

[12] See in the context of human trafficking: the Joint Action which provides a promotion and exchange program (the so-called 'STOP-program', which tries to facilitate the fight of these crimes by creating a framework for training and instruction activities, studies and exchanges, for the benefit of persons who are responsible for taking action against all possible forms of human trafficking and sexual exploitation of children), *Official Journal* No. L/322/7 of 12 December 1996; the Joint Action adding the fight against trafficking in human beings to the operational scope of the European Drugs Unit (EDU), *Official Journal EC*, No. L/342/4 of 31 December 1996; the Joint Action in relation to the measures to be taken to harmonise the fight against trafficking in human beings and the sexual abuse of children, *Official Journal EC.*, No. L/63/2 of 4 March 1997.

situated within the third pillar of the European Union, the areas of justice and internal affairs.

The Joint Action of 24 February 1997 intended to approximate the legislation of the Member States in relation to trafficking in human beings and the sexual exploitation of children more effectively. Next to measures to be taken on a national level, the Joint Action of 24 February 1997 contains a number of provisions concerning international co-operation between Member States, thereby promoting the police and judicial co-operation in this field.

The hope is real that the Joint Action of 24 February 1997 constitutes more than the mere overall result of an ad-hoc policy, and that it may be regarded as a first concrete realisation of the fifteen EU member countries' willingness to pave the way for joint legislation. Within the European Union a fundamental mutual consultation of the Member States is required when dealing with East-European and South-East Asian countries. Isolated projects of EU member countries, set up within the third pillar usually give the impression of being ineffective.

A Pro-Active Approach

Since human trafficking is one of the ways in which migration takes place, the authorities dealing with immigration issues should pre-empt it by taking measures based on co-operation with sending countries and transit countries. Further co-operation in the field of migration between the EU Member States and, for instance, Russia, have to be encouraged. Another positive element that should be elaborated concerns the regular meetings between CIREFI[13] experts of Central and Eastern European Countries, and their participation to the data-exchange related to illegal migration problems. Also the participation of candidate countries in an early warning system for the transmission of information on illegal immigration and facilitator networks, as proposed earlier this year in the CIREFI group, should be encouraged. Finally, the initiative to establish an Europan Centre of Monitoring Illegal Migration and Trafficking in Human Beings has to be supported.

Protection and Reintegration

Protection

The Joint Action of 24 February 1997 encourages the EU Member States to provide appropriate protection for witnesses. In this respect the hearing of witnesses using (audio)visual equipment (with the possibility to distort the sound and the images in order to avoid recognition and thus intimidation) offers a solution not only for witnesses who wish to remain anonymous, but also for known witnesses and especially for victims of human trafficking and crimes of a sexual nature.

---

[13] CIREFI: Centre d'information, de réflexion, et d'échange sur les frontières extérieures et l'immigration.

The initiatives relating to the protection of witnesses, informers, etc. which have been developed within the EU Council of Europe[14] are of particular relevance in the fight against organised crime, and should be expanded. This suggestion also emerged during the preparatory stage of the Tampere Summit.[15] It is obvious that, certainly in cases of trafficking in people or sexual exploitation (of children)[16], providing protection to withness is of great importance.

Reintegration

Fear of repatriation often prevents victims of human trafficking from co-operating with law enforcement agencies. To encourage victims to co-operate the Belgian authorities developed a system which give the victims of human trafficking a temporary residence permit. Usually, this permit is not extended if the presence of the victim is no longer deemed necessary for the inquiry, or after the trial has been completed.

If after having co-operated with the inquiry, the victim expresses the wish, to return to his/her country of origin, support should be given. In this context, reference can be made to the Resolution of 16 December 1998 on the Communication from the Commission on the Council and the European Parliament concerning trafficking in women for sexual exploitation[17] (in particular to its recommendation No 22). The payment of a reintegration bonus in the country of origin can undoubtedly play an essential role in this respect. Since the victims of human trafficking are mostly not entitled to unemployment benefit, as they often work illegally, a reintegration-premium system could be introduced. In order not to send them home with empty hands (knowing that victims of human trafficking are often treated by their family as failures when they go back as poor as they left) the premium would encourage victims to return to their home country and re-integrate into their family.

The return of the victim to the family environment has important advantages. On the one hand, it can have a preventing effect, as it can dispell the myth the of □making easily lots of money abroad.' On the other hand, it is necessary for the self-esteem of the victim.

The best place to work on their self-confidence is the family environment where the person is more than just another victim of human trafficking. However, integration is very difficult if the victim does not meet the expectations of the family. Therefore, giving some kind of re-integration premium would make the way to integration a lot easier for the victim.

---

[14] E.g. The Resolution of 23 november 1995 on the protection of witnesses with regard to the fight against international organised crime, *Official Journal*, nr. 97/C 327/04, 7 December 1995; the resolution of the European Council of 20 December 1996 relating to persons who co-operate with the police in combating international organised crime, Official Journal, nr. 97/C 10/01, 11 January 1997: the draft Recommendation of the Council of Europe on the practical application of the European Legal Assistance Treaty, the Recommendation of the Council of Ministers of the Council of Europe on the Intimidation of Witnesses and the Rights of Defence.

[15] Council of Europe, 9611/99 CRIMORG 83 JAI 65 CATS 13, 12 July 1999, 3.

[16] Recommendation nr. R(97) 13 of the Comittee of Ministers of the Council of Europe.

[17] Resolution about the Communication from the Commission to the Council and the European Parliament concerning trafficking in women for sexual exploitation of 16 december 1998, *Official Journal EC*, nr. C 14/39, 19 January 1998

To prevent abuse and to reduce the 'attraction effect' as much as possible, the development of a formal payment structure is a crucial requirement. Therefore, contacts between various NGOs in countries of origin and target countries should be stimulated. It would also be appropriate to organise meeting, with NGOs and local assistance centres, so that each returning victim can be accompanied home by an NGO.

CONCLUSION

Human trafficking is -- by definition -- connected with forms of international organised crime and take place in the larger context of illegal migration flows. Human trafficking must be analysed against the backdrop of world-wide economic and political changes. It is a structural problem caused by a complex set of economic and social reasons, commonly called 'the gap between the rich and the poor'. It implies that criminals exploit the desire of victims to find a better life in a new country. The central question is how this phenomenon can been tackled without worsening the conditions of the victims.

The findings of the above mentioned research projects point out that control measures alone cannot stop the flow of trafficking in persons. Moreover, a legal approach relying only on one area of legislation (criminal, social, administrative law etc.) would be too narrow. Only a harmonised approach, both in countries of origin and destination, which integrates all relevant parts of legislation and balance punitive measures and human rights can offer multi-faceted responses to the problem.

LITERATURE

Brants, C. and Klip, A., Uitsluiting, criminalisering en migratie. *Recht en Kritiek*, 1997, *nr 4*, 301-314

Bruinsma, G.J.N. and G. Meershoek, Organized Crime and Trafficking in Women from Eastern Europe in the Netherlands, *Transnational Crime*

Buchowska, O., Oleszczuk, J. Garnier, I. Dawid, B. Butterweck and S. Kupryashkina, (eds.), *One Year La Strada. Results of the First Central and East European Program on Prevention of Traffic in Women*, Stichting tegen Vrouwenhandel, September, 1996, p. 27 and Limanowska, B., Trafficking in Women - Report from Poland, in *Sim special*, 17

Caquette, T.M., *Needs Assessment on Cross-border trafficking in Women and Children in the Mekong Sub-region*, Draft prepared for the UN Working Group on Trafficking in the Mekong Sub-region, Bangkok, Thailand, 1998

Derks, A., *Trafficking of Cambodjan Women and Children to Thailand*, IOM, October 1997

De Ruyver, B.; W. van Eeckhoutte, J. Meese, K.van Impe, K. and S.Vanheste, S., *Multidisciplinary research on the phenomenon of trafficking in human beings from an international and national perspective: a pilot study with Poland and Hungary*, Research Group Drug Policy, Criminal Policy and International Crime, Ghent, 1998.

De Ruyver, B. G. Vermeulen, T. Vander Beken, N. Siron, and P. van Baeveghem, *Multidisciplinary research into the phenomenon of transit migration in Poland with a view to the control of human trafficking: a case-study with Poland*, Research Group Drug Policy, Criminal Policy and International crime, Ghent, 1999.

De Ruyver, B., W. van Eeckhoutte, K. van Impe, P. de Somere and M. Delcour, *Research on a multidisciplinary approach to the phenomenon of trafficking in women: a pilot- and case study of the Philippine situation*, Ghent, 1998

Flormann, W., Rotlichtmilieu - Menschenhandel als Teilbereich der Organisierter Kriminalität, *der Kriminalist*, 4/95, 178-179

Franssen, M., *Zicht op vrouwenhandel. Een methodiek van geïntegreerde begeleiding van slachtoffers van vrouwenhandel*, Stichting Tegen Vrouwenhandel (STV), Utrecht, Uitgeverij SWP, 1994, p. 15-16

Frauenhandel und Prostitutionstourismus. Eine Bestandsaufnahme zu Prostitutions- tourismus, Heiratsvermittlung und Menschenhandel mit ausländischen Mädchen und Frauen, Anhang: rechtsexpertise zur Situation in de BRD, Aktionsgemeischaft Gegen Internationale und Rassistische Aubeutung (AGISRA), Trickster, p. 44-48

Gaberle, A., Gruppenkriminalität in Polen als kriminologische und strafrechtliche Erscheinung. In: *Internationale Perspektiven in Kriminologie und Strafrecht für Günther Kaiser zum 70. Geburtstag*, Berlin, Duncker & Humblot, 1998

Galdwell, C.Galster, S. and Steinzor, N., *Crime and servitude: an exposé of the traffic in Women for prostitution from the Newly Independent States*, Moscow, Global Survival Network, 1997, 16-20

Ghosh, B., *Huddled Masses and Uncertain Shores. Insights into Irregular Migration*, IOM, Martinus Nijhoff Publishers, The Hague/Boston/London, 1998

Go, S., The Philippines: A look into the Migration Scenario in the nineties. In: *Migration and Regional Economic Integration in Asia*, Organisation for Economic Co-operation and Development (OECD), 1998

Gramenga, M.A., International Conference on the Trafficking of NS Women abroad. *New Migration Challenges after the Cold War and International Responses*, IOM, Moscow, 3-5 November 1997

Hummel, D., Lohnende Geschäfte: Frauenhandel mit Osteuropäerinnen und der EG- Binnenmarkt, in: *Beiträge zur feministischen Theorie und Praxis e.v.*, Farbo Drück und Grafik Team, Köln, 1993, p. 58-68

Knudsen, A.; Gunnarson, M. and Forster, F., *Ongoing Evaluation of Two Pilot Projects: Return and Reintegration of Trafficked and other Vulnerable Cambodian and Vietnamese Women and Children from Thailand and Return of Trafficked and other Vulnerable Chinese Women and Children from Thailand, IOM, 1997, 27 p.; X., Two Reports on the Situation of Women and Children Trafficked from Cambodia and Vietnam to Thailand*, GAATW/IOM/CWDA, 1997

Kootstra, T., I thought I would be the lady-companion of one man. In: Kootstra, T., Oleszczuk, O.; Dawid, I.; Butterweck, B.; Kupryashkina, S., *One Year La Strada*,

Results of the First Central and East European Program on Prevention of Traffic of Women, September, 1996

Kupryashkina, S., It is not our problem: Society attitudes to prostitution and traffic in women in the Ukraine. In: *One Year La Strada*, STV/La Strada, 1996, 47

Lap-Chew, L. and M. Wijers, M., *Trafficking in Women., Forced Labor and Slavery-like Practices in Marriage, Domestic Labor and Prostitution. Summary of the Preliminary Report*, October 1996, Utrecht, The Netherlands, GAATW/STV, 22

Licuanan, P.B., A.S. Sta Maria, S.M. Candelaria, M.J.N., Real, M.C.G. Bautista, E.L. Beja Jr., E. Porio, C.S. Crisol, and E.N. Paul, *Philippine-Belgian Project Against Trafficking in Women. Final Report,* Ateneo de Manila University, 1998, p. iv-ix

Oleszczuk, O. and S. Buchowska, The Pretty Women Syndrome. In: T. Kootstra, S. Ofreneo, R.E., and R.P. Ofreneo, R.P., Prostitution in the Philippines. In: L.L. Lim, (ed.), *The Sex Sector. The economic and social bases of prostitution in Southeast Asia*, International Labor office (ILO), Geneva, 1998

Phongpaichit, P., S. Pipriyaransan and N. Treerat, *Guns, Girls, Gas and Ganja. Thailand's Illegal Economy and Public Policy*, Political Economic Center, Faculty of Economics, Chulalongkorn University, 1997

Sanghera, F., *In the Belly of the Beast: Sex Trade, Prostitution and Globalization*, Discussion paper for the Asia-Pacific Regional Consultation on Prostitution, February 17-18 1997, Bangkok, GAATW, Canada, 1997

Seshu, M., *Trafficking in Women and Children in the Countries of South Asia*, Regional Meeting on Trafficking in Women, Forced Labor and Slavery-like Practices in Asia and the Pacific, February 19-22 1997, Asian Women's Human Rights Council, 1997

Sieber, U., Internationale Organisierte Kriminalität. Eine Bestandsaufnahme. *Kriminalistik*, 2/98, p. 98-102.

Sieber, U. and Bögel, M., *Logistik der Organisierter Kriminalität. Wirtschaftswissenschaft -licher Forschungsansatz und Pilotstudie zur Internationalen Kfz-Verschiebung, zur Ausbeutung von Prostitution, zum Menschenhandel und zum illegalen Glücksspiel*, Wiesbaden, 1993

Vasquez, N.D., L.C. Tumbaga, and M.Cruz-Soriano, *Tracer study on Filipino Domestic Helpers Abroad. The socio-economic conditions of Filipino domestic workers from pre-departure until the end of their first two-year contract in Hong-Kong*, IOM, Geneva, 1995, p.25-27)

Wijers M. and L. Lap-Chew, *Trafficking in Women, Forced Labor and Slavery Practices in Marriage Domestic Law and Prostitution*, Foundation against Trafficking in Women (STV), Utrecht, the Netherlands

Chapter 5

TRAFFICKING IN MIGRANTS: A EUROPEAN PERSPECTIVE

Andrea Di Nicola
Researcher at Transcrime, Research Group on
Transnational Crime, University of Trento

INTRODUCTION

This chapter seeks to answer questions related the trafficking in migrants in Europe: are there organised criminal groups who are involved in human trafficking, and if so which groups? How do they organise their business? Which routes are most widely used? While answering these questions, I will try to identify, though tentatively, the role played by Western, Central and Eastern European states, sometimes as sending, sometimes as transit or destination countries. The analysis will also try to identify the most common illicit acts performed by organised criminals while trafficking in migrants.

There is reason to believe that this illegal business, when conducted by organised criminal organisations, is very dangerous because it links international and local criminal aspects. The more the traffic is organised, the more it is related to the exploitation of victims in the local criminal markets of destination countries. Trafficked people, once in the host countries, are of then pushed into deviant or criminal markets, such as those of illicit drugs, prostitution, begging or theft. These activities may cover the cost of being smuggled.[1]

The second part of this essay sets some guidelines in order to build up a feasible and comprehensive strategy, at the European regional level, to fight the international migrant

---

[1] Part of the crimes committed by immigrants in host countries can be referred to as the state of dependence and exploitation in which trafficked people are kept by traffickers who help them, at high costs, to enter the desired destination countries. In order to receive payment, traffickers may force clandestine people to engage in criminal activities. See, on this issue, TRANSCRIME, 1996; Savona, Da Col, Di Nicola, 1997: 154-229; Savona, Di Nicola, 1998.

trafficking. In particular, it suggests that interventions should be devised country by country. This should not only focus on criminal law but start from the consideration that some Central and Eastern European countries are the main sending countries, while Western European countries, are mainly receivers of illegal migration.

ORGANISED CRIME AND THE TRAFFICKING IN MIGRANTS IN EUROPE

Perceived differences between nations concerning the welfare of citizens is a main factor contributing to migration. Overpopulation, high unemployment rates, ecological disasters, deprivation of civil rights, political persecution and low standards of living, all lead some to seek a better life elsewhere. All of these also create new opportunities for criminal organisations, which are better equipped to offer alternative migration services. Facing these disadvantages and others, thousands from developing countries wish to flee their birthplaces for better lives in industrialised nations. Of course, the industrialised countries are responding to these emigration pressures to suit their own needs, tightening migration policies in times of high unemployment and making them more liberal when a supply of cheap labour is desired. For example, with high unemployment rates across the continent, Western European countries have enacted legislative restrictions on immigration, and this legislation has stemmed the flow of legal migrants and asylum seekers. Unfortunately, since the desire to emigrate has not been affected by these laws, a strong market for illegal migration has developed, and criminals (particularly organised ones) have begun to service it. If opportunities have increased for criminals with respect to illegal immigration, it must also be noted that the risks associated with these opportunities have remained uniformly low. In many countries, trafficking in aliens is not even considered a crime and in others it is only lightly penalised.[2] This is the case in some Central and Eastern European nations and even in the Western European nations, where sanctions against human smuggling often do not exceed a two year term of imprisonment and sometimes simply amount to fines. Finally, law enforcement standards are low in many countries and 'along with high levels of corruption' help to explain the spread of illegal smuggling (Savona, Lasco, Di Nicola, Zoffi, 1997: 8-9).

As a consequence of all this, illegal immigration represent a huge source of profit for traffickers in Europe as elsewhere. The *International Centre for Migration Policy Development* (ICMPD), considering the fact that in 1993 from 100 to 220 thousand of the illegal immigrants seemed to have used traffickers' services, estimates that the overall gain of the trafficking syndicates operating in Western Europe accounts to between 100 million and 1,1 billion dollars. The global profit margin in this criminal sector for one year is alleged to be around 5 to 7 billion dollars (Widgren, 1994: 5-6). For the year of 1996, estimates of the world business turnover for traffickers was 8 billion dollars (Paiva (IOM), 1996: 382). These huge profits are due to the high prices migrants pay for the

---

[2] For further treatments of this subject, see Belgium, Austria and ICMPD, 1995; Secretariat of the Inter-Governmental Consultations on Asylum, Refugee and Migration Policies in Europe, North America and Australia, 1995a; Siemens, 1996; IOM, 1998: 20.

services they require. The average cost to reach a European country, for instance, is from 2 to 5 thousand dollars (with a maximum 35-40 thousand for Chinese people).

The growing skills and organisation of illegal traffickers[3] are probably the most important development in illegal migration world-wide. This is not to say that 'amateur' smugglers or less organised criminals do not operate in this sector. However, large criminal organisations prevail in the business. Let us see why. Taking advantage of the fact that trafficked aliens who make their way to a new country are often quite vulnerable (because of their limited access to legal income and assistance), some criminal organisations exploit these recent illegal immigrants by introducing them into the drug market, prostitution, begging or theft. This exploitation is likely to leave the recent illegal immigrant enmeshed in the world of crime, although this involvement may be best described as induced rather than freely chosen. Thus, the high rate of illegal aliens involved in criminal activities in host countries can be understood within the context of the following circuit: trafficking leads to exploitation which leads to induced criminality (Transcrime, 1996: 53-72; Savona, Da Col, Di Nicola, 1997: 191-207; Savona, Di Nicola, 1998).

Because organisation in the traffic in migrants is of essential importance, the analysis that follows provide overview of major European-based organised criminal groups involved in this illegal activity.

In the European continent organised groups trafficking in migrants very rarely devote themselves to this activity exclusively. It is more likely that they start this illegal business as a result of the experience built up while performing other kinds of traffics. This applies to the criminal groups that can be defined as opportunistic, i.e. able to shift from one illicit activity to another spreading their operative sectors only on the basis of mere opportunistic criteria. Like legal enterprises, these illicit organisations seek to maximise profits (and the traffic of migrants can bring huge ones) minimising losses (and the traffic of migrants implies very few losses). To minimise losses means to minimise the risk of being caught and convicted and having one's goods seized and confiscated. It means, in the case of conviction, to be reasonably sure of receiving a very low penalty. Organised criminals, being good international entrepreneurs, constantly monitor different opportunities and the risks connected with different crimes in the countries in which they act. They exploit the legislative loopholes and the low qualitative standard of the law enforcement system in some countries. As the trafficking in migrants is increasingly characterised by organisation, we can note an increased flexibility available to traffickers when choosing their logistic bases and the countries to be used as transit points to reach their destinations. In performing this choice, they draw their attention to those countries where criminal legislation is weak, where police control activity is low and possibility of connivance with governments is high. The analysis that follows may possibly clarify these remarks.

Some routes are preferred by traffickers to take their human cargoes to the economic core of Europe. Every route seems to be linked to specific countries and to some Mafia groups.

---

[3] As far as organisation of traffickers is concerned see Salt, Stein, 1997.

The first route was defined for some time as the Balkan route. It is still alive though its traffickers had to modify it as a consequence of the events which took and are taking place in the former Yugoslavia and of the increase in border controls along some European areas. The Balkan route crosses Turkey and the Balkan States, usually terminating in Germany. It has various possible patterns. From Bulgaria it is possible to go through Romania and Hungary terminating in Germany or to enter Macedonia or Albania and there make your way to Italy, where you can stay or continue the journey towards the Federal Republic of Germany or other Western European States. Different kinds of criminal groups act in this way; some of them individually and some in a sort of joint criminal venture. It is an area of interest for the Albanian Mafia, the Italian Sacra Corona Unita and, more recently, for the new and dangerous Greek-Turkish-Pakistani Mafia.

Today there is great concern about the Albanian Mafia, because it combines the traffic in human beings with that of drugs and for its ability to keep immigrants in severe conditions of exploitation, once they reach their destination. In Italy Albanians have established contacts with the Sacra Corona Unita, which controls both the distribution and the exploitation of trafficked immigrants all over Italy and the connected drug traffics. Around 250 illegal immigrants (especially Curds, Pakistani, Iraqi and Chines, though Albanians are sometimes also involved) are thought to be trafficked to Italy every day. In the summer of 1997 estimates were around 5.000 per week.[4] The average cost to be transported from the Albanian to the Italian shores is about 800 US dollars for a foreigner and 400-500 for an Albanian. A further extension of the illegal business of these organisations is represented by the exploitation of Albanian girls in the Italian markets of prostitution[5] and of children in begging.

Once again, along the Balkan route a new criminal joint-venture formed by an illegal strategic alliance among Greek, Turkish and Pakistani criminal groups appears to operate in the field of human smuggling. In Italy there have been new testimonies in recent criminal proceedings that allow us to infer the existence of this connection. This may also be supported by media reports on sea disasters in connection to human traffic and by passengers' stories. The link among the three criminal organisations can also be inferred from the increase in illegal immigration between Turkey and Greece.[6] Istanbul is said to be a gathering point for illegal migrants, most of all of Asiatic origin. From the Turkish capital some migrants are transported to coastal towns (such as Izmir, Kas, Kousadasi), where they are shipped in boats leading towards the Aegean islands, easily reachable

---

[4] See Italy: New Law, Albania. In: *Migration News. Europe*, vol. 5, n. 3, March 1998.

[5] See, for instance, Eastern European Newsletter, vol. 10, n. 20, 26 September-12 October 1996, as cited in IOM, *Trafficking in Immigrants. Quarterly Bullettin*, n. 13, Geneva, December 1996; IOM - Migration Information Programme, 1996a; Tantalo, Merzagora Betsos, 1997.

[6] In the last few years diplomatic contrasts between Turkish and Greek authorities have arisen right because of this question. For example, in April 1996, a Greek police patrol boat fired at Turkish fishing boat that was believed to clandestinely transport Iranian refugees towards the Greek territory. Turkey lamented that the Greek action had not taken place in Greek territorial waters, while the government of Athens accused the Greek one of "protecting slaves' dealers", turning a blind eye on traffickers (P.J. Smith, Smuggling People into Rich Country Is a Growth Industry. In: *International Herald Tribune*, 28 June 1996). See also Incidents - Turkey-Greece. In: IOM, *Trafficking in Immigrants. Quarterly Bullettin*, n. 16, Geneva, September 1997.

from the Turkish coasts. Other immigrants are packed into trucks or other means of transportation and cross the land borders between Turkey and Greece. The joint-venture among Greek, Turkish and Pakistani criminals focuses its attention on particular ethnic groups (mainly Asian, Kurd and Middle Eastern people) and it is very powerful, thanks to its ability to infiltrate the legal systems of their counties and to its significant relevant contacts in different European areas. The Greek-Turkish-Pakistani Mafia prefers sea shipments, very often using 'old crocks' bought for the purpose[7]: traffickers get migrants to flow from many smaller boats into a bigger one, which transports them over long stretches of water. They are then regrouped into lighter boats to facilitate their landing on destination shores. The preferred landing points are usually in Italy, mainly in Sicily or Calabria.[8] Malta is also used as a sorting point.

The second preferred route is the Baltic route. It spreads from Asiatic countries, through Russia and the Baltic states, to Scandinavian countries and, from there, often trough Poland, to the core of the European Union. It has been increasingly exploited since the collapse of the Soviet Empire.[9] The poverty of controls, the inadequate criminal response, and the high corruptibility of officers make countries such as Russia, Lithuania, Latvia, Estonia and Bellorussian strategic crossroads to gain access to richer European countries (Ulrich, 1995). For example, according to the German government (The Government of the Federal Republic of Germany, 1994: 3), the traffic in migrants in Russia[10] has been facilitated by rules on visas and on entry permits not properly in line with Western European countries' standards and by corruption among police officers. The Russian Mafia, which is a clear example of opportunistic organised crime for its ability to adapt to new criminal needs and perform new activities, is taking advantage of the situation. Moscow has emerged as a transit conduit for those illegal migrants wishing to find their way towards the West. An estimated 300 thousand immigrants, coming from developing countries, are believed to be illegally present in the Russian capital waiting to be smuggled into Western Europe (Ulrich, 1995: 10-11). Several investigations have revealed that Russian criminal groups are also involved in the traffic in women towards Western Europe.[11] Traffickers seem to be often protected by the police, by members of KGB and the FSB (the National Investigative Agency) and they can easily falsify visas and other documents.[12] There is also evidence that criminals succeed in obtaining

[7] A boat of medium dimension costs, at the used boat market, around 50 thousands US dollars and every journey it brings in about one million of dollars (just calculating 250 passengers at an average cost of 4 thousands dollars each). Only one journey is widely sufficient to refund the price of the ship and to be safe from the risks coming from the freezing and confiscation of the good.

[8] See D. Frisullo, Buon Natale Clandestino. In: *Narcomafie*, anno V, *n. 9*, September 1997, pp. 3-5; D. Frisullo, La holding degli schiavisti. In: *Narcomafie*, anno V, *n. 9*, September 1997, pp. 6-9.

[9] See, among others, IOM - Migration Information Programme, 1997.

[10] On the traffic in migrants which involves Russia see Center for the Study of Transnational Crime & Corruption at American University, 1999.

[11] The traffic in Central and Eastern European women towards Western European countries is a phenomenon that, in the last years, has become more and more alarming, assuming bigger and bigger proportions. See, on this topic, IOM - Migration Information Programme, 1995; 1996; 1996a.

[12] See Caldwell, Galster (of the Global Survival Network) in collaboration with the International League for Human Rights, 1997: 3-4.

authentic passports of many countries of the former Soviet Union (The Government of the Federal Republic of Germany, 1994: 3).

Traffickers wishing to reach Western Europe also use some Central European countries (such as Bulgaria, Czech Republic, Poland, Romania, Hungary) as transit or gathering points waiting for a further movement. This might happen because of the loopholes or lack of criminal law provisions in these countries[13] and/or because of their lax visa regulations and/or for the inadequacy of border control activities. By controlling the trafficking operations from these nations, traffickers guarantee themselves a substantial impunity. Cities such as Prague and Warsaw (see Salt, Stein, 1997: 475) have become gathering points for many migrants waiting to move towards the West and centres where documents used for trafficking purposes are counterfeited (IOM, 1994: 11). If, for instance, we look in greater detail at the situation in Poland, we see that this is both a sending and transit country, especially as far as women are concerned. 'Trafficking in Poland has acquired the character of organised crime proceeding according to the same principles and methods used in the traffic of weapons, nuclear material, cars and drugs, even if on a smaller scale. Criminal rings of four to five traffickers with German-Polish cross-border links sometimes also operate on larger trafficking rings. It is precisely the increasingly organised character of the crime that makes traffickers powerful and a threat for female victims'. (Commission on Human Rights, 1996: n. 59).

The Strait of Gibraltar is another gateway towards Europe. It is exploited by African criminal groups that are certainly far less stable than the Russian Mafia or their Turkish/Greek/Pakistani counterpart. Anyway, they represent a real threat because, they simultaneously engage in drug smuggling[14] and encourage trafficked people to work in the drugs markets of the destination countries.

At the end of this brief overview it is worth underlining the variety of illicit acts that can accompany the trafficking in migrants. These acts go far beyond the simple activity of transporting migrants and violating immigration laws. They include the counterfeiting of documents, the corruption of public officers, the use of accomplices offering food and lodging to illegal immigrants, the exploitation of trafficked people once they have reached their destination (in the black labour market, in prostitution rings, in the drug market, in theft, and in begging). These illicit acts are linked among themselves by what could be defined as 'vertical interdependence'. Vertical interdependence arises when organised criminals or other criminal subjects, with the aim of committing a final offence, go trough a series of intermediate or instrumental crimes: in order to finalise a crime of particular importance (in terms of effects or gains), a chain of offences is committed. It is a typical *modus operandi* of organised criminals: it can be recognised in illicit activities other than the trafficking in migrants and shows that a process of

---

[13] See Belgium, Austria and ICMPD, 1995; M.A. Siemens, 1996; Belgium, Poland and IGC, 1996. See also IOM, *Trafficking in Immigrants. Quarterly Bulletin*, Geneva, *n. 12*, September 1996.
[14] From 1993 Spanish officers estimate that about 1.000 people are drawn in the attempt of crossing the Strait of Gibraltar (Illegal Immigration: Spain/Marocco. In: *Migration News. Europe*, vol. 5, *n. 3*, March 1998). In relation to the traffic from the African continent see D.A. Kornbluth, 1998: 174-175.

specialisation is occurring in criminal organisations (Adamoli, Di Nicola, Savona, Zoffi, 1998: 16-18).[15]

BUILDING A GLOBAL STRATEGY AT THE EUROPEAN LEVEL

The analysis carried out so far highlights how some Central and Eastern European countries act as major starting, transit and/or gathering points for illegal migrants. In other words some European states can be considered weak spots of a protective net built around Europe.

It might be useful to explain why traffickers prefer some countries to others in which to conduct their operations. In this respect, the following aspects should be considered. There are legislative loopholes in the criminal law, legislation is often ignored, the police lack resources, corruption is rife, and socio-economic conditions are poor. In other words, countries lacking legislation on trafficking in migrants or failing to implement such legislation, and countries where corruption is widespread are highly exposed to criminal entrepreneurs engaged in illegal migration.[16] On the other hand, rich European countries, are rapidly closing their borders, and by introducing more restrictive policies they are encouraging the use of traffickers. Western European countries also lack serious structured polices concerning the planning of legal migration flows.

As a consequence of all this, almost every European state seems to have its own responsibilities. This is the reason why, at the European level, it should be understood that the only way to try and tackle this problem is to design a global response, agreed upon by several countries collaborating together to reach a common result. Consequently, in Europe like elsewhere, the most correct strategy against the traffic in migrants would seem to be a mixture of prevention and control policies harmonised at the regional level. That is to say rich and poor European countries should perform different but important roles, accepting their different responsibilities and their respective areas of intervention. In other words, it would be appropriate that some European countries intervene in the field of the criminal law or in that of law enforcement, while others focus on admission policies or, more generally, on the reduction of criminal opportunities.

Let us try to analyse a possible European strategy.

With regard to the criminal law, efforts should be made to harmonise the legislation and law enforcement strategies among European states. Traffickers should find their roads blocked by a regional wall constructed by standardised criminal law. This means that a similar level of sanctions all should be applied, with penalties reflecting the gravity of this illegal behaviour. The types of legal definition should also be similar, with a view

---

[15] Legislator, in the field of the traffic in migrants, such as in other organised crime activities, when using criminal law, should become aware of these interdependencies in the a view of an effective and efficient criminalisation (see next paragraph).

[16] From the analysis on the phenomenon of the traffic in migrants above carried out, Baltic States and many Central and Eastern European countries have emerged as points of origin, of gathering or of transit of migrants. From these states traffickers control the trafficking operations for they are reasonably sure to have a substantial impunity. The same could go for countries such as Albania or Turkey.

to improving the co-operation in the field of judicial and police matters. This development should be relatively smooth in Western European countries, where adequate rules are already in place. However, difficulties may be encountered in Central and Eastern European countries, where legislative loopholes exist. Therefore, differentiated efforts should be made by European countries, though harmonisation should be the common task. Furthermore national legislators should try to design criminal legislation which consider the 'criminal interdependencies' which take place in such traffics.[17] The trafficking in entails corruption of officials, the forgery of documents and, exploitation of women and children. Consequently, these should be regarded as that these further aggravating circumstances of the main offences, i.e. the crime of trafficking in migrants. Particular attention should also be devoted to the establishment of efficient confiscation systems. In order to pursue this goal, especially in the New Independent States, financial transparency should be seen as a powerful preventive tool (Global Survivor Network, 1997).

Criminal law in the book, anyway, is useless if it is not implemented. Too often we witness laws which are only symbolically implemented. They represent mere declarations, sometimes enacted only to please the international or the national community. The problem is serious, most of all because of the likelihood that a few of the poorest European countries have little resources to be used in police activity. The only instrument to get rid of this difficulty is represented by police co-operation, first and foremost intended in a sense of material co-operation. Rich European countries should provide poorer ones with the necessary instruments (in terms of resources, technical instruments, skills) to develop serious law enforcement policies.

In any case, the traffic cannot be stopped by resorting solely to the criminal law. Preventive measures should support the criminal law in the fight against big criminal organisations with a view to reducing criminal opportunities. In the field of these prevention policies, rich European countries should play a prominent role. Here below are a few examples.

Governments of rich European states should enact policies that make would-be migrants aware of the serious risks they face when they trust in traffickers and in alternative, illicit ways of migrating.

All countries touched by trafficking routes should act, at the national and regional level, to reduce the infiltration of organised crime in the legal arena and do their best to limit opportunities for corruption, possibly through a system of incentives for public officers, a constant monitoring of their activities and an increase in their professional standards.

All countries, particularly the wealthier ones, should 'promote' the morality of employers, through tight controls over their activities and incentives encouraging them to comply with labour legislation. This would reduce the number of entrepreneurs who resort to traffickers as a means of finding low-cost 'black' labour.

All receiving countries should avoid producing those 'factors of social construction' which associate migrants with deviance and criminality (Pastore, 1995). States, through

---

[17] See paragraph 2 in the end.

institutional measures and immigration policies, may influence the dynamics of traffic and exploitation of immigrants.

For example, sudden and unconditional closure of borders can increase the number of persons requiring traffickers' services.

In countries which do not provide irregular residents with a minimum standard of social welfare trafficked immigrants may resort to criminal groups to obtain such welfare. These groups, in turn, will strengthen their control over illegal immigrants.

To conclude, every country should consider modifying criminal law, police control strategies and policies and aim at reducing opportunities for criminals. Simultaneously, countries should combine prevention and control, and harmonize meansures at the regional level. This should involve all European states in an attempt to design policies which are specific nationally and effective internationally. Shared responsibility and joint actions are, therefore, the keywords in the fight against the traffic in human beings.

LITERATURE

Adamoli, S., Di Nicola, A., Savona, E.U., Zoffi, P., *Organised Crime Around the World*, Publication Series No. 31, European Institute for Crime Prevention and Control, affiliated with the United Nations (HEUNI), Helsinki, 1998

Belgium, Austria and ICMPD, Harmonization of Legislation to Combat Trafficking in Aliens, report prepared for the *Third Meeting of the Expert Group of the Budapest Group*, Budapest, 15-16 June, 1995

Belgium, Poland and IGC, *Anti-Trafficking Model Legislation. Report of the Working Group of the Budapest Group*, Oslo, 3-4 October, 1996

Caldwell, G., Galster, S., (of the Global Survival Network) in collaboration with the International League for Human Rights, Crime & Servitude: An Exposé of the Traffic in Russian Women for Prostitution, paper prepared for the Conference on *Criminal Justice Issues in the International Expoitation of Women and Children*, U.S. Department of State, U.S Department of Justice and the Federal Judicial Center, Washington, 7 April, 1997

Center for the Study of Transnational Crime & Corruption at American University, *Organized Crime Watch - Russia*, vol. 1, *n. 2*, February 1999

Commission on Human Rights (U.N. Economic and Social Council), *Report of the Special Rapporteur to Poland on the Issue of Trafficking and Forced Prostitution of Women*, Whashington, 10 December, 1996

Global Survivor Network, *The Trafficking of NIS Women Abroad, An International Conference in Moscow*, Moscow, 3-5 November, 1997

IOM (International Organisation for Migration), Trafficking in Immigrants: Characteristics and Trends in Different Regions of the World, paper presented at the *Eleventh IOM Seminar on International Response to Trafficking in Immigrants and the Safeguarding of Migrant Rights*, Geneva, 26-28 October, 1994

IOM (International Organisation for Migration), *Analysis of Data and Statistical Resources Available in the EU Member States on Trafficking in Humans, Particularly in Women and Children for Purposes of Sexual Exploitation*, Geneva, 1998

IOM - Migration Information Programme, *Trafficking and Prostitution: the Growing Exploitation of Migrant Women from Central and Eastern Europe, Budapest*, May 1995

IOM - Migration Information Programme, *Trafficking in Women to Austria for Sexual Exploitation*, Budapest, June 1996

IOM - Migration Information Programme, *Trafficking in Women to Italy for Sexual Exploitation*, Budapest, June 1996a

IOM - Migration Information Programme, *The Baltic Route: The Trafficking of Immigrants Through Lithuania*, Budapest, January 1997

Kornbluth, D.A., Illegal Migration from North Africa: The Role of Traffickers. In ISPAC, *Migration and Crime. Proceedings of the International Conference on 'Migration and Crime. Global and Regional Problems and Responses'*, Courmayeur, 5-8 October, 1996, Milan, 1998

Paiva, R.G. (IOM), Multilateral Efforts to Combat Trafficking in Immigrants: An International Agency Perspective. In: ISPAC, *International Conference on 'Migration and Crime. Global and Regional Problems and Responses'*, Courmayeur, 5-8 October 1996, Milan, 1998

Pastore, M., *Produzione normativa e costruzione sociale della devianza e criminalità tra gli immigrati*, Quaderni I.S.MU. 9/1995, Fondazione Cariplo - I.S.MU., Milan, 1995

Salt, J., Stein, J., Migration as a Business: the Case of Trafficking. *International Migration*, vol. 35, *n. 4*, 1997

Savona, E.U., in co-operation with Da Col, G., Di Nicola, A., Migrazioni e criminalità in Europa. In: L. Tomasi (ed.), *Razzismo e società plurietnica. Conflitti etnici e razzismi giovanili in Europa*, Franco Angeli, Milan

Savona, E.U., Di Nicola, A., Migrazioni e criminalità. Trent'anni dopo. *Rassegna Italiana di Criminologia*, vol. IX, *n. 1*, 1998

Savona, E.U., in co-operation with Lasco, F., Di Nicola, A., Zoffi, P., Globalisation of Crime. The Organisational Variable, paper prepared for *The 15th International Symposium on Economic Crime*, Jesus College, Cambridge (UK), 14-20 September, 1997

Secretariat of the Inter-Governmental Consultations on Asylum, Refugee and Migration Policies in Europe, North America and Australia, *Summary Description of the Legislation on Alien Trafficking in States in Europe, North America and Australia*, Geneva, December 1995

Siemens, M.A., European Responses to the Phenomenon of Illegal Migration: National and International Initiatives, paper presented at the International Conference on *Migration and Crime. Global and Regional Problems and Responses*, Courmayeur, 5-8 October, 1996

Tantalo, M., Merzagora Betsos, I., Immigrazione femminile e vittimizzazione possibile. Riflessioni per un'analisi fenomenologica, paper presented at the XI National

Congress of the Italian Society of Criminology on *Nuove sfide per la criminologia: migrazioni, violenza giovanile, didattica*, Gargnano del Garda (Brescia, Italy), 21-24 May, 1997

The Government of the Federal Republic of Germany, International Cooperation in Fighting Illegal Immigration Networks, paper presented at the *Eleventh IOM Seminar on International Response to Trafficking in Immigrants and the Safeguarding of Migrant Rights*, Geneva, 26-28 October, 1994

TRANSCRIME, *Migrazione e criminalità - La dimensione internazionale del problema*, CNPDS, Milan, 1996

Ulrich, C.J., *Alien Smuggling and Uncontrolled Migration in Northern Europe and the Baltic Region*, HEUNI Paper N° 7, Helsinki, 1995

Widgren, J., Multilateral Co-operation to Combat Trafficking in Immigrants and the Role of International Organizations, paper presented at the *Eleventh IOM Seminar on International Response to Trafficking in Immigrants and the Safeguarding of Migrant Rights*, Geneva, 26-28 October, 1994

Chapter 6

DRUG TRAFFICKING IN POLAND

K. Krajewski

Adjunct Professor of Criminology
at the Jagiellonian University of Cracow, Poland.

INTRODUCTION

Before 1989 communist Poland, like many other countries of the eastern block, remained to a large extent separated from the phenomenon of international drug trafficking. This situation resulted from a number of factors. First of all, countries behind the iron curtain were isolated from the outside world by extremely tight border controls. Secondly, Poland was surrounded by other members of the 'socialist brotherhood', i.e. had no common border with any western country. It meant that German Democratic Republic to the west, Czechoslovakia to the south, Soviet Union to the east, and Baltic See to the north constituted a kind of the first line of defence against any 'bad' influence from the West, drugs included. Third, because of all this, it made very little sense for any domestic or foreign criminal group or organisation, to attempt to import and sell drugs, or to use Poland as a transit route. It would have been just too difficult and risky, unless local authorities, first of all communist secret services were somehow interested and involved in such an activity, and organised it or provided protection. For many years it seems that this was the case in Bulgaria, but rather not in Poland, which does not mean that secret services of the communist Poland were not involved in variety of other criminal activities of more or less organised, commercial nature. Because of unconvertible currency and extremely low average income (as calculated according to the black market exchange rate), there was also little chance for international criminal groups involved in drug trafficking to obtain a meaningful profit margin from selling drugs, taking into account that the profits should compensate for much high risks and special difficulties connected to trafficking in this part of Europe. It would also have implied additional difficulties with laundering the profits in Poland or transferring them abroad.

THE DRUG PROBLEM BEFORE 1989

All this did not mean that during this period there was no drug problem in Poland. Just the opposite was the case, particularly since the middle of the seventies (Gaberle 1986, Krajewski 1997). At the beginning of this decade an able student of chemistry from Gdańsk developed simple technology of producing strong narcotic drug of an opiate type from the poppy straw, which was at that time easily available from any Polish farmer, often free of any charge, as farmers were happy to get rid of the stuff which they were not able to utilise in any other productive way. This drug called 'Polish heroin' or *kompot* was easy to produce without any special laboratory equipment, chemicals difficult to obtain or special knowledge or expertise in chemistry. Anybody could produce it right in his own kitchen. Despite primitive method of production 'Polish heroin' constitutes a very strong and addictive opiate drug, which quickly leads to the psychological and physical dependence, identical with that resulting from using morphine or heroin. Additionally, however, this substance is also very toxic, as it contains many by-products from the unsophisticated production technology.

All this resulted during the seventies and eighties in the development in Poland of a substantial subculture of opiate addicts. The real dimensions of the problem could be estimated at that time only very roughly, because of the lack of serious and broad epidemiological research (as a matter of fact this is also the case nowadays). Anyhow, the number of people who had any contact with drugs (although not necessarily 'Polish heroin'), had been estimated in the eighties to be somewhere between 500 thousand and 1 million, the number of occasional consumers to be between 150 and 300 thousand, and the number of actual addicts between 20 and 40 thousand. For a country of about 36 million inhabitants in this period these numbers were not insignificant and indicated that consumption of drugs and drug addiction constituted a serious social problem, although still much less serious than the traditional alcohol problem.

The drug problem in Poland had also certain distinguishing features, which differentiated it strongly from the analogous phenomenon in the west. Despite serious problems on the demand side, the supply side remained for many years absolutely different from the situation on the 'mature' western drug markets. In fact there was no drug trafficking, neither domestic, nor cross-border. In other words, production, smuggling, distribution and dealing with drugs for profit by the people who are mostly not consumers themselves were practically non-existent. Such situation resulted from the fact, that 'Polish heroin' constitutes a home-made drug, which was produced at that time almost exclusively by addicts themselves for their own needs. If drugs were provided to other people, they were provided by addicts to other addicts as a form of favour among colleagues with the eventual expectancy of some sort of the reciprocity in the future, and the profit motive was usually absent. In other words the supply of drugs constituted at that time an internal matter of the addicts' subculture. It means that from the point of view of the classification proposed once by Dorn and South the predominating mode of drug dealing at that time constituted so called 'mutual societies' (Dorn, South 1990).

Because of the above mentioned features, the drug problem has been perceived in Poland for many years from the rather specific perspective, namely almost exclusively as a problem of demand which required preventive and therapeutic measures, with consumers constituting the main object of attention. Relatively little attention has been paid to the supply side of it. The only exception constituted the introduction of special provisions to control growing of poppy by farmers. As a matter of fact, for a few years after the new law on prevention of drug addiction has been introduced in 1985, cases of illegal, i.e. without special permission, cultivation of poppy constituted the largest group (up. to 70%) of drug offences registered by the police (see table 3). Persons convicted by the courts under the provisions of this law, mostly peasants, were however hardly criminal entrepreneurs. They had sometimes no idea about the new provisions or just disregarded them, as they were used to grow poppy for baking and cooking purposes since generations. And although during the eighties it was possible to observe a very slow emergence of the phenomenon of commercial production of 'Polish heroin', i.e. by individuals or more or less organised groups with the purpose of selling it to addicts, what meant the establishment of the foundations of the ' real' black market, this process before 1989 was rather very slow and did not change significantly the picture of this phenomenon.

THE CHANGED SCENE AFTER THE FALL OF COMMUNIST REGIME

More significant changes have been brought about by the fall of communism. This event also meant, among others, opening of the borders. This resulted in significant changes of the Polish internal drug market and also in coming into being of the phenomenon of the cross-border drug criminality, which at present seems to constitute quite serious a problem.

The main change on the internal drug market consisted in the loss by the 'Polish heroin' of its almost monopolistic position as a source of the problem. Although consumption of this drug still predominates within Polish addicts' subculture, its production and distribution do not constitute any more an exclusively internal affair of this subculture. At present these activities have to a high degree been commercialised and dominated by profit oriented individuals and groups. In the time span 1993 - 1996 several big laboratories producing daily some hundreds cubic centimetres of 'Polish heroin' have been destroyed by the police. The number of cases of illegal production of drugs registered by the police, great majority of which are cases of producing ' Polish heroin', remains on the other hand (with the exception of the year 1993) rather stable (see table 3). Also the population of consumers of this drug seems to remain fairly stable during last ten years. According to the recent estimates (1997) the number of opiate consumers in Poland (depending on the method used) amounts to something between 8,300 and 40,000 persons, the best estimate being probably something like 20,000 (Sierosławski and Zieliński 1997).

There are also two other drugs which play nowadays an important role on the Polish internal market, namely amphetamine and cannabis. Reasons for special concern in recent years gives first of all amphetamine. As Poland became in the nineties one of the major European producers of this drug (see below), some part of the output is being distributed within the country. Especially the media are full of alarmist reports about growing consumption of amphetamine, first of all among students in high schools but also schoolchildren in primary schools. According to these reports in many schools dealers distribute this drug free of charge or for a very low price with the purpose of creating future demand. Such reports, based mostly on personal evaluations of teachers or police officers, must be approached, however, with due caution. There is no doubt that media reporting about this issue are sometimes extremely sensationalist, creating moral panic and scare. On the other hand some data provided by the public opinion research may give grounds to serious concern. For example a survey conducted in the year 1994 by CBOS (Centrum Badania Opinii Publicznej - Centre for Public Opinion Research) confirmed that in recent years drugs became easily available in Poland. 45 % of questioned students of high schools (research has been conducted on a national, representative sample) said that they know or could learn without any difficulty where to buy drugs. Also the number of students of such schools admitting taking drugs has almost doubled in the first half of the nineties (Ślusarczyk 1996). While in 1992 5 % of the high schools students admitted to taking drugs, in 1994 10 % of them made such admission. However, the most popular drug constitutes according to this research cannabis, and not amphetamine (CBOS 1994). Other illegal drugs, like heroin, cocaine, ecstasy and LSD do not seem to play a significant role, which does not mean that they are absolutely absent. As a matter of fact in the previous year there was plenty of publicity in the media about growing problems with 'brown sugar' heroin, consumption of which constitutes allegedly a special problem in Warsaw. The main reason for this relative unimportance of the 'classic' hard drugs constitutes probably the fact, that most of them are still too expensive for average recreational user.

The ambiguity of the situation may be confirmed by some other official statistics. First of all it is important that the number of deaths by overdoses, an important measure of the dimensions of the drug problem, despite some significant growth at the beginning of the nineties, remains since a few years relatively stable (table 1). On the other hand the number of addicts registered by the police because of the commission of an offence has been growing steadily in the 1990s (table 2). Also the number of drug trafficking offences and offences of providing or selling drugs to others registered by the police has been growing (table 3). Especially the time span 1996 - 1998, brought about significant changes in the structure of the registered drug offences, as the above mentioned supply side offences started to dominate over cases of illegal cultivation of poppy and illegal production of drugs, which predominated earlier. However, this may also be interpreted as evidence of the growing demand followed by the supply of illegal drugs. It may also confirm opinions about the growing professionalisation of dealing with drugs on the Polish internal market, which is increasingly being taken over by well organised networks of dealers active in youth and student clubs, coffee shops, but also in the vicinity of schools. On the other hand this growth has been by no means constant and stable. Just the opposite: we could observe rather quite significant fluctuations, which may mean that patterns of law enforcement and intensity of police actions against trafficking and dealing play a very important role here. For example the sharp increase in the year 1996 of the number of the registered cases of providing and selling drugs to others has to be attributed first of all to the fact that special police drug squads have been established in that year in few major cities.

Table 1. Deaths by overdoses of drugs in Poland in the years 1990 - 1996.

Year	1990	1991	1992	1993	1994	1995	1996
Number of cases	98	130	167	150	151	177	157

Table 2. Addicts registered by the police because of committing criminal offences.

Year	1990	1991	1992	1993	1994	1995	1996
Number of addicts	13,950	14,480	15,335	16,597	17,363	18,200	19,868

In sum, it seems, that the Polish consumer market, although it underwent in recent years significant changes, remains still quite different from the situation in most countries of Western Europe. Also dimensions of the drug problem, despite its significant growth since 1990, are still relatively small. All this means, that problems which Poland is facing since some time on the supply side of the drug problem most probably do not result from the growing domestic demand. However, all this does not mean that the situation may and will not change in the near future. Prognoses are here rather unfavourable.

CHANGES ON THE SUPPLY SIDE

After 1989 two other aspects of the drug problem in Poland underwent more significant changes. Both of them involve the supply side. First, Poland became one of the most important European producing countries of amphetamine. Secondly, Poland became also an important, although probably not the most important, transit country for smuggling drugs to Western Europe (Hołyst 1993, pp.85 - 88, Hołyst 1994).

Table 3.Drug offences in Poland registered by the police in the years 1985-1998.

Year	Altogether		Illegal growing of poppy		Illegal production of drugs		Illegal production of devices used to produce drugs		Smuggling of drugs		Trafficking with drugs		Providing or selling drugs to others		Possession of drugs	
	N	%	N	%	N	%	N	%	N	%	N	%	N	%	N	%
1985	1763	100.0	1218	69.1	277	15.7	71	4.0	4	0.2	53	3.0	140	7.9	-	-
1986	6260	100.0	4879	77.9	817	13.1	135	2.2	7	0.2	126	2.0	296	4.7	-	-
1987	4709	100.0	3765	79.9	583	12.4	75	1.6	2	0.0	34	0.7	260	5.5	-	-
1988	3177	100.0	1940	61.1	1003	31.6	63	1.9	4	0.1	38	1.2	139	4.4	-	-
1989	2279	100.0	1156	50.7	568	24.9	32	1.4	5	0.2	25	1.1	493	21.6	-	-
1990	1128	100.0	382	33.9	557	49.4	34	3.0	1	0.1	77	6.8	77	6.8	-	-
1991	2735	100.0	1712	62.6	589	21.5	60	2.2	6	0.2	24	0.9	128	4.7	-	-
1992	2554	100.0	1631	63.9	521	20.4	94	3.7	23	0.9	45	1.8	340	9.4	-	-
1993	5569	100.0	3577	64.2	1280	22.9	123	2.2	21	0.4	207	3.7	361	6.5	-	-
1994	3927	100.0	3040	77.4	387	9.9	85	2.2	20	0.5	107	2.7	288	7.3	-	-
1995	4284	100.0	2780	64.9	392	9.2	97	2.3	69	1.6	215	5.0	731	17.1	-	-
1196	6780	100.0	2634	38.5	459	6.8	135	1.9	97	1.4	397	5.9	3058	45.1	-	-
1997	7915	100.0	2518	31.8	701	8.9	116	1.5	148	1.9	847	10.7	3507	44.3	78	0.9
1998	16432	100.0	1195	7.3	574	3.5	190	1.2	252	1.5	1957	11.9	10762	66.5	1502	9.1

Source: Statistical Yearbooks of the Polish Republic.

It seems that there were a few good reasons for Poland becoming such an important producer of amphetamine. First of all it was probably the geographical position of the country bordering on Germany, and offering relatively simple and short routes for smuggling the product. Secondly, Polish police and other services (e.g. customs) lacked at the beginning of the nineties almost any experience in fighting production and smuggling of drugs, what made such activities relatively safe or at least probably much safer than in the west. Third, substances used to produce amphetamine (so called precursors) were not subject to any monitoring or legal control[1], and could be easily produced domestically or imported for a low price from the countries of the former Soviet Union, usually from Ukraine. Fourth, there was a surplus of highly qualified chemists, Polish or from the countries of the former Soviet Union, sometimes even scientists with academic degrees, who were available, usually because of low wages, to use their skills in this market. The last factor constitutes probably the main reason for a very high quality and purity of the amphetamine produced in Poland (Adamoli et al. 1998, pp.50 - 51). There was for example a famous case of a former university employee with the doctoral degree, who developed his own technology of producing some precursors of amphetamine of extremely high purity. His laboratory operated quite legally, he has been paying taxes, and did not attempt to hide his activities.

It is impossible to estimate the amount of amphetamine produced in Poland, there is little doubt that Poland has a significant share in the European market. About 50 % of amphetamine confiscated in Sweden is of Polish origin. It means that as the result of the competition between the Polish and Dutch producers of the amphetamine, the Dutch could have lost about 30 % of that market. In Germany the share of the Polish supply is smaller and amounts to about 20 %. Generally it is estimated that between 10 % and 25 % of the amphetamine sold in Europe is produced in Poland (Ślusarczyk 1996, p.79; Serdakowski 1997, p.228), which means that Poland may successfully compete with the Netherlands for primacy in this area[2]. Polish amphetamine is produced primarily for export and smuggled out of the country, usually either to Germany or to Sweden. At the beginning of the decade it was produced even exclusively for export. It was probably the large supply of Polish amphetamine which contributed to the rapid fall of prices of this drug on the European markets in the nineties: from 8 - 10 thousand US $ per kilo in 1993 to 2,5 - 2,8 thousand in 1995 (Serdakowski 1997, p.227). Only since about 1992 - 1993 some part of this production started to be distributed within the country. It is difficult to estimate what percentage of the entire output is being distributed domestically. However, it seems that still most of the product is exported. It is also impossible to give exact numbers of laboratories producing amphetamine as estimates vary here widely. For example Polish police estimated that in the year 1992 there were about 200 such

---

[1] This has been changed by the new law on counteraction against drug addiction passed by the Parliament in April 1997, which entered into force on October 15th, 1997. For more detail on it, see: Krajewski (1999).

[2] It seems that Polish producers are making some inroads with their amphetamine even in the Netherlands itself. In September 1999 Polish media reported broadly on the case in which Polish police dissolved in the city of Łódź in central Poland a criminal group which cooperated closely with the Dutch drug dealers. According to these reports Poles exported their amphetamine to the Netherlands and received in exchange cannabis.

laboratories concentrated most probably in the vicinity of big cities like Warsaw, Gdańsk, Łódź, Lublin, Katowice and Bydgoszcz, but also Wrocław, Poznań and Szczecin. Especially the surroundings of the last city, major see port on the German border, seem to constitute a problem, as it is also an important point on the smuggling route. On the other hand according to the estimates of the German *Bundeskriminalamt* there may be even 500 such laboratories in Poland (Serdakowski 1997, p.227). Compared with these estimates the results of the efforts by the Polish police to curb production of amphetamine seem to be meagre and absolutely unsatisfactory. In 1994 only 3 such laboratories have been destroyed, in 1995 - 8 and in 1996 - 6. The number of registered cases of producing drugs, after reaching absolutely unusual peak in the year 1993 dropped slightly, and in the years 1994 - 1996 was even lower than before 1992 (see table 3). It has risen than in 1997 only to drop again in 1998. However, as it was mentioned before, the great majority of these cases are cases concern the production of 'Polish heroin' and not amphetamine. The main reason for this, no doubt, is the fact that production of 'Polish heroin', especially by addicts themselves (which still exists) and small entrepreneurs not connected to organised groups, is much easier to detect for the police[3].

POLAND AS A TRANSIT COUNTRY

A new phenomenon in Poland constitutes also organised transit of drugs. As mentioned above drugs passing illegally Polish borders are usually or primarily not destined for domestic consumption. Poland constitutes here only a transit route for drugs destined to the western Europe. Sometimes it happens that parts of the smuggled transports are distributed within the country. Such distribution, however, seems not to play, as it was mentioned earlier, a very significant role on the domestic market. The main drug being smuggled through Poland seems to be heroin transported on the land route from Turkey or even from Iran, Afghanistan and Pakistan. There were few reasons for Poland becoming such a transit route for smuggling heroin. First of all the war in former Yugoslavia disturbed the traditional Balkan route (Adamoli et al, p.50) which existed before the fall of communism and which was controlled to a certain extent by Bulgarian secret services. Second, as Russian organised criminal groups started to get more and more involved in drug trafficking, it was only natural for these organisations smuggling Asiatic heroin through the territory of the former Soviet Union to use also Polish territory. Third, Polish customs and border guards had previously almost no experience in fighting such activities, which made the Polish route, and also the route through other former communist countries, relatively safe. Also opportunities of bribing customs and police officers or other officials (usually seriously underpaid) are probably much greater in these countries compared to the Western Europe.

---

[3] It is necessary to mention also cases of smuggling ' Polish heroin' out of Poland, mainly to Germany, to Berlin. It is called there *polnische Suppe* (Polish soup) and is being smuggled in Coca Cola bottles, as there is no difference between colour of both liquids. This smuggling appears however, to have rather weak connections with organised crime and constitutes rather individual entrepreneurship of individual Polish 'tourists'.

It seems, that there are three major routes of smuggling drugs which go through the Polish territory (Serdakowski 1997, p.233; Kreuzer, Thamm 1997, 187-332). The first one begins in Turkey and using the land route through Bulgaria and Romania or the sea route to Romania passes then through south-western Ukraine or Hungary and Slovakia to southern Poland and to Germany. The second route originates also in Turkey, crosses the Black See to Ukraine and leads through Belaruss and central or northern Poland to Germany. Finally, the third one originates in Central Asia or in Far East and through Russia or Russia and Ukraine joins the previous one. Although these routes seem to be of very great importance, they do not constitute probably the only and most important smuggling routes in Eastern Europe. Of even greater importance may be the route through Romania, Hungary and Czech Republic to Germany. The classic Balkan route seems to regain its importance recently too. Smuggling of heroin from Turkey takes place very often under the cover of legal activities conducted by legal firms engaged in textiles importation and exportation and owned usually jointly by Poles and Turks. In such cases drugs are usually hidden in trucks, sometimes without any knowledge of drivers. Also tourist buses are used for such purposes. Other method employed by Turkish groups uses Polish-Slovak border. Drugs are smuggled by car to Slovakia, repackaged and than carried by individual couriers crossing the border illegally, usually in the mountains.

Poland is also used as a transit route to smuggle marihuana and hashish, primarily by the see route to the Polish ports on the coast of the Baltic See and subsequently on the land route to Germany. Drugs originate usually from Central Asia and Near East or from North Africa. During last years Polish customs confiscated a number of times spectacularly large amounts of marihuana and hashish, smuggled usually in containers brought by ships to Polish ports.

Finally since a few years Poland seems to be used increasingly as a transit route for smuggling cocaine, again mainly to Germany. Here again two possible routes are used: either by sea to the ports on the Baltic coast (Gdynia, which has major container port seems to be used particularly often), or by air to Okêcie, international airport in Warsaw. At the airport both methods, individual couriers swallowing packages with drugs and larger transports using air-cargo are used, when cocaine is involved. Such activities seem to be controlled first of all by Cali cartel. For example in 1997 a major cell of this cartel has been dismantled by the police in southern Poland.

According to the data of Interpol in the years 1992 - 1995 the following amounts of drugs have been confiscated in Poland or in neighbouring countries as a results of attempts to smuggle them to Poland or out of Poland: 35 tons of marihuana, 24 tons of hashish, 1500 litres of hashish oil, 3,3 tonnes of cocaine, 590 kg of heroin, 195 kg of amphetamine and about 2 000 litres of BMK (Serdakowski 1997, pp.234-235). Table 4 shows the amounts of smuggled drugs confiscated by the Polish customs service on the borders and by the police on the Polish territory in the years 1991-1996, and table 5 provides more detailed data on that subject for the year 1998 only. As in many other countries these numbers are fluctuating very strongly, as the effectiveness of the agencies dealing with smuggling of drugs is by no means constant. For example since the year 1990 the amounts of the confiscated drugs were increasing year by year, only to drop rather spectacularly in 1996. The same tendency may be seen also in the increasing numbers of the drugs smuggling cases registered by the police (table 3). This was especially the case in the years 1997 and 1998, although the overall position of such offences in the structure of drug criminality remains rather insignificant. These tendencies seem to constitute rather the result of the increased efficiency of the Polish police and customs services and increased co-operation with such agencies in neighbouring countries, and not necessarily of the increasing flow of smuggled drugs through the Polish territory[4] Intensification of Poland's efforts to control and curb the flow of drugs through its territory resulted also, no doubt, from its current status as the country associated with the European Union and aspiring at the future full membership (Dorn 1996). Also financial help and know-how provided by the EU and by Germany was here of great significance. Despite all that it must be assumed that perceived and real risks connected with being involved in any form of drug trafficking are in Poland probably still lower than in most Western countries. Also prospective profits may be much greater than in the West (especially when measured by the local standards), what creates strong incentives to engage in such activities (see: Dorn et al 1998).

Table 4. Confiscations of drugs in Poland by the police and custom services in the years 1991 - 1996 by types of drugs.

	1991	1992	1993	1994	1995	1996
Heroin (kg)	13.0	5.8	12.5	64.3	66.3	33.3
Cocaine (kg)	110.0	48.8	104.5	523.5	383.2	8.5
Hashish (kg)	-	3.1	6592.0	12.0	10001.3	5.2
Marihuana (kg)	-	6.5	566.0	164.0	2086.6	2018.5
Amphetamine (kg)	5.0	10.0	25.4	16.3	12.9	13.5
LSD (portions)	-	-	-	-	-	1300
MDMA (tablets)	-	-	-	-	-	1000

Source: Serdakowski (1997), p.239.

It is also necessary to mention that since the year 1990 one can observe increased involvement of the Polish nationals as drug couriers, i.e. in smuggling drugs to or out of countries other than Poland. The dimensions of the known aspect of this problem in recent years are illustrated in table 6. The majority of such cases involve Polish citizens engaged in smuggling of amphetamine either to Sweden or to Germany. There are however also known cases of using Polish couriers to smuggle heroin from Turkey or cocaine from Colombia and Brazil to Western Europe. Most of the couriers are people in difficult financial situation (for example unemployed), who in this way want to get out of financial trouble, or people who want to earn quickly sums of money very substantial for Polish conditions. On the other hand Polish couriers have an opinion of being very cheap.

---

[4] It is necessary to remember also that the growth of the amounts of seized drugs constitutes since many years all-European tendency. See Farell et al (1996).

Table 5. Confiscations of drugs in Poland in the year 1998 by types of drugs and agencies involved.

Type of drug	Police	State Security Office	Custom Services	Border Guards	Together
Amphetamine	43,265 kg	-	1,600 kg	6,638 kg	51,503 kg
Ecstasy	1796 tabl.	-	-	-	1796 tabl.
Cocaine	9,225 kg	0,100 kg	8,130 kg	3,702 kg	21,157 kg
Heroin	41,93 kg	0,120 kg	23,79 kg	3,133 kg	67,405 kg
LSD	11199 trips	-	3703 trips	-	14902 trips
Hashish	2,400 kg	4,800 kg	0,873 kg	0,103 kg	8,176 kg
Marihuana	57,170 kg	-	4,260 kg	1,103 kg	62,146 kg
Herbal cannabis	1832,600 kg	-	70,201 kg	1,500 kg	1904,361 kg
' Polish heroin'	394 litres	-	-	-	394 litres
Poppy straw	6870 kg	-	-	1,700 kg	6871,700 kg
Hallucinogenic mushrooms	3,600 kg	-	0,838 kg	0,370 kg	4,475 kg
Sterides	527590 ampoules	-	-	-	527590 ampoules
BMK	88,5 l	-	-	-	88,5 l

Source: Data of the Drug Unit of the Main Headquarters of the Police.

Table 6. Polish citizens arrested abroad for smuggling drugs and amounts of drugs seized by them.

	1991	1992	1993	1994	1995
Number of cases	14	17	38	51	90
Number of persons	23	30	51	76	156
Heroin (kg)	22	20	56	147	447
Cocaine (kg)	43	8	63	1369	118
Hashish (kg)	-	2850	4505	1506	9775
Marihuana (kg)	-	-	8	-	2082
Amphetamine (kg)	15	34	81	67	102
Together	80	2912	4713	3089	12524

Source: Serdakowski (1997), p.235.

INVOLVEMENT OF POLISH AND FOREIGN CRIMINAL GROUPS

Production of drugs, especially of amphetamine, and the smuggling of them out of Poland or through its territory are since 1989 usually subject to control by organised Polish and international criminal groups. Such activities require usually prior investments (for example in laboratory equipment and chemicals), preparations, organisation and co-operation of many persons. They require also, first of all in cases of smuggling, contacts with analogous groups abroad. This type of organised criminal activity was rather unknown in communist Poland, although it would be wrong to claim that organised criminal groups did not exist at that time at all. Many such groups being active currently have their roots and origins in communist period. Their members were involved at that time first of all in illegal currency trade, various forms of trade on the black market (which flourished because of the permanent shortages of basic consumer goods) or smuggling of goods from abroad. They had also probably quite often various links to the communist secret services. After 1990 these people and groups started to constitute a 'hard core' of the Polish organised underworld.

For example in the year 1996 there were more than 377 organised criminal groups active on the Polish territory which were known to the Polish police and which had about 4750 known members[5] However, it is necessary to stress that the Polish police seem to use for registration purposes a broader definition of the organised criminal group than for example definitions used by German *Bundeskriminalamt* (Levi 1998) or by the Expert Group on Organised Crime of the Council of Europe (Adamoli et al 1998, p.9). In other words it seems that above data include most criminal groups independently of their internal structure, eventual hierarchy, division of labour etc.[6] Nevertheless, most of these groups (about 212) were Polish, i.e. they were composed exclusively of Polish members. Remaining groups (158 with estimated membership of 522 persons) were of mixed membership, i.e. consisted of Poles and representatives of other nationalities. These groups involved nationals from 37 countries of the world, first of all, however, citizens of the countries of the former Soviet Union (39%, primarily Ukrainians and Russians) and Germans (14%). There were also 7 known groups of purely foreign character, involving among others Armenians, Albanians and Vietnamese.

Organised criminal groups in Poland engage in variety of activities, three most important being production, trafficking and smuggling of drugs, smuggling of arms, explosives and stolen cars and money laundering. Most of the groups do not limit themselves to or specialise in just one kind of criminal activity. However, usually it is possible to point out to some sort of predominating or most important area of activity. Producing, smuggling and trafficking with drugs constituted such predominating kind of engagement for about 66 groups known to the police in the year 1996, i.e. less than 20 % of the total number.

These very scarce data on Polish organised crime groups, together with the data on the numbers of illegal laboratories producing amphetamine, suggest that there are relatively many groups active within the field of drug trafficking. It may lead to the conclusion that despite the stereotypes about organised crime in Eastern Europe (Adamoli et al. 1998, p.49), this trade is rather not highly centralised and monopolised, as

---

[5] According to the data for the year 1993 (see Ptywaczewski 1997), there were 293 such groups with about 4 000 members. It does not mean of course that this phenomenon is growing so quickly. It is rather police's knowledge which becomes still better. In 1998 the number of groups known to the police was already 644.

[6] For more details on the term criminal group in Polish legal and criminological literature, see Gaberle (1998).

it is also the case in many western countries (Becchi 1996; Dorn, South 1990). Just the opposite, namely a very chaotic and highly competitive market, may be the case. Such opinion may be supported by the rather high rates of violence connected with organised crime in Poland and recent 'gang-wars' which include sometimes spectacular incidents reminding of the 'St.Valentine's Day Massacre'. If, as some claim, the principal function of 'Mafia' is the enforcement of contracts (Reuter 1983), Polish organised crime may be at the moment, as a matter of fact, pretty disorganised. However, with the current state of knowledge and research it is impossible to tell something more exact about the nature of the competition among organised groups involved in drug trafficking and the nature of this market in Poland.

According to the police Polish criminal groups are organised in a rather simple way and do not have a very complicated structure. They have always a leader and few additional members belonging to the collective leadership. Other members, called sometimes 'soldiers', are usually not 'constant' or 'full' members. They are rather hired to do a concrete job. Usually a more elaborated structure have groups involved in producing drugs. Here clear cut division of labour constitutes a rule. Members involved in supplying chemicals, actual production of drugs and their distribution usually, for security reasons, do not know each other, what makes destruction of entire organisations particularly difficult. Smuggling of drugs requires also preparation of many separate stages of the entire operation which sometimes takes place in many countries. Because of this international connections, with criminal groups in other countries are necessary. It seems that such structures in Poland are connected very often to the people having some sort of contacts with traditional producing countries in South America or in Asia. Such role may be played by foreigners living in Poland (students, businessmen, spouses of Polish nationals), or Poles having some contacts abroad, as a result of marriage, studies, business connections, tourist travels and similar. It is also well known, that groups active in Poland, especially in producing amphetamine, use as a distributors Polish nationals living permanently abroad. The last situation is especially often the case in Sweden. Finally, there are cases of organising smuggling of drugs through the Polish territory without engaging in any contacts with local, Polish criminal groups.

Although it seems that the Polish police gain still greater operational knowledge about the structure, membership and operations of criminal groups involved in drug smuggling and trafficking in Poland, this knowledge is of course confidential. What is known officially (see: Pływaczewski 1995, Pływaczewski 1997) is sometimes quite superficial and empirical research on criminal groups is almost non-existent. Because of this it is difficult to say something exact and beyond what is known publicly through the media. That such groups have international connections is certain. Apart from 'Russian Mafia' such contacts seem to exist first of all with Italian (Mafia and N'dranghetta), Turkish and Colombian (Cali cartel) groups. In last two cases among the common activities drug trafficking predominates.

It is also very unclear to what extent Polish and foreign groups are intertwined with legal businesses and enterprises. It is certain that there is a lot of economic crime in Poland and other post-communist countries, where transformation to market economy and privatisation create sometimes especially suitable conditions for that type of crime

(Jasiński 1996). More or less illegal business operations, transactions and fraud by people operating otherwise legitimate enterprises are however something different from engagement in purely illegal activities connected to drugs. There is very little public knowledge about interconnections between such legal and illegal activities. However, it may be assumed that people engaging in drug production, smuggling and trafficking belong rather to the category of a *crime*-entrepreneurs and not necessarily to *criminal* entrepreneurs (van Duyne 1996), what means that drugs business has more similarities to the 'classic' underworld than for example alcohol smuggling, which constitutes a very problematic form of the trans-border economic crime in Poland. On the other hand, it seems that money earned on drug trafficking is invested in legal businesses and enterprises. According to the opinion of the police sources such investments take place first of all in restaurants, night clubs, hotels and recreational complexes. The exact nature and dimensions of the problem are however not (at least publicly) known. There is also very little known about eventual connections of organised crime with the worlds of politics, administration, media and similar.

Polish media use quite often the word 'Mafia' to describe organised criminal groups active in Poland. They do it however without exact knowledge of the meaning of this word in criminology and such use does not prove that real Mafia-type structures exist already in Poland. There is no doubt that leaders of the organised criminal groups, especially those who are active within a variety of economic structures, may attempt to contact politicians and public officials with the purpose of influencing their policies and decisions in a way which would be advantageous to their interests. In exchange they may offer a variety of gratifications, like cash, shares of companies and similar. The extent of this phenomenon is however extremely difficult to assess. It is also particularly difficult to ascertain whether such activities are undertaken only or primarily by groups engaged in economic crime (which are usually somehow integrated in business circles) or also by groups of purely criminal character, engaged for example in drug trafficking. Three years ago the State's Prosecution Office prepared a report on this subject, which was however not made public. According to the police information informal and operational knowledge about it in only very few cases may constitute a good enough ground to institute an official investigation and criminal proceedings. Nevertheless in 1996 there were only 18 cases of corruption revealed by the officers of the organised crime units.

Although laundering of money (Pływaczewski 1996), drug money included, of both domestic and foreign origin, is considered to be the widespread phenomenon in Poland exact knowledge about this phenomenon is very limited. Nevertheless Poland, like many other east European countries, is considered to be a money laundering paradise. According to some estimates about 2 billions US $ have been laundered in Poland since 1990. The estimates of the Supervision Division of the Polish National Bank are much more pessimistic. According to them there are between 2 and 3 billion US $ laundered yearly in Poland. What share of these money constitute drug money is an absolute mystery. The results of repressive measures in this area are extremely meagre. According to the police data in the year 1996 there were for example only 8 revealed cases of ' legalising' illegal property. Although since 1994 Polish criminal law contains provisions criminalising various forms of money laundering, which were broadened and improved in the new criminal code which is in force since 1. September 1998, there were no convictions for this offence yet. There are also some reporting procedures required by the Banking System Act of 1992 and the instruction of the President of the Polish National Bank from the same year requires all banks to register all cash operations above certain value and to identify and register persons conducting such operations. However it seems that many banks are not very eager to cooperate on such matters. Because of this special legislation on preventing money laundering through banks and other means is currently being prepared. It will include, among others, the creation of a special agency with the task of monitoring all financial operations above certain limit.

CONCLUSIONS

Polish drug market underwent in the past ten years significant changes. It evolved from rather unsophisticated and simple pattern of 'mutual societies' dealing primarily with home-made stuff of 'Polish heroin', towards more developed and western-style structures dominated by profit oriented criminal groups. This approximation to the situation in the west does not mean however that there are no significant differences. From this point of view Poland may be treated still as some sort of 'emerging market'. Such opinion is based first of all on the fact that opiate-users' subculture is still dominated by 'Polish heroin' and not real one. Also other hard drugs, like cocaine, seem to play a marginal role. It is only cannabis and amphetamine which during the 1990s gained a significant position on the domestic market as a new drugs of choice among Polish consumers. All this justifies the opinion that Poland still does not belong to important consumer countries. This may end however even in the near future.

The reason for much more serious concern gives the development of Poland's position as a major producing country, first of all of synthetic drugs, and an important transit country. Here the role of Polish organised criminal groups acting as actual producers of drugs or intermediaries in international smuggling is of great importance. It seems however that drug trafficking constitutes by no means an exclusive area of activities of such groups. It is difficult to tell something more detailed on the nature of this international drug market in Poland. Quantitative data, gathered by criminal justice and other crime control agencies are of very limited character, and they are notoriously unreliable. Qualitative data based on research (and not on usually secret operational knowledge of the police) are almost non-existent. However, it may be assumed that, as in may other countries of Europe, drug trafficking takes place on a very segmented and competitive market, which is not dominated by some sort of monopoly.

In sum, it seems that research on organised crime in general, and patterns of drug trafficking in particular, research leading to more comprehensive knowledge about these phenomenons, will constitute the major challenge for Polish criminology during the next decade.

LITERATURE

Adamoli, S., Di Nicola, A., Savona, E.U., Zoffi, P., *Organised Crime Around the World*, Helsinki, HEUNI 1998.

Becchi, A., 'Mafia-dominated drug Market?'. In: N.Dorn, J.Jepsen, E.Savona (eds.) *European Drug Policies and Enforcement*, Basingstoke-New York, Macmillan Press Ltd., 1996.

CBOS *Młodzież i używki (Youth and legal and illegal drugs)*, Warszawa, CBOS, 1994.

Dorn N., South N., Drug Markets and Law Enforcement, *The British Journal of Criminology*, 1990, nr. 2, 171 - 188.

Dorn, N., Borderline Criminology: External Drug Policies and the EU. In: N.Dorn, J.Jepsen, E.Savona (eds.) *European Drug Policies and Enforcement*, Basingstoke-New York, Macmillan Press Ltd., 1996.

Dorn, N., Oette, L., White, S., Drug Importation and the Bifurcation of Risk: Capitalisation, Cut Outs and Organised Crime, *The British Journal of Criminology*, 1998, nr.4, 537-560.

Duyne van, P.C., The Phantom and Threat of Organised Crime, *Law and Social Change*, 1996, 341-377.

Farell, G., Mansur, K., Tullis, M., Cocaine and Heroin in Europe 1983 - 1993: A Cross-national Comparison of Trafficking and Prices, *The British Journal of Criminology*, 1996, nr. 2, 255-281.

Gaberle A., Die Vorbeugung gegen die Drogensucht in Polen - zum Gestez von 31. Januar 1985, *Jahrbuch für Ostrecht*, 1986, 307-323.

Gaberle A., *Patologia spoteczna (Social Pathology)*, Warszawa, Wydawnictwo Prawnicze 1993.

Gaberle A., Gruppenkriminalität in Polen als kriminologische und strafrechtliche Erscheinung. In: H.J.Albrecht, F.Dünkel, H.J.Kerner, J.Kürzinger, H.Schöch, K.Sessar, B.Vilmow (eds.) *Internationale Perspektiven in Kriminologie und Strafrecht. Festschrift für Günther Kaiser zum 70. Geburtstag*, Berlin, Duncker & Humboldt, 1998.

Hołyst, B., *Narkomania i przestępczoœæ (Drugs and Crime)*, Warszawa, Polskie Towarzystwo Higieny Psychicznej, 1993.

Hołyst B., Drugs and Crime in Poland, *Eurocriminology*, 1994, 141 - 167.

Jasiński, J., Crime in Central and East European Countries, *European Journal on Criminal Policy and Research*, 1996, nr.1, 40-50.

Krajewski K., Recent developments in drug policies in Poland. In: L.Böllinger (ed.) *Cannabis Science. From Prohibition to Human Right*, Frankfurt a.M., Peter Lang, 1997.

Krajewski K., Die Reform des Betäubungsmittelstrafrechts in Polen, *Zeitschrift für die gesamte Strafrechtswissenschaft*, 1999, nr.2, 539-557.

Kreuzer, A., Thamm, G., Erscheinungsformen von Drogenkriminalität und verwandtem abweichendem Verhalten. In: A.Kreuzer (ed.) *Handbuch des Betäubungs-mittelstrafrecht*, Munich, Verlag C.H.Beck, 1997.

Levi M., Perspectives on 'Organised Crime': An Overview, *The Howard Journal of Criminal Justice*, 1998, *nr.4*, 335-345.

Pływaczewski, E., Economic and Organised Crime. In: J.Jasiński, A.Siemaszko (eds.) *Crime Control in Poland*, Warsaw, Oficyna Naukowa, 1995.

Pływaczewski, E., Organised Crime in Poland, *The Kanagawa Hogaku (The Review of Law and Politics),* 1997, *nr.3*, 367-388.

Pływaczewski, E., Zur gegenwärtigen Stand der Bekämpfung der Geldwäsche in Polen. In: H.-J. Hirsch, P.Hoffmañski, E.W.Pływaczewski, C.Roxin (eds.) *Neue erscheinungsformen der Kriminalität in ihrer Auswirkung auf das Straf- und Strafprozeßrecht*, Białystok, Temida 2, 1996.

Reuter P., *Disorganized Crime. The Economics of the Visible Hand*, Cambridge, Mass.-London, The MIT Press, 1983.

Serdakowski J., Zorganizowana przestępczość narkotykowa w Polsce (Organised drug criminality in Poland). In: W.Pływaczewski, J.Świerczewski (ed.) *Policja polska w walce ze zorganizowanñ przestêpczości (Polish police against the organised crime)*, Szczytno, Wydawnictwo Wyższej Szkoły Policji, 1997.

Sierosławski. J., Zieliński A., Comparison of different estimation methods in Poland. In: *Estimating the Prevalence of Problem Drug Use in Europe*, Luxembourg, European Monitoring Centre for Drugs and Drug Addiction Scientific Monograph Series, 1997.

Ślusarczyk B., Narkomania w Europie w 1995 r. (Drug addiction in Europe in 1995), *Przeglad Policyjny (Police Review)* 1996, *nr 4*, 79-80.

Chapter 7

CRIME ACROSS THE BORDER
FINNISH PROFESSIONAL CRIMINALS TAKING
ADVANTAGE OF ESTONIAN CRIME OPPORTUNITIES

Mika Junninen & Kauko Aromaa[1]

THE PROBLEM

Cross-border crime in the case of Finland of recent years has typically been understood in terms of Russian and Estonian criminals entering the Finnish crime scene. This one-sided understanding of the matter has, among other drawbacks, hampered the development of a balanced police approach to the cross-border crime scene. The Finnish-Estonian[2] border is a sea border: the traffic takes place over a few main ports, the leading passenger ports being Helsinki (pop. 530,000) and Tallinn (pop. 500,000), some 70 kilometres apart. The annual number of passengers crossing the Gulf and entering each country is approaching 3 million (2.2 M in 1996, 2.5 M in 1998). The passenger flow is dominated by Finnish rather than Estonian travellers. Since 1995, no visa is required[3]. Estonia is also a transit country from Russia, Poland, Latvia, Lithuania to Finland and vice versa[4].

As the border between Estonia and Finland also represents a relative poverty border, it is attractive for the smuggling of certain commodities from the low-price area to the

---

[1] This report is based on the Master's thesis (sociology) of Mika Junninen: Ammattimaiset rikoksentekijt Virossa 1991-1998, University of Helsinki, Institute of sociology, 1999. The present document is edited by Kauko Aromaa. The project has been partially supported by the National Research Institute of Legal Policy, the Finnish Ministry for Foreign Affairs and the police department of the Ministry of the Interior. A more extensive report will published in the National Research Institute of Legal Policy series Research communications.

[2] The population of Finland is 5.1 million, of Estonia 1.5 million.

[3] No visa between Finland and the Baltic countries (for citizens) is required as of May 1st, 1995.

expensive one. Income differences also mean that police, customs and border controls of the Estonian side may be unusually vulnerable to corruption. Further, Estonia of the 1990s, with a newly established and/or reformed control apparatus and incomplete legislation has been widely understood as a country where traditional as well as organised crime have been growing (cf. Aromaa & Ahven 1995, Lehti 1997, Aromaa 1998, Markina 1998), implying control problems and, thus, favourable crime opportunities.

ADVANTAGES OF GOING TO ESTONIA

Estonia 'particularly Tallinn' is relatively easy for Finns to enter as they can conduct the main part of their business in Finnish. It is specially attractive for Finnish offenders. There is no mutual extradition agreement between the countries[5], Estonia has not joined the Schengen agreement and is not a member of the EU. The local authorities do not know him in the first place, and they are easier to neutralize than in Finland. Estonian police are often judged to be less efficient and more easily corrupted than their Finnish colleagues. Also, the lack of relevant legislation facilitates many criminal projects. It is easy to make contacts with foreign, in particular with Russian criminals in Estonia. As a consequence of pre-1991 Soviet penal policy, Estonia hosts Russian ex-convicts who have good connections with Estonian Russian criminals (Lehti 1997).

This raises the question to what extent Finnish (semi)professional criminal operators are taking advantage of this situation and to what extent they represent the organising and financing party. Estonian agents wishing to operate in Finland often cannot manage the situation on their own, but are instead in need of support from Finnish partners. Their acquaintance with Finnish circumstances, but also their relatively greater wealth (involving ability to invest) and technological and strategic know-how, make it likely that the role of Finnish agents becomes quite central.

SOURCES

The data of the research have been obtained by means of qualitative interviews with a total of 20 Finnish and Estonian police and customs representatives, including police liaison officers placed in the other country. The interviews were performed in March-May 1998.

The researcher was also granted access to Finnish non-public police files where unverified or other temporary police intelligence is stored. This information comes from various, sometimes anonymous sources and serves as supportive or initial data for further

---

[4] Finland has entered bilateral crime prevention agreements, among others aimed at facilitating police cooperation across the borders, with Russia (as of 17.2.1994), Estonia (as of 12.10.1995), Latvia (as of 5.3.1997), and Lithuania (as of 24.10.1997).
[5] Between the Baltic countries and Finland, the general European extradition rules apply.

investigations. In addition, Finnish pre-trial investigation records were available. The files covered the period 1993-1998 (the first years are incomplete).

The definition of (semi)professional involvement cannot be very clear-cut. The purpose was to exclude amateur-level small-time and non-continuous smuggling (of tobacco and alcohol, primarily). Our tentative criteria of (semi)professional crime refer to offences that are *planned* and involve *considerable* material values, and that, if found out, would be sanctioned with *imprisonment*.

FINNS IN THE ESTONIAN CRIME SCENE

According to Estonian police records, 41 Finnish offenders have been apprehended in 1993-1998 for crimes committed in Estonia. The annual number of Finns registered as permanent residents in Estonia was about one-hundred; however, unofficial estimates of the number of Finns staying in Estonia on a permanent basis are much higher, a minimum of several hundreds.

The recorded number of offences committed by Finns in Estonia is equally low. From 1993 to mid-1998, this number has varied between 5 and 8 annually. In the Finnish police records, Finns were suspected of having been involved in nearly 700 offences on the Finland-Estonia axis, and almost 200 other persons, known as offenders by the Finnish police, had been observed to have contacts with Estonian and Russian offenders in Estonia. Additionally, over 200 enterprises were suspected of acting as a front to criminal activities.

In routine checks by the Finnish border control, annually one thousand Finnish persons are stopped. Of those to be arrested immediately, the informant said that they are persons trying to avoid a sentenced prison term, escaped convicts and criminal patients, persons who have broken against parole rules, persons to be taken to court or apprehended as suspected offenders, or youths who have escaped from a remand home.

Finnish citizens wanted by Finnish authorities are able to stay in Estonia because of deficiencies in the cooperation between Finnish and Estonian authorities. The policemen interviewed thought that Finnish wanted persons would be rather easy to apprehend in Estonia, considering that they carry on openly and visibly in the country. The risk of apprehension of a Finnish offender who visits Estonia was estimated to be low. Estonian police were judged to be quite inefficient. The Finnish offender was thought to be the safer the better relationships his Estonian partners had with Estonian police and other authorities. Corruption being relatively widespread in Estonia, the problems arising from apprehension may be neutralized in advance by bribing certain central persons. This may, however, also be done after the problem arose:

'. . .if you are part of a criminal organisation then this group will pay to get the man out. Estonian police is such a young organisation . . . They are young people and they are still learning how to do police work. Knowing how small Tallinn is... and how small the

Estonian underworld is, you cannot avoid thinking that criminals have good relationships with police . . .' (I 4)[6]

Estonian police were assessed to suffer from an attitude problem, based on their low salaries, poor working facilities, the low esteem of police work, threats and other pressures from organised crime etc. The staff turnover is large and the accumulation of experience and professional skills suffer from this. Many young policemen are 'bought' to work for private security, a flourishing industry.

The capacity of clearing crimes was assessed to be rather weak. The register of wanted persons is still on a manual basis, the register of court decisions is decentralized and the fingerprint register was only recently transferred into a computer system. Estonian police report that they clear 30 % of recorded offences. However, it has been documented that they only record a fraction 'according to one estimate, 40 %' of all reported crimes. In the face of this, the actual clearance rate is very low.

> '. . . homicides, violent crime, and robberies are considered as real crimes. Resources are concentrated on these, and they also clear these offences quite well . . . Narcotics crime . . . . only very recently have they begun to take this seriously, and now they have started to allocate people to this sector. But as far as economic crime is concerned, they're still in the very beginning . . .' (I 2)

SMUGGLING BETWEEN FINLAND AND ESTONIA

The massive traffic between Finland and Estonia provides ample opportunity for smuggling. From Estonia to Finland, smuggling involves, e.g., metals, hormones, arms/weapons, alcohol and tobacco, narcotics and pirate products[7]. From Finland to Estonia, stolen goods are known to have been smuggled.

Most of the persons apprehended in Finland because of smuggling have been Estonian citizens. Finns have mainly been involved in the project as organisers and financiers. In Estonia, it is easier and cheaper than in Finland to hire a driver for the smuggling vehicle or a person who will carry drugs on his person. The commission paid to the courier is maximally a few thousand FIM. This may be equivalent to the annual income of an Estonian, whereas for a Finnish person, the same amount is not even one month's salary. The following categories of smuggled merchandise have been reported.

---

[6] Case descriptions are reported according to two standards. Expert interviews are cited ad verbatim, and descriptions taken from police files are reproduced in a manner where such details are changed or omitted that might make it possible to identify the source of the information

[7] Smuggling of people from or over Estonia to Finland has not been observed but may, of course, take place. Isolated instances have been reported from Russia to Finland, and from Baltic ports to Sweden. It is, however, a flexible matter, whether entering the country with false documents should be understood as smuggling people. This is likely to take place to some extent, travellers with false documents being stopped at the borders regularly: part of the documents are manufactured and sold as a business. Concrete smuggling of people may not be in great need if the forged document method can be applied successfully.

Metals

Between 1992 and the end of August 1998, 21 Finnish persons have been involved in smuggling metals from Estonia to Finland. Finnish metal business started with the imports of scrap metal and radioactive metals. The heyday of the metal trade was in 1992-1994. After 1995, the metal business has been smuggling of gold (import to Finland without paying the VAT).

There are no active metal mines in Estonia. After 1991 metals came from the obsolete Soviet military bases in Estonia, sold by the members of the military corps. However, imports of metals to Finland continued even after the local military bases had been emptied. Subsequently the merchandise came from Russia over Estonia to Finland and third countries.

From 1992 till 1994 Finland was an important transit country of rare metals. Finnish agents 'individuals and companies' handled radioactive metals to third countries. Part of the metals was temporarily stored, while the Finnish middlemen arranged for certificates to the metals, then being able to move the metals freely around. Thus, 'customs have since 1994 investigated a series of aggravated tax frauds where . . . persons imported, on behalf of their companies, in 1992-1995 from Estonia over Helsinki scrap metal that actually was platinum, palladium, nickel, copper and brass. Over 200 separate loads of metal have been imported, altogether over 5,000 tons. At the customs, the metals have been reported for only a fraction of their real value, part of the metals have not been reported at all. Also forged sales documents have been used... The real value of the metals has been over 100 million FIM. The value of unpaid import taxes exceeds 9 million FIM . . .' (Criminal investigations of the customs, 1997).

This citation refers to one of many similar cases, where Finnish agents have bought the metals legally but have failed to pay excises and also misinformed the customs as to the type and amount of the metals. Such tax evasion was said to have been very common.

More recently VAT fraud scams with gold traffic to Finland have been detected. In the police files, seven Finnish persons have been identified as gold importing suspects. The following example describes a rather large operation.

Example (1996): One Finnish, one Estonian and one Israeli citizen are suspected of having 450 kilos of gold imported from Estonia without a customs declaration. Couriers have carried the gold through customs on the 'green line', thus evading the VAT (approximately 8 million FIM). A Finnish company engaged in trade in valuable metals has bought from companies X Ltd. and Z Ltd 450 kilos of gold imported from Estonia as VAT-paid merchandise. Six Finnish men are identified as suspects in the operation. Prosecution has taken place.

Hormones and Medicaments

The police registers identify 23 Finnish persons as suspects of smuggling hormones and medicaments from Estonia to Finland or selling these commodities. This activity is mainly carried out by single individuals or groups with a few members. Smuggling is facilitated by the circumstance that Estonian pharmacies sell without a recipe or with a bought recipe (these are on sale informally or at certain physicians) chemicals that are not available or hard to come by in Finland: some hormone preparations and drugs classified as illegal narcotics in Finland. Smuggling these products is profitable even without sophistication and in small amounts.

The following case illustrates a more sophisticated pattern which is repeated in many examples in the police registers. Two companies, one in Finland and one in Estonia, are used as the fronts and the instruments for multiple crimes. The companies are also used to launder the profits as the bookkeeping is manipulated to transform illegal sales into legal incomes.

> Example (1993): A Finnish man A and his Russian-born wife B own companies X Ltd. in Finland, and Y Ltd. in Estonia. X Ltd. is reported as dealing in escort services, security guard services, model services, and dance group agent services. A was apprehended in Helsinki as he was trying to smuggle about 30,000 hormone tablets from Tallinn to Finland... In a search of A's home, military material from Estonia was found. Also, a visa application for four Estonian women was located.

Arms/Military Materials

The police sources identify 23 persons involved in smuggling or selling firearms or explosives between Estonia and Finland. Mostly, they have offered firearms for sale in the Finnish black market. There are, however, also observations of Finnish operators exporting modern weapons to Estonia, to the Estonian underworld.

> '. . . a Finnish company sold legally weapons to the Estonian army with documents from the Finnish army headquarters . . . but the weapons were then taken to Estonia past the customs, using this bribe system developed by the Estonian partner, and the weapons were then sold directly to the Estonian home guard and also to the underworld. The whole party was more than one thousand modern western handguns, but also pump shotguns and other such popular stuff... There are charges against these bribed customs officials, and also one Finnish person is charged of complicity[8]" (I 20).

Usually Finns have brought Russian surplus weapons from Estonia to Finland, acquired in the Estonian black market. The availability of army weapons is comparable with the situation in metals stolen from the Russian army. The weapons emerging in the world market have first been stolen from Russian army bases in Estonia and subsequently from Russia. For example, in 1993 a Finnish man offered for sale: 58 ton tanks, two air radars, 4 field artillery guns with 9 or 11 meter barrels and 22 anti-aircraft guns with a solid carriage. In another case, a Finnish man cooperated with a German and two Estonians, offering assault rifles etc. to the Finnish market.

Finnish customs have received several tip-offs of weapons entering Finland and of Finland being used as a transit country. Customs have, however, only found one larger

---

[8] The case is presently (Oct. 1999) on trial in Tallinn.

party of weapons in Finland. Usually, the weapons entering Finland come in small amounts, one by one[9]. Finnish authorities belittled the role of Finnish citizens in the arms trade. The informants pointed out that the Finnish black market for firearms is quite small.

Alcohol

Ample mention was made of Finns being involved in alcohol imports from Estonia to Finland. In the police records, 114 Finns were registered as suspected of professional smuggling of alcohol from Estonia (73) or selling such alcohol in Finland (41). In this count, each person appears only once, by the focus of their activity. In practice, many persons are active in both roles.

Overall, the professional smuggling of alcohol is understood as taking place in two different modes:

- professional smuggling of spirits in large amounts;
- professional smuggling of alcohol in small quantities by couriers, the recipients of the commodity organising and running the operation.

Professional smuggling of alcohol is rather profitable. For example, the price of a litre of spirits imported from Holland is about 20 FIM in Estonia. In Finland, it can be sold at about 150 FIM (retail price). Part of the difference is spent on expenses, including bribes. These expenses are estimated at approximately 30 FIM per litre, making a 100 FIM profit per litre. A truckload, or 10,000 litres thus yields a profit of one million FIM.

The actual import was often said to be made by couriers who were Estonians and Estonian Russians. Finns were typically described as organising and ordering the commodity on the Estonian side, and running the sales network in Finland.

Example (1997): The yard of the home of a Finnish man A has been used to store spirits. There has been several thousands of bottles in plastic sacks. The commodity may be corn spirits. It has been brought from Estonia on a truck, unloaded in a garage, and moved in plastic sacks to the place of storage. The alcohol has been sold to restaurants in cities of the west coast. The Finnish men A, B, C and D are involved in this. Many truckloads of alcohol have been brought to Finland in this operation.

The alcohol business contains elements of professional organised activity. However, the ties between group members do not seem to be very strong or permanent. The organisation can be described as several persons operating together in the same smuggling and sales network, their role differentiation being unclear. There may be roles such as the establishing of contacts and making deals, financing, storage, and organising the transport of the alcohol to the retailers.

---

[9] Swedish customs have uncovered several shipments of weapons presumed to be intended for the Swedish market.

More sophisticated patterns have been detected too. Here, the operation also contains ways of converting the illegal income to legal money.

Example (1998): Two Finnish men A and B have run an organisation that has smuggled several thousand litres of American 'Royal' spirits from Estonia to Finland. The two men are also involved in company X Ltd. Company X Ltd. is active in real estate and construction. Part of the financing is from the spirits business. The person responsible for the company is a Finnish man C, the shares are owned by C, B, and a Finnish association of which A is the president. A is also engaged in importing timber from Russia, using a tax haven company Y Ltd. A Finnish man D is acting as financial adviser and accountant; D has previous experience in economic crime.

A further similar operation is unveiled through a simple mistake:

Example (1994): In an industrial hall, a truck and a steel container were found with 2,520 litres of 96 % Royal spirits. Interrogations of an Estonian Russian apprehended here revealed that the spirits have been brought to Finland on the truck a little earlier. The truck has been loaded with leather couches, and with these, 7,560 litres of spirits have been imported. A large part of the alcohol has already been distributed to many different areas. Out of the 7,560 litres, 3,840 litres could be confiscated. Five Finnish men and three Estonian Russians are identified as suspects.

Example (1995): At least nine truckloads of construction stones have been imported to Finland, the recipients being X Ltd. (2 loads) and Y Ltd. (7 loads). Further, at least two truckloads of construction board have been brought in, addressed to Z Ltd. In the town named, no Z Ltd. was known, and the Estonian truck driver thus could not find a place where to leave the cargo. He took his truck to Tampere customs chamber where the truckload was found to have been constructed so that it could hold 8,016 litres of Royal spirits. Similarities in the spirits and in details of the operation make it likely that the illegal spirits brought in truckloads to another town belong to the same smuggling series. Five Finnish men and five Estonian Russians have been interrogated, suspected of professionally smuggling and distributing the alcohol.

In a further example, also other commodities are dealt with, and the Finnish operators have not needed to travel to Estonia to organise the transports:

Example (1993): Two Estonian Russian men living in Finland have imported at least 1,815 one-litre bottles of Royal spirits. 489 litres have been confiscated from an industrial hall in central Finland, owned by a Finnish man. A Finnish man living in Helsinki has bought a large part of the spirits and distributed it, mainly around a city of the west coast. In the industrial hall, also 154 cartons of Marlboro and North State cigarettes were confiscated. The Estonian Russians have sold at least 200 cartons of cigarettes. In the basement of the home of one of the Estonian Russians, 33,490 doses of Methandostrenolon, an anabolic steroid, were confiscated.

Cigarettes

In the police records, 20 Finnish persons were identified as organisers, interme- diaries, or recipients in cigarette smuggling from Estonia to Finland. The tobacco has been imported by the truckload, the whole operation typically concentrating on this commodity. The profitability at present prices is obvious, with retail prices of about 50 FIM per carton in Estonia against over 200 FIM in Finland.

Example (1998): A Finnish woman A is going to Tallinn one morning, returning the following day. She has manufactured a new smuggling vest to replace the one she has lost to the customs previously. Sometimes, she has a 3-year-old daughter with her, sometimes she is with other women. She may change her appearance under way. She usually carries 5-10 litres of alcoholic beverages and a lot a cigarettes.

As of recently, statements have been made to the effect that cigarette smuggling is developing to a more professional and voluminous level. The amounts of contraband cigarettes confiscated by customs have grown by a factor of 30 over five years, from 23,460 cigarettes in 1992 to 7,096,558 in 1996. In these seizures, the suspect has usually been an Estonian driving the car or the truck. Often, the owner or the recipient of the contraband have remained unclear, the Estonian drivers being reluctant to tell who hired them. (Criminal Investigations of the Customs, 1996). The larger parties appear often to be in transit to the Swedish market (cf. Persson 1999).

Narcotics

The number of persons suspected of smuggling or selling narcotics from Estonia increased slowly in the first half of the 1990s, from just a few persons to 32 in 1995. In 1996, the number doubled (67) and has remained around that level since. The growth of the figures is attributed to improved border controls; customs and police had both received tip-offs according to which large amounts of narcotics were coming in from Estonia.

'. . . This Estonian connection was found out quite suddenly in 1996. We began to get information . . . according to which imports from Estonia have grown radically. We . . . had not succeeded in confiscating much from the Estonian traffic, so we started to work on this . . . when we then had done some profiling, towards the end of the summer, we got seven serious narcotics offences in three weeks.' (I 13).

Interviews suggest that Estonia has become an important source and transit country for amphetamine, metamphetamine and ecstasy coming to Finland. Also heroin and hashish are mentioned. Regarding amphetamine, Estonia has become the most important source country. Compared to other options (such as Italy or Holland, and even Poland), the manufacturing of amphetamine is cheaper and safer in Estonia. The geographic proximity makes the smuggling route easier and less risky than the alternatives. Also the price difference between Estonia and Finland makes trade in other narcotics attractive; Estonian prices seemed to be around one-third or one-fourth of the world market prices and profits are easily made.[10]

> '. . . you buy a kilo of hashish for 8,000 FIM and sell it in Finland for 50,000 . . . Depending on how you choose to travel, it's a maximum of five hours, before you have that 42,000 profit in your hands . . .' (I 4)

Finns are mainly connected to the Estonian narcotics business in the phase, when the merchandise is delivered to Finland. Finns are professionally involved as financiers and wholesale operators, who transfer the narcotics to the retail level. The role of the Finns is seen as being quite central in the narcotics trade from Estonia to Finland.

> 'They organise the narcotics flow to Finland . . . Estonians may be involved in that they decide where the stuff comes from and when it comes. And there are a few who are even able to organise the delivery all the way to Finland as a sort of full service package. But usually . . . a Finnish criminal has been the brains, he has gone and collected the money and organised the whole operation. So these Estonians are acting more as couriers . . .' (I 8).

Narcotics also represent a more attractive commodity than alcohol, having a favourable price/volume ratio. The high value contraband can be smuggled in small quantities by couriers, who are not hard to recruit in Estonia at the present income level. Carrying one party of 200 grammes, the 'mule' earns a sum equivalent to several months' salary. Also, an Estonian first offender (no previous offences in Scandinavia) only receives a five year entry ban. The number of persons known or suspected of large-scale activities is not very large: two groups or a handful of men are mentioned.

Part of the narcotics involved has been manufactured in Estonia. Other Eastern European countries 'Poland, the Czech republic, Latvia and 'Lithuania are also contributing. Also, there have even been suspicions of Finns being involved in the manufacturing, as a couple of 'kitchen laboratories' have been detected. Manufacturing is relatively easy since the precursor chemicals may be bought in Estonian pharmacies. Confiscations of such chemicals have also been made by the Finnish police.

Some indications of threats against Finnish and Estonian authorities have been reported, amphetamine smugglers and dealers attempting to neutralize control.

> Example (1998): Suspicions were presented of narcotics being smuggled in the passenger traffic from Estonia to Finland, packed in 600 gramme cans of chicken conserve. The cans had Russian labels. The smuggling is suspected as being organised by an Estonian criminal group. The group has a dangerous reputation, and it is said that local police do not dare to interfere.

---

[10] The Europol Drugs Unit price comparison of 1996 states that, for example, the price of amphetamine in the wholesale market was 110-150 FIM/gramme, and 200-400 FIM/gramme at street level, whereas the Estonian prices reported in our sources in the same year were 30-45 FIM/gramme.

Narcotics cooperation between Estonian and Finnish criminals has been reported. The cooperation and the volume of smuggled narcotics has increased steadily. In 1999, the first Finnish organised group importing narcotics from Estonia has been apprehended and brought to trial. The group operated independently in Estonia, with good relationships with the highest leaders of Estonian organised crime. In the light of our data, this group is not going to remain the only one. Already in 1997, two similar groups were known to operate in Estonia following a similar pattern. In the course of 1999, two other major cases of this type have been in court in Finland. Preliminary intelligence about both was already in the police registers used for the present study.

Pirate Products

Pirate products imported from Estonia to Finland were usually imitations of brand clothing, CD records, video films, and computer programs. The brand clothing is believed to be mainly exported to Russia. In examples found in the police records, part of the products have remained in the Finnish market, typically distributed on flea markets and by newspaper advertisements. The AV products are targeted to the Finnish market exclusively.

Stolen Property

Smuggling stolen property is one of the very few crimes where the direction is from Finland to Estonia. Car break-ins, house burglaries and bicycle thefts are often suggested to have increased in Finland in recent years partly because of Estonian demand of commodities derived from such sources. The police registers included 60 persons suspected of taking stolen property from Finland to Estonia between 1991 and the end of October 1998. The culprits have usually been in groups of a few persons who have stolen the goods on their own or bought them from others. A common feature is that somebody has been known to buy stolen property in Finland and to sell it to Estonia. The amounts of merchandise and the time span of the operations are so large that we may speak of organised crime.

Example (1997): The Finnish man A receives stolen property that he stores on his farm in Eastern Finland. At a few months' intervals, a truck arrives from Estonia to pick up the goods. The previous load has been taken in July, the next one in September; this time, A has also gone to Estonia, returning alone a week later. Another Finnish suspect has a warehouse in Turku. He transports stolen mountain bicycles to Tarto on his trailer. The car has Estonian plates.

ECONOMIC CRIME

Economic crime encompasses defrauding the public fund (in Finland as well as in Estonia), committing commercial fraud schemes, which victimize private persons as well as corporations and turning ill-gotten profits and other undeclared moneys into legitimate income, brief: money-laundering.

Making Money

Finns have been committing economic crimes and frauds in Estonia. Estonia, with its opportunities of a growing economy, has attracted Finnish speculators. According to Finnish police intelligence, 89 Finnish persons have been involved in economic crimes in Estonia; three money laundering groups had a total of 51 members.

Making 'new' money in Estonia denotes fraudulent economic activities and dealing in counterfeit money in which Finns have been involved in Estonia. Subsequently, this new money is transformed into 'old' money by resorting to money laundering that is performed by means of fraudulent constructions or bankruptcies.

Finns have been dealing in counterfeit money in both countries. In 1994-1996, 23 persons, ten of them Finns have been involved in manufacturing or distributing counterfeit money. The money was manufactured in Finland and marketed in Estonia. The whole boom lasted for only three years. The money was not marketed directly in Finland. Instead, it was taken to Estonia first. This may have been done in order to conceal the origins of the money. As described in the following example, money counterfeited in Finland was indeed imported back to Finland from Estonia. Counterfeit money has been found in many parts of Finland in large amounts, and high values.

> Example (1994): Police received a forged 20-dollar banknote that had come from the Finnish man A. According to him, there was a party of banknotes worth 3 million USD in one city. The money comes from Estonia where an amount equivalent to 16 million are still for sale, the price being 1,50 FIM/banknote. A is looking for a market for the 20-dollar bills.
> Two Finns have been apprehended and imprisoned in Estonia for circulating counterfeit money, the volume encompassed several millions even in their case. A further case description identifies still another person, a Finnish man A who was released from prison in the spring and has been reported to have circulated forged 50-dollar banknotes in Tallinn. The money is said to be in Finland, a total of 100-200 kilos. For the bills, A is asking one-third of their nominal value. In Finland, A is suspected of customs fraud in connection of car imports, and insurance fraud related to a car.

Frauds schemes are another way of making new money, used by Finns in Estonia. Advanced fee fraud, credit frauds, and selling non-existent commodities have been ways in which Finns made money at the expense of Estonians. According to the Finnish police files, such crimes, fraudulent bankruptcy, deefrauding banks and tax evasion schemes have been attributed to 43 Finnish persons who in this context have been moving money between Finland and Estonia or out of Estonia to third countries.

The frauds Finns make on their own are often copies of frauds of which they have earlier been victims themselves in Western countries. As was stated in several interviews, most new forms of economic crime are first developed elsewhere than in Finland and Finns are defrauded as they enter big money business. Then, they pass the damage around.

In another case, six Finnish men have been identified, together with an Italian businessman. The fraud has been carried out by using cheques with which the men have attempted to raise substantial sums of money from an Estonian bank. The men have been in the possession of several other cheques of foreign banks.

The second case, rather similar, uses a forged payment order: A Finnish man A was apprehended in Tallinn as he tried to cash a foreign currency cheque in a bank. The cheque was given by a Hawaiian bank, in Italian lire, worth 2,75 million FIM. The Estonian man B had received the cheque in Stockholm from an Italian man. The intention was to move the money to the account of Finnish man C in the same bank (C has several entries in Finnish police registers). Finnish men D, E and F have organised the operation (all three also have dozens of entries in Finnish police registers). They are suspected of having still another similar cheque in their possession, worth 30 million FIM.

Variation of this example are abundant, like the scam seducing an Estonian to enter a programme that enables investors to participate in foreign deals in debenture loans from big European banks at a low price with a tax-free interest of 60 % (one million USD as minimum subscription). The money went to Switzerland.

A simple, but well organised fraud case, requiring good faith from the Estonian party, is one of many similar plots. In such plots, the victim has been made to pay money against promises that subsequently were never fulfilled or delivered.

Example (1993): The Finnish man A, representing the foreign-registered company Z Ltd. made a contract of delivering 100,000 tons of sugar to company X Ltd. in Tallinn. A had informed company X Ltd. that sugar can be bought in Europe at 266 USD/100 tons, if the contract could be entered immediately. According to the contract, the sugar was to be delivered to X Ltd. within two weeks after the payment was deposited on A's bank account. One week after the payment, the Finnish man B, then representing Z Ltd. towards X Ltd., informed X Ltd. that the sugar could not be delivered. More than a month after the sugar had been paid, A and B participated in a negotiation with Tallinna Pank that had been entrusted by X Ltd. to collect their debt. Director C representing the bank demanded that the sugar deal should be cancelled and that Z Ltd. must return the 266,000 USD, to which A consented. However, the money was not returned for several months. X Ltd. transferred the debt to be collected by a Finnish agency. As the agent contacted A he said that he has no knowledge whatsoever of any sugar deals.

A further variant of making new money in Estonia are the timber deals, which turned out to be extensive long firm frauds, victimizing various Baltic entrepreneurs.

Transforming 'New' Money into 'Old' Money

Transforming "new" money into "old" money in the present sources is equivalent to what is often called money laundering in other contexts. The main method is to invest in legal business. Investments in legal business are often followed by operations where more 'new' money is created (frauds, tax evasion and evading other revenue). Finns have used Estonia as a money laundering base, circulating and reinvesting their capitals either to Estonia or over Estonia to third countries.

> 'In Finland, you first go bankrupt, clean the estate and go to Estonia, contact some so-called businessman friend and say that here is this much money, could this be invested somewhere. Over there, the Estonians... find use for the money, in the restaurant business, the hotel business, real estate deals. Still better if the money goes abroad as that may give some profits in return. Narcotics are one good investment. It's always possible to find launderers to cash . . . Right now there are several Finns laundering through other business, money that has been acquired by some economic crime..." (I4).

A first provision is that several companies are available through which the money may be circulated. Therefore, there is a market for Estonian companies and Finnish dealers of Estonian 'shell' companies (3000 FIM) have been identified.[11]

The police files contained a total of 233 different companies, Estonian and Finnish, which were suspected of being involved in criminal activities. An interesting example is a group of 30 Estonian companies where the persons registered as liable for the company were 30 Finnish pensioners, who had never heard of the matter. The real owner was a Finnish man with a heavy criminal background.

In all of the 233 companies implicated in the police registers, at least one of the persons liable for the company was a Finn. In more than 90 per cent a Finn was the only person registered with the company. In case of bankruptcy the company assets are easily moved to Estonia, beyond the reach of debtors.

The next example also gives an idea of the criminal surroundings in which such businesses operate. This is not the only example of connections to motorcycle gangs[12] by Finnish and Estonian criminals since three different motorcycle gangs have been observed to be travelling to Estonia buying drugs. Also the connection of prostitution to other criminal activities in Finland is mentioned in this example.

> Example (1997): The Finnish man A together with his relatives owns two restaurants in Helsinki. He also owns restaurants in Tampere, Estonia, and Russia. There are suspicions that the restaurants are used for money laundering and prostitution. The man is about to move his operations to Estonia. He is also familiar with motorcycle gangs, eastern crime, and prostitution.

---

[11] In later years, Estonian consulting companies have made similar businesses. Such enterprises have been subjected to investigations by Finnish tax authorities in 1999.

[12] Motorcycle gangs (Hell's Angels, Bandidos and others) are active in all Scandinavian countries, suspected and at times established to engage 'besides gang warfare' in illegal activities such as narcotics business, debt collection, protection racket, and traditional property crime.

The dominant pattern is that Finns have made money relying on deficiencies in Estonian legislation. People making 'new' money have been creative in getting rich at the expense of loopholes in the law and the good faith and the lack of knowledge of their naive (Estonian) victims. Also, among those trying to make 'old' money, there are competent bankruptcy speculators (long firm fraud) as well as unlucky small-time entrepreneurs who have believed they can have a new start in Estonia.

Customs Frauds

Export-related customs frauds across the Finnish-Estonian border is mostly taking place in double invoicing practices and in failure to pay the VAT. One of the well-known forms of customs frauds is the export of VAT-subjected merchandise from Finland to Estonia. No export actually takes place. Making use of fictitious or forged customs documents and driving empty trucks to Estonia, the VAT returns have been fraudulently received from Finland. The merchandise if any is distributed in Finland.

> '. . . chocolate was supposedly being moved by the truckload and they pretended they sold it to Estonia. So this way they got all possible returns when it was exported over there. That chocolate bar then cost about one FIM when the normal price was ten. The truck went over and came back and the profit was huge when they then sold the stuff here in Finland . . .' (I 4).

In the police registers, ten persons are identified in 1995-1997 who have been suspected of similar scams. The activity may have been much more voluminous and the number of people involved may have been much larger, but not very much hard evidence is found.

Also, exporting tax-free alcohol and beer in Finland has been profitable. The scam has been simple. A typical arrangement was as follows: the agents reported that they are exporting tax-free beer and vodka to Tallinn, and paying for the load in advance and arranging their own transports. They were supplied with 12,000 litres of Finnish vodka and 300,000 cans of Finnish beer. A retail organisation started only for this purpose distributed the merchandise mainly in the region of Helsinki. In this case alone, the revenue losses of the Finnish state were about 4,5 million FIM. The criminal profit was estimated at about 1,7 million FIM.

In another project, the same pattern was used to acquire a 36,000 kilo tax-free party of sugar, half of which was immediately sold to a supermarket in the Helsinki region. In this operation, an intermediary company was used, making up a bill in which the VAT was included. In this way, the illegal origins of the sugar could be concealed. Persons or groups operating in such tax evasion plots have registered paper companies in Estonia and Lithuania in order to facilitate their 'exports' and to conceal traces and identities of persons involved.(Annala 1994).

In imports to Finland, the VAT frauds have been most common in merchandise that is highly taxed: alcohol, cigarettes, valuable metals, and, to some extent, foodstuffs.

Characteristically, companies that have imported metals to Finland have been active for only a few months, during which time as much metal as possible has been imported from Estonia. Then the company has been transferred to someone else's name. The import company has changed hands repeatedly, making it easier to conceal the persons responsible and to destroy the paperwork. The customs value has been reported at 10-20 per cent of the real value. In the customs declarations, the amount of the metal has been under-reported using forged sales documents. In the domestic business taxation, the monthly reports and accounts have been neglected and the taxes have not been paid. This has often been already part of the original plot. The persons reported to the company register as being liable for the company have been straw men, having no wealth or income to collect the unpaid customs fees or taxes. The company importing the metal has immediately sold the merchandise and unloaded it directly at the client's warehouses. The payments have been exchanged in Finland into US dollars. Only after this, the loads have been paid to the representative of the supplier in Finland, or the importer has taken the dollars to Estonia. (Annala 1994).

'EXPORTS' OF CARS

Finns have participated in the illegal export of cars to Estonia in two manners. The first is mostly not genuinely 'professional': private citizens have gone to Estonia to sell their car, and subsequently have reported it stolen. The Finnish police registers report 20 persons as suspected of this kind of insurance fraud. Secondly, Finnish auto theft groups have delivered cars stolen upon order from Finland to Estonia. The Finnish police registers mention five such groups, the central operators in these have been a total of 15 Finnish persons.

Selling Finnish cars in Estonia and reporting them stolen is concentrated in the time span 1993-1995. No more incidents turned up after the theft insurance clauses were changed in 1996 to the effect that selling the car is not any more profitable.

The more systematic operation is revealed in cases in which a group steals cars in Finland and takes them to Estonia. The Estonian client has ordered, for example, three multi-purpose cars from a Finnish car theft group. They deliver the cars to Estonia directly from Finland or over Sweden.

The Finnish police registers identify at least five Finnish groups engaged in exporting several dozens of cars to Estonia. The cars were either stolen or rented.

The car business, whether private or professional, is history by now.

'. . . in 1992-1994, we had several of these Estonian car leagues and Finnish car thieves who sold the cars to Estonia. A lot of insurance frauds and the cars went . . . to Russia, they were driven over Narva . . . and this was quite big. I was investigating these things one year, at least 70 cars. They were already registered in Estonia, we could not get them back . . . We only could take back cars that did not have an Estonian registration . . . that's in the past now . . . a small number are going across, they're found out by the manufacturing numbers on the border now . . .' (I 4)

SEX BUSINESS

The low income level in Estonia has been made use of by Finns also in the area of commercial sex. The typical story is that Estonian girls have been persuaded to come to Finland for payments that are rather large compared with normal incomes in Estonia. The largest profits remain with the Finnish pimp[13]. The front is, for instance, erotic dance.

The Finnish police registers identify 93 persons in Finland who, between 1993 and the end of August 1998, had mediated, invited, or housed Estonian prostitutes. Finnish men are the persons typically implicated. Finnish men are also involved in Estonian sex business. In one entry, a Finnish man starts and manages brothels in Estonia. The main mode of operation in which Finns are participating is, however, mediating prostitutes to Finland and to different parts of the country, indicating that the activity is widespread, usually involving small scale enterprises.

> Example (1998): Two Estonian girls on the Finnish West coast are available for money. The price is 950 FIM/hour, including sauna and sex, or only sex at 500 FIM/hour. By the highway, a sign was put up, stating "BROTHEL, 500 FIM/HOUR", with a telephone number. The number belongs to a woman living on the west coast. The sexual services are offered by two Estonian women B and C from Tallinn. The flat in which the services are rendered is owned by the Finns A, D and E (two women and one man). These had rented the apartment to the Estonian woman F.

Another significant form of sex business from Estonia to Finland that Finns have been engaged in is the manufacturing and import of sex videos from Estonia[14]. Finns have been manufacturing this type of video films in Estonia. The Estonian shame culture prevents the activity from being found out, and before 1996, Estonian law was quite weak on sex offences. Also, the salary level made it easy to recruit actors.

OTHER CRIME

The following cases complement the general picture emerging from the previous incidents. They reveal a variety of crime opportunities, ranging from forced 'protection' to direct theft and mugging. What make them noteworthy is the mixed Finnish-Estonian criminal partnership.

> A Finnish man is extorting protection money from a Finnish company in Tallinn. He is adopting an Estonian mode of crime and using it in the local setting against his own

---

[13] Prostitution in not a crime in Finland, but procuring is.

[14] The criminal character of such projects is based on Finnish legislation regarding video films and pornography. The present stipulations only allow the distribution of video films that are rated to be suitable for persons aged 16 or older, meaning in effect that the distribution of all hard core pornography on video is illegal. Besides this, child, animal and violent pornography are totally prohibited, as well as extreme violence, whether on video or film. The production of pornographic video films is much cheaper in Estonia than in Finland. This is the case with child pornography, as well. It is also reported to be much easier to obtain models for the latter variety in Estonia than in Finland.

countrymen. Another Finnish man A (with many entries in Finnish police registers) is in Tallinn involved in an illegal debt collection and protection racket. A is operating with companies registered in tax havens. He is extorting money from a Finnish company selling Finnish products in Tallinn.

Another case of protection racket involves a mixed ethnic group. In the bar of hotel Palace a Finnish man A, together with a few Estonians, had approached a Finnish entrepreneur B. They had asked for 7,000 FIM per month in protection money as 'insurance', in order to be able to safeguard the existence of B:s company.

The next case is of a different character - a Finn, together with Estonian colleagues, is mugging other Finns in Tallinn. The group would not be of interest if it did not also involve corruption, as an Estonian customs officer is cooperating, putting the victims into the ferry back to Finland.

Example (1995): A Finnish tourist at the Viru hotel was approached by a Finnish man aged 40-50 years who boasted how easy it is to make money in Tallinn. He explained that they watch Finnish men who are strongly intoxicated, pick them up in their car that has been camouflaged as a taxi, and drive towards the harbour. On the way, the passenger is robbed. Then, he is taken to the passport inspection to "the bald inspector". The inspector takes the passenger inconspicuously to the ferry.

SUMMARY AND DISCUSSION

Between 1991 and the end of August 1998, the registers of the Finnish police identified 817 Finns who were suspected of crimes between Estonia and Finland. If also those 174 Finns are included who have a criminal background in Finland and have been observed in Tallinn in the company of Estonian criminals or who have invited Estonian criminals to Finland (up to 1995 when invitations were required for visas), the total number adds up to 991. The different registers used may overlap to some extent, 20-30 per cent according to police estimates. At any rate, this is considerably more than the figure (41) reported by Estonian police. The figures, of course, are not comparable as Estonian sources refer only to crimes investigated by local police.

Our sources also contained information of a total of 233 companies in which Finns have been active and where there is reason to suspect illegal activities. Many of these companies are paper companies, fronts for illegal action. In Estonian and Finnish company registers, they are reported as making legal business. In reality, the turnover may consist of providing prostitutes, dealing with alcohol and drugs or metals, arms trade or supplying stolen cars. Money obtained through these operations is laundered by fictitious invoices and the inflation of the legal turnover. As of the summer of 1999, investigations of an Estonian consulting company have revealed dealings in several hundreds of Estonian paper companies that have been sold to foreign, often Finnish parties who have used these to open anonymous bank accounts, helpful for money laundering and tax evasion.

The illegal activities recorded in the police and customs sources made available for the present study are to a great extent relatively small-scale crime enterprises or one-time fraud projects, in which the typical number of involved persons is small and the timespan of each project is less than one year. Systematic, long-term activity is suspected or observed mainly in the context of manufacturing, smuggling and distributing narcotics, alcohol and cigarettes for the Finnish market and of VAT frauds. Even in these cases, the timespan of each observed project has rarely exceeded one year. However, it often seems that the same persons are involved in one project after the other, indicating a permanence of the criminal activity that exceeds the lifetime of any single project. The opportunistic nature and the flexibility of the operators in many of the observed projects are reflected in the merchandise involved.

What remains an open question is related to the sources used in this study: to which degree is the crime profile found a consequence of the prevailing way police and customs representatives understand the phenomenon of 'professional or organised crime', and to what extent is it a reflection of objective characteristics of this phenomenon[15]? Both police and customs see only fragments of the targets and their own preconceptions of the phenomenon must influence the ways in which they interpret their own observations. In traditional police work, investigations normally do not reach much beyond the immediate event and therefore interesting and relevant traits related to the possible organisation involved in the single crime may remain unnoticed. Thus, the finding may not reflect more structured, more permanent, or more professional operations. Also, as police and customs are usually concerned with concrete cross-border events, they may, indeed, be rather weak in observing operations of a more abstract character. Further research is needed to provide answers to this dilemma. For the time being, the findings may be compressed in four observations:

1. (Semi)professional and organised crime by Finnish operators in the Finnish-Estonian border setting involves quite a large number of people as compared with what is reported in regular law enforcement sources. The largest single group of activities consists of smuggling narcotics, alcohol and tobacco to Finland. On the other hand, the operations observed represent a broad variety of crimes, committed by taking advantage of the cross-border opportunities created by differences in the standards of living, in legislation, and law enforcement practices at both sides of the border. The Finnish participants are often the main beneficiaries, and are typically in a dominant role.

2. Nevertheless, the bulk of the observed activities is not highly professional, does not involve large, permanent, or hierarchically structured criminal organisations. It is, rather, carried out by variable, flexible, opportunistic project groups. These groups do often operate in ways that involve the use of companies as fronts or as

---

[15] There is a further problem with the sources: the non-public police files consulted are not complete in the sense that individual crime investigators who are expected to feed in the 'tips' use the system in a rather variable way. A concrete illustration of the nature of this problem is that many of the persons interviewed for this study described incidents that could be expected to be found in the tip information system, but could not be found, since the experts had kept the intelligence to themselves. Discussions we have had with many other persons knowledgeable of the register practices have confirmed that such selectivity is widespread.

vehicles of the crimes. Corporate crime, however, is not observed in any significant scale in this context.

3. Companies (very often paper companies) do appear in relatively large numbers on the suspect-list of police and customs. It is not often that these are investigated in depth, at least judging from the data available to us. Only very recently □in the summer of 1999 have the Finnish tax authorities organised systematic control attempts where the attention is directed at Estonian paper companies and their Finnish owners. This would indicate, as was the case with the control of economic crime and the grey economy developed in Finland over the 1990s, that there would be a powerful argument for the tax authorities to become more systematically linked to the control activities of the traditional control agencies, in this cross-border case customs and police. The argument is in particular based on the fact that police, even if trained in company law and bookkeeping, are not too familiar with many relevant aspects of company behaviour. The investigation would therefore be likely to benefit greatly of improved cooperation and intelligence-sharing with tax authorities. This might prove to be particularly fruitful in proactive control, today a rare activity if judged by known results. Also, as our own data prove, police have not made much systematic use of the flow of intelligence concerning companies involved in suspect operations. Such intelligence in effect often remains hidden in their own records. It is conceivable that so-called crime analysis would be positively rewarding in this area and even more so if combined with systematic cooperation with tax investigators.

4. Our observation is that cross-border police cooperation has not developed efficient procedures. Much effort has not put in correcting this state of affairs. Finnish police sources also indicate that the passivity is mutual. On the Estonian side, this is probably linked to a resource problem, a training deficit, and, to some extent, also a corruption problem. On the Finnish side there is a language problem, but also a problem of tradition. Finnish police are not yet accustomed to work together with the Baltic (or Russian, at that) police forces. This refers to the lack of personal relationship networks of the kind that Finnish police representatives often say exist with the Scandinavian neighbours, Sweden in particular. These have remained underdeveloped and would require systematic investments, joint projects etc. The liaison officer networks with the Baltic countries and in Russia are a laudable and necessary first step, but not a sufficient surrogate for a more extensive cooperative network.

Also shortcomings in judicial cooperation may exist in the cross-border crime scene. However, these are difficult to observe because so few serious professional criminal cases ever come to court. Therefore, the police forces are presently the key for improvement.

LITERATURE

Annala, E., *Tavaran tuontiin ja vientiin liittyvä ammattimainen rikollisuus.* Helsinki, Tullihallitus, tutkintatoimisto, 1994.

Aromaa, K., Ahven, A., *Victims of Crime in a Time of Change.* Helsinki, National Research Institute of Legal Policy, Research Communications 19, 1995.

Aromaa, K., The International (Crime) Victimisation Survey in Finland, Estonia, Latvia, and Lithuania 1995-1997. In: K. Aromaa (ed.) *The Baltic Region. Insights in crime and crime control.* Oslo, Scandinavian Studies in Criminology, Vol. 15., 1998, 82-103.

Hirvonen, M., *Viranomaisyhteistyön kehittäminen, selvityshankkeen väliraportti* [Interim report of an investigation for improving authority cooperation]. Helsinki, Valtiovarainministeriö, 1999.

Lehti, M., *Viron henkirikollisuus 1990-luvulla.* Helsinki, National Research Institute of Legal Policy, Publications 148, 1997.

Markina, A., Organised Crime in Estonia: A National and International Issue. In: K. Aromaa (ed.) *The Baltic Region. Insights in crime and crime control.* Oslo, Scandinavian Studies in Criminology Vol. 15., 1998, 183-194.

Niemi, Hannu (1999). Ulkomaalaisten rikollisuus. In *Rikollisuustilanne 1998. Rikollisuus ja seuraamusjärjestelmä tilastojen valossa.* Helsinki, National Research Institute of Legal Policy, Publications 165, 1999, 120-130.

Persson, L.G.W., *Den organiserade cigarettsmugglingen - från ax till limpa. Kontrollnivå och lönsamhet vid organiserad cigarettsmuggling.* Stockholm, Brottsförebyggande rådet, 1999.

Tullihallitus: *Tullirikostutkinta 1996* [Criminal investigations of the customs]. Helsinki, Tullihallitus, tutkintatoimisto, 1997.

Tullihallitus: *Tullirikostutkinta 1997* [Criminal investigations of the customs]. Helsinki, Tullihallitus, tutkintatoimisto, 1998.

Chapter 8

Organised Economic Crime Problems in the Ukraine[1]

I. Osyka

Researcher of the Department of Criminalistics of the
University of Internal Affairs which is a part of the Ministry of Interior
of Ukraine; Senior Lieutenant of Militia.

Introduction

Ukraine, like other countries of Eastern Europe, has been changing its economic system from a command to a market economy. Ukraine became an independent State only in 1991, and is currently experiencing many difficulties in its economic and legal development. An important element is formed by certain kinds of economic activities that turned out to be unprotected in terms of legislation and administrative regulations. Evidently, the absence of legislation encouraged the development of quantitative and qualitative changes of criminality, including 'organised' financial, computer and economic crimes (the latter including pollution and environmental offences).

According to the data given by the Ministry of Internal Affairs (further MIA), the economy has been criminalised extensively. The analysis of the structure and dynamics of economic crime shows the strong growth rate of registered economic crimes from 1992 until 1998. For instance, in 1992 in Ukraine, 36,866 economic crimes were registered, rising to 65,322 in 1998, a rise of 73.9%. The growth rate of all crime in the country is just 20.4 % for the same period, though from a higher base rate. It is of course possible that some of this rise may be artificial, reflecting increased policing activity responding in turn to social concern rather than the underlying crime itself. However,

---

[1] The paper is based on the analysis of the state of organised crime in the Ukraine conducted by the Head of Co-ordinating Committee In Fighting Corruption and Organised Crime, run by the President of Ukraine, who is at the same time the Director of the just founded National Bureau of Investigations. The analysis was published in the journal *The Law of Ukraine*, nr. 1, 1998, 26-32.

there are no obvious changes in policing patterns, especially of a proactive nature, that could account for a large proportion of this increase in recorded economic crime. New developments connecting economic crime with aggression have been revealed too.

The main reasons of the substantial increase in crime in the Ukraine have social-economic roots. We can highlight such reasons as an inconsistency and subsequently a slowing down of the process of social and economic reforms; the presence of considerable overt and hidden unemployment; reduction in living standards of the majority of population; lack of solution of the problems of property ownership; disorder in the process of privatisation; lack of co-ordination within the inland revenue, financial, investment, industrial, customs and excise and many other elements of the economic policy of the State.

The active development of market relations, the appearance of new forms of property, and new opportunities in the sphere of private business have also been reflected in the structure and dynamics of economic crime. We also have many 'white spots' in the legislation, especially in the field of civil, economic and fiscal law, Criminal and Criminal Procedural Law, which are abused very actively by criminals to launder their illegal proceeds and commit various forms of economic crime. During the process of the 'great privatisation', the controlling share-holdings in those industries that are most important for the State could turn out to be held by criminals.

A Shadow Economy

According to the assessment of specialists the share of the 'shadow economy' has increased to 60 per cent of the State's gross revenue. Criminals own a considerable capital, using corrupted State executives: they are striving for political power, possibly to influence the economic and political development of the State, but certainly to influence the local environment so as to minimise threats[3]. Illustrations at the local level include the murder of the Editor of an Odessa regional newspaper in 1997, and attempts to kill two more journalists and the kidnapping of another in Odessa. These crimes allegedly were part of the sharing of power between the mayor of Odessa and the Head of Administration of the President in the Odessa region, who are supported by leaders of organised criminal groups which are operating in the Odessa region. But at the national level, it is arguable that some are interested in what they can steal from internal investment due to loose laundering controls.

The existence of such a large share of 'shadow economy' in the total Gross Domestic Product may slow down the process of development of private business, which still has a rudimentary. This shadow economy is not just a black market: it includes the circulation of dirty money and fiscally undeclared goods and services. It is alleged by the tax authorities that 9 out of 10 existing companies are involved in tax evasion, which is not surprising given the 98 per cent tax rate [3]. In this economic landscape criminals and legitimate soon detect a common interest: on the one hand there is the entrepreneur who needs cash and on the other hand, there is a criminal who owns considerable amounts of cash and needs bearer bonds to use it in legal business. This exchange of interest allows them to by-pass the banking system. There is little doubt that legitimate business is losing the competition with crime-entrepreneurs, because the latter have more financial resources. This situation is furthered by poor control of civil servants, caused by the high level of corruption and the absence of any civil and financial regulations against money laundering. Investment of laundered money into the licit enterprises provide an opportunity to return the capital in a legitimate way, generating an inexhaustible source of 'clean' money (for covering of routine expenses), whether from (tax evading) business or crime [4]. In short, there is a strong counterforce against the survival of legitimate entrepreneurship in Ukraine, where criminal capital drives out legitimate business.

CORRUPTION

Corruption is the one most important cause of the increase of crime in the Ukraine. It is not exclusively connection with organised crime. All criminal groups which operate all over the country have some kind of protection, which actually enables them to operate over a long timespan with little or no problems from law enforcement. In Russian slang, such protection is called 'roof'. This word reflects perfectly the functions of such protection. The 'roof' can be provided by an executive representing a variety of powers, including law enforcement officers. Another meaning of 'roof' could be a person who is respected in the criminal society and again has an influence on somebody from executive power or enforcing bodies: a sort of 'fixer'. The main role of the 'roof' is to help criminals to cover their criminal activities, avoid criminal liability and punishment, hide criminal proceeds, and enjoy some privileges.

In 1997 the Police and Service of security of Ukraine (further SSU) recorded 2,679 crimes that are defined as a corruption: bribery, abuse of power and position, activities directed against the interests of service. This figure is considerably bigger in comparison with 1996. The government is working very actively under the law and administrative aegis of the National Programme Fighting Corruption in the State. The realisation of the Programme has already had some results, but they remain insufficient. The level of corruption is still very high.

There were three main flaws in the State's policy and activities toward fighting corruption. The first one is domination of power and administrative measures rather than prevention, especially situational prevention. 'Actually we are fighting the consequences but not with conditions', stated V. Durdinec. The second flaw is the anti corruption legislation, which is poorly drafted and supported, while officials are reluctant to take action because of the fear of sanction for making a mistake in their investigation. And finally, there is the benign sentencing levels for corrupt executives. Quite often the Deputies of different levels are beyond the reach of the law and law-enforcement agencies, because 'intelligence' is not evidence according to the Criminal Procedure Code and because of the absence of funds for a proper implementation of the witness protection programme, plus possible police corruption. Permission of the Parliament is required before a Deputy can be arrested. This was refused in the obvious cases like an MP who smuggling $26,000 out of the country; another MP who illegally set up currency bank accounts abroad, committed embezzlement and abuse of power and position; and another who beat up a colleague. Such situation creates a serious threat for the political integrity and economic security of the State. In addition, it will demoralise active law enforcement officers, aggravating the situation.

ORGANISED CRIME

The most dangerous manifestation of economic crime is its organised form, a view appreciated by Parliament and Government. Many steps have taken made towards combatting organised crime in the Ukraine. In June 1993 the 'Administrative-and-Law Basis of Combatting Organised Crime Act' was adopted by Ukrainian Parliament and signed by the President. Article 1(1) of the Act defines organised criminality as a 'Totality of crimes which are committed in connection with the creation and activity of an organised criminal group'. Article 1(2) states: 'Types and the main features of these crimes as well as criminal-and-law measures against the person who has committed such crimes are defined by the Criminal Code of Ukraine'. But unfortunately until now there is no definition of organised criminal group in the criminal Code. There are some definitions which concern criminal activity if a group of persons is involved. In the theory of the Criminal Law, the *group of persons* is defined as a unit of 2 or more persons conspiring for co-operative criminal activity (to commit one or more crimes); there is also a definition of *banda* (art.69 of CC): a group of *armed* persons who conspired for the same aim for *long term* criminal activity; the group *inside the prison* population which conspired to commit a crime inside the prison or to defy prison authority (art.69-1 of CC); and illegal armed formation as a group of persons *hired* and *armed* by somebody with aim of protection of somebody's interests (art.187-6 of CC). The characteristics of crimes defined in articles 69,69-1, 187-6 of CC is that criminal liability is provided even for membership of such groups. For the Criminal Law it does not matter whether the members together or somebody separated from the group committed a crime or not. The *existence* of such groups and *membership* of it is a crime in itself.

However, the organised criminal group in the sense of the above Act should be treated in a different way because of the different social danger, characteristics and the nature of organised criminality as a whole. There are a lot of discussions about the definition of organised criminal group in the theory of Criminal Law now. We can provide the most wide-ranging one: an organised criminal group is a *stable* unit of 2 or more persons conspiring for co-operative criminal activity (to commit one or more crimes). The stability of a group means close connections between the members of the group, different roles in criminal activity, division of labour, the planning of criminal activities and special regulations of their behaviour such as jargon, special body language, share of power, individual responsibility for different kinds of criminal and routine activity of the group, different 'social levels' of members of the group, clear hierarchical structure of the group, behaviour in the case of arrest of one of the member of the group, punishment for giving evidence against other members of the group or other collaboration with the Police. There is also a legal definition of organised criminal group which actually is being used by MIA, SSU and other law-enforcement agencies in their tasks and criminal statistics. This definition is contained in the paragraph 25 of the resolution of Supreme Court of Ukraine 'About the court practice cases of crimes for gain committed against private property' adopted on December 1992. The resolution defines organised criminal group as a *stable* unit of 2 or more persons *specially* organised for *co-operative* criminal activity.

The above mentioned definitions still do not reflect the social danger and particularities of *organised* criminal activity, which appears to be nothing more than a small, well organised group of persons. In our opinion, the lack of mentioning the connection of organised criminal group with state's officials of different levels or their membership in the organised crime group is a serious defect.[2] The *element of corruption* should be considered a conerstone in the definition of organised criminal group in terms of our understanding of organised criminality and its social danger: such a definition of an organised criminal group was adopted in Poland in 1996.

RESPONSIBLE ORGANISATIONS COMBATTING ORGANISED CRIME

The Act also required to set up special subdivisions to fight corruption and organised crime in the organisation of the Ministry of Internal Affairs and Service of Security of Ukraine. Thus, in 1993 the Department in Fighting Organised Criminality was founded in the MIA. The staff of the Department consists of experienced professionals from the Criminal Search Service and The State Service in Fighting Against Economic Criminality. The Department deals with armed bandit groups (gangs) and organised criminal groups which commit crimes in the sphere of economy. It also has a special armed emergent department called 'FALCON' that deals with the release of hostages and arrest of armed criminals. In the structure of the SSU, the Department In Fighting Corruption has also been founded.

The Act also established the Co-ordinating Committee in Fighting Corruption and Organised Criminality, which consists of heads of law-enforcement agencies of the State, excluding the General Prosecutor, though he/she and his/her Deputy take part in sessions of the Committee according to the Act. The Committee is responsible for fighting organised crime and corruption all over the country. Its functions according to the Act are:

- co-ordination of and assistance to all agencies which are involved in fighting organised crime;

---

[2] The state's official is a person with power or political influence in the State from the President, MP to local government member or ordinary police officer level.

- working out of the strategy and recommendations concerning tactics of fighting organised crime;
- organisation of liaison and co-operation with corresponding foreign agencies and international organisations in fighting organised crime;
- preparation of annual and special reports (information) about the state of organised criminality in the Ukraine, the main directions and results of fighting organised crime and their presentation to the President and Parliament;
- disposal of the Fund of assistance of fighting organised crime and corruption.

ORGANISED CRIMINAL GROUPS

Organised criminal groups in the Ukraine dominate in spheres of black market such as drug dealing, illegal car trading and particular varieties of smuggling. They control illegal migration of population, firearms market, and 'white slavery', including the 'sale or rent' of women and children. Organised criminal groups that have foreign roots are especially dangerous for the public security, because those with international connections have more escape ways abroad, knowing that the Ukrainian authorities have still little capacity for international co-operation. They also possess quality equipment that is seldom available to the modest forensic facilities (and skills) of the police. Sometimes, foreign killers are hired to operate in Ukraine: in 1995, a Polish 'contract killer' who had been hired by one leader of a Ukrainian organised criminal group to kill a businessman who refused to pay for 'protection' of his company, was arrested in Ukraine.

The nature of organised economic crime in Ukraine represents an interaction between violent and non-violent (white-collar) criminals. The latter hire increasingly the 'services' of violence-prone criminals to help them make money. Such interaction may lead to an enduring cooperation and subsequently 'mixed crime enterprise' of traditional and 'new' white collar criminals, example a company director, professional killer and having a state executive or law-enforcement officer as a 'roof' as a result of bribery, violence or threat of violence.

Given the above examples in Odessa, and the attempted murder in 1997 of an MP at Donetsk airport because he was investigating abuses in the coal industry, we have every reason to suggest that 'heavyweight' criminal organisations are enforcing their connections with the help of some political connections and power structures using a su bstantial amount criminal capital, pressurising certain politicians, State's executives, and law-enforcement officers with help of blackmail, threats, bribery, and violence.

Is organised crime growing? At any rate, between 1995 and 1998 the quantity of discovered organised crime groups has risen sharply with 67 %. (Though given the breadth of definition not too much should be read into this apparent rise.) In 1998, organised groups were held responsible for 9,273 crimes including 648 facts of different kinds of larceny, 553 facts of embezzlement and 216 briberies were committed by organised criminal groups in 1998. If crimes are divided depending on field of commission, 750 crimes were committed in credit-and-financial sphere, 133 in sphere of international economic activity, 59 in sphere of privatisation and 573 in commercial structures.

ENTREPRENEURSHIP

The activities of organised crime groups in the area of private business is a considerable problem for Ukrainian law-enforcement. Private business is a new and profitable field of economic activity for Ukraine. Therefor criminals are trying to have an influence on entrepreneurs and to build up power in this field. Organised criminal groups which operate in area of private business usually resort to extortion against entrepreneurs using violence or threat of violence, damaging or over distracting the business or property. Quite often they are 'employed' by some dishonest directors or owners of companies or entrepreneurs to help them to retrieve their debts or 'maintain' their local business monopoly by frightening off the competition. They also could propose their expensive services for the 'protection' of beginners in the branch of commerce. The refusal of such services sometimes could cause extortion with violence or threat of violence or attacks against property, goods and business.

The money and property obtained by extortion can also be used to invest in business crimes. For example recently, the organised criminal group which consists of more then 10 persons, headed by the director of one joint-stock company, was detected and its have been members arrested. The criminals dealt with extortion for hire in sphere of private business. As a result of their criminal activity they held passports, statuses and financial documents of companies, companies' blanks, invoices, samples of their seals and stamps. Moreover, they used all these documents and equipment to commit additional crimes. They committed long-firm frauds using forged documents and presented the banks' and companys' documentation as a guarantee of their creditworthiness and identity. However, after they received the goods, they sold them elsewhere and disappeared or made false excuses.

Recent changes and supplementations to the Criminal Code of Ukraine, like the use of threats to require performance of civil obligations such as debts (art.198-2 of CC), and inadequate performance of public duty by officials (art.155-8 of the CC), the formation of illegal armed groups (art.187-6 of the CC), in my opinion confirm the seriousness of the situation in the sphere of private business, since in practice, the Ukrainian Parliament does not like to pass merely symbolic laws.

CREDIT-AND-BANKING SYSTEM

The largest increase of crime was recorded in the credit-and-bank system, where the occurrence of crime is difficult to register. During 1998, almost 8,539 crimes, including larceny with an extremely high financial damage, have been registered in this field. The total amount of the damage in the financial field was estimated at approximately more then 17 millions hrivnas (approx., 6 million): a sum which has to be set in the context of the poor financial state of the Ukrainian economy.

There is also a disorderly situation in the banking system. In 1998, 225 commercial banks and 2,377 of their branches were operating in Ukraine, but all but two of these were formed after liberalisation of the economy. In 1995 362 offences have been registered, increasing to 533 in 1996 in this field, but jumping up to 6,312 crimes in 1998. According to V. Durdinec, the main reason for such a relatively high crime rate is the existence of 'black holes' in legislation which concern the regulation of bank activities as well as of regulations covering credit, investments, international money transfers, and electronic money transfers. However, the main crime contributing factor is an absence of any clear and effective control mechanism of the activity of commercial banks on the part of the National Bank of Ukraine (further NBU) and its Departments in the all regions of Ukraine.

The NBU is insufficiently active in their use of powers to licence banks, while there is no specific anti-fraud monitoring policy, nor is there any sign of any major speeding up of activity. Only in the legislative sphere have some activities been noticed. There are a few bills such as the 'National Bank of Ukraine Act', 'Changes and additions to the 'Banks and banks' activity Act', which have been sent to the Parliament by the Board of Directors of the NBU. The NBU established the Department of Banking Supervision, including regulations about liaisons with law-enforcement bodies. But proper and effective practical implementations remain problematic, as for example effective liaisons between the Ministry of Internal Affairs, the National Security Service and the National Bank of Ukraine in the field of fighting organised economic crime.

MONEY LAUNDERING

Though there is no evidence about how much money is laundered, either generally (van Duyne, 1994, 1999) or in the Ukraine particularly, banking is obviously a sphere where substantial domestic and international laundering can take place. There are some strong channels inside the system that exist for the creation of favourable conditions for companies and individuals to transfer bearer bonds into local cash and then to transfer this into foreign currency with the aim to bring it abroad and use it in some overseas 'shadow economy'. With this aim a considerable quantity of so called 'one day' companies appeared, using people with false identity and forged documents: the number of such companies discovered rose from 210 in 1996 to 280 in 1997.

Analysis of practical experience shows that banks have an interest in the existence of such fraudulent companies, partly to avoid credit risk but sometimes to obtain a 'cut' in the proceeds for the bank employees personally. For example, one criminal group in one of the regions of Ukraine during 1996-1997 with support of one of the commercial banks in Ukraine and commercial banks in Byelorussia, Poland, the Baltic Countries and Germany used front firms to transfer and withdraw from bank accounts more then $ 1.7 million. According to the assessment of specialists 'though it is unclear how they could be so precise' about 9 out of 10 existing companies use illegal transfers of money (such as under-invoicing for goods exported and over-invoicing for those imported) with the aim of tax evasion. Criminals transfer huge amounts of the money using so called 'loro' (overseas personal) accounts. In 1996, money transfers amounting to more than 250 millions hrivnas (approximately $ 81 millions) were discovered, but in 1997 such 'loro' accounts with a total sum of almost 50 millions hrivnas (approximately $ 16.6 millions) have been discovered. This may reflect declining law enforcement capability, but it may also represent a possible decline in transfers. The branch of one of the banks in one region of the Ukraine made 61 transfers of currency abroad, totalling more then 5 million hrivnas (± $ 1.6 million), without the licence of the National Bank of Ukraine (NBU).

The question of repatriation of stolen funds that have been exported is still very important for Ukraine, since the amount of money is believed to be very substantial. Attention is being paid to how these funds can traced be before leaving the country and how to get the money back. About $ 1.5 billion has been returned in recent years, including just $ 19 million in 1997.

THE STATE FUNDS AND BUDGET SPHERE

The problems of financial resources fraud and abuse of credit are still sharp. Some banks are lax in checking the financial state of the companies that wish to borrow money, either because of incompetence (and lack of transparency) or because of corruption. The funds then disappear and may be lost to the economy. The inspection which has been conducted by the State Control-and-Inventory Service into almost 500 banks and their branches testifies to this. For example one bank gave a credit for $ 200,000 to one private company and another one for almost $ 850,000 to another private company and in both cases the money was embezzled or stolen.

The State also suffers because of the lack of the control of the return to the state's budget of expenses connected with the use of the export credit guarantee obligations of the Cabinet of the Ministers. In October 1997, $ 236 million have been paid from the State's budget as a result of non-fulfilment of the debtors' obligations which were guaranteed by Cabinet Ministers: only 3 out of 14 debtors repaid the budget. During 1997, the State Control-and-Inspection Service conducted inspections into more than 64,000 companies and organisations and in a third of them, abuses, embezzlements and thefts were discovered to the total amount of 1.6 billion hrivnas (± $ 530 million). As a result of the investigations, 350 million hrivnas (± $ 116 millions) were returned into the public funnds, but the problem and the risk remain serious. The individual responsibility for use of the public funds of top and middle management, as well as executives of the controlling bodies, should be enforced. Recently adopted 'Changes and additions to the Criminal and Criminal Procedural Codes of the Ukraine as for enforcement fighting offences in budget sphere Act' should create favourable conditions for these regulatory efforts.

PUBLIC SECTOR COMPANIES

Activities of organised (multi-offence) crime groups inside the companies of the Ministry of the Coal Industry have become widespread recently. For instance more then 900 crimes have been registered in just one coal mining region during 1997, almost half of them committed by organised crime groups. At present almost 30 high level executives are under investigation (1998). The damage caused by these offences is more than 1 million hrivnas (± $ 330 000). The sorts of crimes include bribery, embezzlement, tax evasion, illegal trading in stolen coal. There are also unsafe working conditions, because of shortage of funds due to these frauds.

The field of the natural energy resources also needs to be protected against criminal encroachments. There are some positive results in this field. During 1997 more than 1.8 thousand offences for economic gain connected with fuel materials and more than 1,000 concerning other energy resources have been cleared. More then 2,500 crimes were detected in the natural gas-and-power complex. The number of detected offences which connected with the markets in spirits, energy, gas, sugar are considerable. A considerable number of offences are committed during the importation of fuel and oil materials. Quite often these shipments go to the Ukraine accompanied by forged documents. Substantial sums do not flow into the public fund because of tax evasion: to this we must add hrivnas 100-300 million from the total amount of yearly sold fuel and oil materials. Furthermore, these proceeds, which were obtained from the sale of this and other smuggled goods, are laundered with the help of accounts of the front firms opened in commercial banks, and are reinvested in other criminal enterprises or bribes to officials.

PRIVATISATION

Discussing the problems of economic and organised criminality in the Ukraine, we also have to emphasise the field of privatisation. There is a substantial danger, that the process of changing of forms of property into private hands is increasingly corrupted. This threat has been confirmed by multiple inspections which have been carried out by the Prosecutors Office in September and October of 1997.

Criminals actively abuse the absence of a control system of privatisation process for their own criminal benefits: in 1997, some 1,870 crimes were discovered. There is also no control of the formation and use of the State Fund of Privatisation, created for support by granting credit to recently privatised companies to help them in their development. The Fund of the State's Property was established to sustain the process of privatisation, but bribery became routine and no-one was able to establish how much State property had been sold and for what prise. Many abuses were discovered as a result of inspections by the State Inspection Service and State Tax Administration. Instead of supporting the companies which have been recently privatised, as legally required, the money from the Fund was spent on purchases of flats, houses, cars etc. Credits to the private firms and 'loans' to the staff of the organs of the privatisation (which later were discharged from the out-of-budget funds) to the total amount of more than 10 million hrivnas (± $ 3.3 millions) have been provided illegally.

It is no secret that criminals are trying to purchase highly profitable companies, real estate and other assets, using the crime-moneys they gained from drug trafficking, sale of stolen vehicles, tax evasion and other criminal activities.

INTERNATIONAL CRIMINALITY

As argued above, organised crime groups, operating in the economic sphere, quite often have international connections. Ukrainian criminals want to invest their criminal money somewhere abroad, or place the money into the accounts in foreign banks. Their behaviour is understandable: they are afraid of losing their money. Ukrainian currency is not strong and the economic situation is very far from stable. Consequently, for the combat of organised crime, it is very important to have international co-operation with the former communist States as well as with law-enforcement agencies of the developed countries. For Ukrainian law-enforcement, it is very important to stop the drain of capital abroad. At the same time law-enforcement agencies of other countries are trying to protect their economies from 'injections' of crime-money. Some steps towards cooperation have already been made. The Ukraine have signed international agreements with the governments of Russia, Byelorussia, Moldova, Hungary and the UK in fighting crime. These agreements should be extended and used actively.

The role of Legal Attachés in the Ukrainian Embassies overseas in defending the country against cross-border organised criminal groups and terrorists is also very important at the present. In this field, we are going to implement actively the experience of the USA's law-enforcement agencies, especially FBI. Alternatively it could be effective to establish an international liaison office in the structure of National Bureau of Investigations and give the officer some international powers and competencies. But the most effective level of international co-operation in the field of fighting economic organised crime may be police-to-police contact, though this is a matter for the future.

FUTURE MEASURES FOR COMBATING ORGANISED CRIME IN UKRAINE

The facts mentioned above confirm the perspicaciousness of the decision of the President of Ukraine to create a National Bureau of Investigations (NBI) as a special State organ which will have tasks of detection and investigation of organised crime, corruption and other serious crimes, concentrating the efforts and abilities of special sub-divisions of the Ministry of Internal Affairs (MIA) and the Service of Security of the Ukraine (SSU). Currently we need such an organisation as an NBI, because the work of the MIA and SSU is hampered by lack of mutual assistance powers in their constitution.

The unification of the special sub-divisions of the MIA and SSU into the one structure of the NBI will create favourable conditions for the work of these sub-divisions in combatting organised crime without duplicating the work of the other law-enforcement agencies. Fighting organised crime also needs a proper scientific basis, for example in relation to data about the methods by which crimes are committed in the private business sector, criminalistics methods of investigating economic crimes, criminological characteristics of organised crime, criminalistics characteristics of organised criminal groups which operate in the economic sphere. The Inter-administrative Scientific and Research Centre In Problems Of Fighting Organised Criminality is finishing at present the elaboration of the draft of the new text of the strategy and tactics of fighting organised crime and corruption in modern conditions. The basic research of the social-and-criminological characteristics of so called 'fifth power' in the Ukraine has been started. But the most important stage of all scientific researches is their practical implementation. This could be a problem.

CONCLUSION

The economic crime situation in Ukraine is quite complicated and extensive. The unmistakable apparent rise of economic crime creates a need for clearly focussed, evidence-based preventative and repressive law-enforcement strategies. We need to react quicker and apply efficiently intelligence on known organised crime groups rather than waiting until their crimes are completed. Otherwise, if left to themselves, we may end up with something approaching the Italian situation prior to the *mani pulite* ('Clean Hands') investigations, where the State was affected by organised crime, in alliance with politicians. Some of our legislation looks good on paper, but there are inadequate resources and a lack of co-ordination for effective implementation.

The problem of economic crime prevention 'including anti-laundering measures' needs more attention from the legislator, the executive powers, and law-enforcement agencies. The mutual evaluation regime instituted by the Council of Europe and the harmonisation with EU policy will undoubtedly take place, but currently and historically, all prevention policy efforts in the Ukraine is confined merely to the adoption of changes and additions to the Criminal Code. This needs to be supplemented by proper Civil and Administrative Law structures, to make it clear what activities are supposed to be protected by law. There should also be effective provisions for situational crime prevention in the economic area, backed by legal sanctions and properly administered, for those who attempt to evade controls.

LITERATURE

Duyne, P.C. van, Money-laundering: estimates in fog. *The Journal of Asset Protection and Financial Crime*, 1994, *nr. 1*, 58-76

Duyne, P.C. van and H. de Miranda, The emperor's cloths of disclosure: hot money and suspect disclosures. *Crime, Law and Social Change*, 1999, *nr. 4*, 1-27

V. Durdynec 'Fighting of criminality must be universal and effective'. *The Law of Ukraine*, 1998, NR. 1, 26-32. Journal and number of issue are in Ukrainian.

Statistical report of the Ministry of Interior for 1998; analysis of the state of criminality in Ukraine for the period from 1992 to 1997 conducted by Criminological Laboratory of the University of Internal Affairs.

Fighting of smuggling: problems and ways of resolvement. Analitical developments, propositions of scientists and practicians. Value 10. Kiyiv, 1998, 229-233. The issue is in Ukrainian.

Materials of the workshop dedicated to the problems of fighting organised and economic crime in the Ukraine. - '*Bulletin of the Academy of Law science of Ukraine*' nr. 4(11), 1997, 15-21. Journal and number of issue are in Russian.

Volobuev A.F. Criminalistics characteristics of larcenies in the sphere of entrepreneurship. *Bulletin of the University of Internal Affairs*, 1997, nr.2, 26-37. Journal and number of issue are in Ukrainian.

Materials of the newspaper '*Facts*' for March of 1998 The issue is in Russian.

Report of the Department of the MIA in Kharkiv region for 1997. The issue is in Russian.

Chapter 9

CREDIT CARD FRAUD IN INTERNATIONAL PERSPECTIVE

Michael Levi
Professor in Criminology at Cardiff University, Wales

INTRODUCTION

Despite the advances of Victimology, very few victims are able to exert as much control over the circumstances of their victimisation as can credit card companies. Sometimes acting collectively, sometimes as an aggregate of individual responses, they control who has legitimate access to their products, how much (up to a point) people may legitimately obtain in goods and money, and which outlets can be authorised to process transactions. Of course, individuals can affect their crime risks by where they live (not always a voluntary choice), where and when they go out, what they wear and with whom they travel. But this is not quite the same level of control as in banking. However, the difficulty card companies are in is that they are in the business of profit maximisation and, unless they are going for deep exclusivity (such as store-cards that can be used only in one store such as Harrods), if they do not 'get about', facilitating the obtaining and use of their particular card(s), they will lose money. The intra-organisational conflict between conservatism and 'victim-precipitation' is therefore quite strong. Furthermore, retailers who are the point at which most fraud occurs, are interested in their *own* profit maximisation, not inherently in helping the banks to the detriment of their customers. If a control measure slows down the customer through-put in a supermarket, for example, they feel that they are losing money or producing a less harmonious environment for repeat customers which will have a bearing upon their profits. Then they may resist the bankers' proposals or demand lower costs for processing as compensation.

CROSS-BORDER CARD FRAUD

It is also vital to understand that there are local, national and international aspects to the credit card market. The card issuer may be in Prague, while the card may be stolen or card number 'borrowed' in London and Rolex watches bought with it in Geneva. Time-space distinction has a special meaning here, where speed of transportation and the development of truly global transmission networks such as Visa, Mastercard, and American Express (or Europay, MasterCard's partner at the European level) create the possibilities of international credit spending, both legitimate and fraudulent, while most police forces remain able to function only with difficulty outside the boundaries of the nation-state. In Federal jurisdictions such as Germany, police liaison and formal powers can be even more problematic. In this arena, however, one must beware of mis-interpreting data to over-state the extent of trans-national organised crime. To illustrate, about a quarter of fraud on UK cards occurs outside the UK, mostly in France and Spain, creating the basis for international crime scares. But this is mainly where British tourists have their cards stolen on holiday, their cards being readily used before the card can be rendered ineffective, rather than the result of large-scale international crime networks which do exist, as we shall see. Even looking at genuine cross-border fraud, where the fraudster or a member of the crime network crosses a national boundary in order to commit fraud, ease of access to crime opportunities may be unaffected by the boundaries of the nation-state: distances between, say, London and Aberdeen are much greater than between London and Paris or Brussels. So where time is of the essence, what difference does it make that national borders are crossed, depending upon how much visitors are slowed down by customs? The Channel Tunnel has made even England closer in rail and car time to the Continent, and the Schengen customs-free zone speeding mobility, with credit card fraudsters unlikely to be targets for human or electronic surveillance. Indeed, the train takes no more time from London to Brussels or Paris than it does from London to Liverpool (and is more reliable). Consequently, the term 'trans-national' or international criminal has more rhetorical than actual meaning in this setting, unless one has intelligence that there are significant movements of cards or card numbers across particular frontiers for some strategic purpose, such as making it even less likely that the police and/or prosecutors can be bothered to pursue a case, or to facilitate finding corrupt or simply negligent merchants.

Research (Levi et al., 1991; Levi and Handley, 1998) illustrates that British retailers are far from vigilant in, for example, checking signatures. Nevertheless, there certainly is *some* risk: retailers are paid £50 for capturing cards and may be made to pay if the signature is grossly divergent from that held on record (or if the goods are ordered by phone and not sent to the true card-holder). However, from my direct observations and interviews, French merchants, who are used to a very low domestic fraud rate because of the connection of their 'smart' card with a Personal Identification Number (PIN) at the point of sale, are not at all interested in matching signatures against those on the card. This is very convenient for those using British-issued cards, which until 1999 have not had an embedded microchip to commit fraud in French shops. Thus, victim-offender-third party relationships make the dynamics of credit card fraud more interesting and complex than in many areas of crime: here, the 'third party' is not merely the bystander or the purchaser of stolen goods (Freiberg, 1997; Sutton, 1998), but the retailer who sells the goods and is seldom directly the defrauded party.

Some stimulating and analytically sophisticated work by Tremblay (1986) and by Mativat and Tremblay (1997) seeks to account for changes in the level and nature of credit card fraud in Canada. *Inter alia*, it is argued that prior to 1992, most credit card fraud was on stolen cards and was fairly local/regional in nature. However, after 1992, some people from mainly ethnic minorities, Malaysian Chinese, at that time (see also Newton, 1994, for analysis in Europe) - discovered international counterfeiting possibilities. This did not displace the previous frauds using lost and stolen cards, despite the greater profitability and longer 'window of opportunity' offered by counterfeits compared with other types of fraud: rather, it represented a move by criminal incomers, mainly those who had not previously engaged in such frauds. There was, one might develop from their argument, a status and competence differential that separated the technical sophisticates from the more routine working class subcultures of theft. The same sort of people used stolen cards and used 'altered' cards, defined by them as removing the original data and by heating the plastic and replacing it with new valid data on cardholder name, account number and expiration date, plus perhaps these data on the magnetic stripe. However, the ready availability of compact and efficient embossing devices did not provide a big enough difference in pay-off to motivate offenders to switch their techniques.

Although I have not sought to obtain the same depth of fine-tuned data on a regional level that Mativat and Tremblay had, I have obtained grosser time-series data world-wide for one major card network (which will remain anonymous, but I have no reason to suppose that other patterns are likely to differ), and I will use these data to develop and update their work, as well as to discuss my findings from recent interviews with a selection of credit card and check fraudsters in the UK and from a recent review of changes in check and plastic card fraud prevention in the UK (Levi et al., 1991; Levi and Handley, 1998; Levi, 1998). My objective is to look at the interaction between offending and what is largely private sector crime prevention, especially in the UK, where fraud against the corporate sector is *not* one of the risks that the police want to manage (Ericson and Haggerty, 1997; Levi and Pithouse, forthcoming). Indeed, the reason why there were so few cases of merchant collusion in the police files studied by Mativat and Tremblay may be that such cases consume a lot of police time and are difficult to prosecute. Lack of interest from the police and the slow speed of the criminal justice process encourages credit card merchant acquirers to use tools under their control: in this case, they have the ability to can 'incapacitate' the merchant (at least under his or her current name!) by taking away their ability to process card transactions.

THE EXTENT OF THE CRIMINAL MARKET FOR PLASTIC FRAUD: DECONSTRUCTING THE VICTIMISATION DATA

Using the nation-state or even the county/urban police force as a unit for crime or offender measurement risks hiding important local differences in crime rates. However, given that people are often interested in precisely such aggregate national rates, let us start with these units of analysis. Between the end of 1996 and the end of 1997, Canada's global share of credit card fraud has been rising, and rising faster than any other area of the world except Latin America: confirmed fraud on Canadian issuers is 7.3 % of the world total, compared with 5.7 % in 1996, and a rise of two fifths in one year was only partly masked by a rise in sales volumes of one eighth. The result was that in terms of confirmed fraud as a percentage of sales, Canada was higher than any other region, with 0.15 per cent, with the US at a modest 0.10 per cent, Western Europe at 0.04 per cent and even Latin America at 0.13 per cent. In terms of counterfeit fraud, during 1997, Canada was even more prominent relatively, topping the world criminal charts at 0.08 per cent of sales, compared with 0.02 per cent for the US, 0.01 per cent for Western Europe and 0.05 per cent in Latin America. Canada was twice the world average for counterfeit losses that year.

However, in the global card market, where retailers act merely as proxies for card issuers, the corporate victims may not 'live' where the crimes occurred: for the latter places of crime occurrence, we must look at transaction data from the financial institutions that 'acquire' the merchants' card slips in exchange for fees. From these data, we see, for example, that Canada still was high on the counterfeit scale, sharing with Latin America the distinction of being the only parts of the world where losses from counterfeit cards exceeded those arising from the use of lost and stolen cards (combined). Counterfeit losses occurring in Canada rose 85 per cent between 1996 and 1997, the quarterly analysis showing a major escalation from September 1996. Mativat and Tremblay (1997) do not distinguish between the country of card issue and the country in which the losses happen ('acquiring' country or region, in business terms). However, the data show that 92.1 % of losses from *counterfeits* 'acquired' in Canada were on Canadian-issued cards; 4.5 % on US-issued cards; with the remainder being on cards issued in the EU (1.3 %); Asia-Pacific (1.6 %) and Latin America (1.6 %). The pattern is similar for fraudulently used cards as a whole, with 90.3 % of losses in Canadian acquirer cases being on Canadian cards and 6.4 % being on US cards. So the level of international activity is modest and it appears to be based largely on convenience. Within Canada, Ontario accounted for around half the total fraud transactions, Quebec being one fifth; for counterfeit only, the ratios were similar, with Quebec slightly more prominent. Ontario, Quebec and British Colombia accounted for 93 % of counterfeit transactions and 83 % of all non-counterfeit fraudulent transactions, lending support to the hypothesis that little sophisticated crime occurs outside urban regions.

Mativat and Tremblay (1997) make much of the fact that larger runs of fraud, creating greater profit potential, are made possible by counterfeiting. Although it has not been possible for me to replicate their break down of counterfeits into altered cards and complete counterfeits -and only some pure counterfeits require merchant collusion- I do have better cost data per sub-type of fraud than they do. This reveals that after cards stolen in the mail, counterfeits do produce the second highest losses (averaging US$1,051 per account in Canada): lost and stolen cards cost only 60 % and fraudulent applications cost 85 % of the counterfeit average. There were fewer differences in length of run of account: fraudulent applications understandably yielded by far the longest runs, at 29 days average, followed by counterfeits (18 days), but even stolen cards averaged 14 days. Cards taken in the post averaged only 11 days use, indicating risk-averse offenders' awareness of the limited time before which the cardholder connects to the card issuer and complains that s/he has not received it. The reason why counterfeit cards generate more losses than do lost & stolen cards is the fraudsters feel confident to make larger transactions on the former. Expensive watches and luxury items are preferred by counterfeiters, in the knowledge that that the cardholder does not know that his identity has been 'borrowed' and is chosen as a high net worth individual whose credit limit will stand the purchases. Mativat and Tremblay (1997) suggest that 'gold card' patrons of car rental firms are particularly sought after targets for 'identity duplication', but hotels also are sources of rich data about cardholders that can be used not only to get card details but also place and date of birth, address, etcetera, which would defeat most suspicions.

ORGANISING CREDIT CARD FRAUD: A PROCESS MODEL

The following factors influence how many people offend and how they organise themselves:

- the levels, social distribution and organisation of criminal activity that already exists in any given environment;
- the social and technical skills available in relation to the control obstacles in place at any one time; and
- the motivation levels of those who contemplate fraud.

The first aspect obviously is highly variable, both within countries and between them. The third aspect has both a personality and a general culture and economic set of influences, with higher inequality (and absolute poverty) lending stimulus to crime. However, whatever the motivation and whatever the criminal ambience, the opportunities and setting for crime depends on how common credit and other card facilities are, and what is done about them by the businesses. Although the card transaction networks are global, and 'bolt-on' services offered by the networks include fraud risk management ones on the basis of parameters selected by card issuers, some of the factors that influence prevention -retailer checks, policing responses, stolen goods markets- are local or national. Thus, even if motivation and criminal structure levels were identical, one might still expect some variation in credit card fraud rates, depending on local 'barriers to entry'. Most research suggests that most offenders lack imagination and technical innovation skills (Shover, 1996): this could be one aspect in which conventional criminological 'control theory' discourses about low self-discipline by offenders make sense. Inertia also plays a part: Mativat and Tremblay (1997) suggest that Quebecois fraudsters were reluctant to shift from using stolen cards to altering cards, despite the ready availability of cheap and compact encoding and embossing equipment, although there may have been some point on the ease and reward axes at which they would have made the change. Perhaps inertia was 'rational selection', since stolen cards were so readily available, and their perceived (and actual) risk of prosecution was low.

A different 'take' on the organisation of crime is to break it up into different analytical functions, which may be carried out by the same people (vertical integration) or different people (horizontal integration):

- Finance the start-up costs of business. In the case of credit card fraud, such initial costs typically are low, except for good quality counterfeiting, where factory costs and perhaps corruption need to be funded.
- Obtaining cards or (depending on merchant collusion and the nature of outlets, such as remote terminals that merely require encoded data on a magnetic stripe that will 'pass' electronically- instruments that will function as cards);
- Obtaining money or goods from the cards; and
- Selling the goods for money or social prestige.

Avoiding capture and conviction may also be an important goal, depending on how risk-averse the potential offender is, though in social psychological terms, plastic fraud may be preferred to non-fraud crime because offenders usually get at least some money before they are arrested.

In a pilot study to explore some features of motivation, 'learning and markets in plastic fraud, I and some associate conducted semi-structured interviews with twenty-eight fraudsters in various parts of England and Wales, found by 'snowball' sampling. I have no reason to suspect that these interviewees present a distorted portrait of opportunity structures or constraints for fraud. Six in-depth interviews were conducted; the other interviews were more superficial. As a partial check, I interviewed several heads of police 'check squads' from around the UK about fraudsters' lifestyles. Typically, both police data (on check fraudsters, since few forces in the UK deal with credit card fraudsters) and interviews suggest that plastic and check fraudsters' personal mobility tends to be within 'their' region, varying from a city to a fifty-mile radius using the motorways to facilitate rapid turnover. (For further details of this study, see Levi, 1998.) 'Pure' counterfeiters tend to be international. Apparently by accident, one off-duty Kent policewoman discovered a group of Chinese parcelling out a suitcase full of gold cards on a train. In 1992-1993, there was a big increase in international counterfeit fraud, but -due partly to some action taken against factories in the Far East and police action in France- this subsided somewhat. However in the UK, in 1998, the 'full counterfeit' cards are still being produced in the Far East by Chinese groups, while groups operating out of

Sri Lanka are re-encoding their own cards with numbers obtained from genuine cardholders and are using these 'skimmed' cards.

OBTAINING CARDS

Logically, cards usable for fraud can be obtained by the following means:

- Using false data or impersonation of genuine persons to obtain a genuine card from one or more issuers (applications fraud);
- Theft, burglary or robbery from cardholders. The 1996 British Crime Survey found that seven per cent of burglary victims had credit cards stolen and four per cent had a check book stolen, that 1 in 10 car thefts involved thefts of bags or purses, and that 1 in 12 people had been mugged (Sutton, 1998: 75);
- Stealing the card in transit from the issuer to the cardholder;
- Manufacturing counterfeit cards that would deceive legitimate merchants, using numbers copied from genuine cardholders or generated by algorithm programs obtained from the Internet.
- Making 'white-cards' and encoding the magnetic stripe with details from a genuine card-holder and/or embossing the relevant details on the older, 'zip-zap' machines that are not connected to electronic terminals: because of their crudity, these require collusion with a retailer, at whatever level of seniority, though the retailer may find itself 'charged back' the losses if it cannot prove that the counterfeit was of high quality. Some retailers are set up partly to process such transactions, and may be planned to go 'bust' like the long-firm frauds studied by Levi (1981): they get the money from the merchant acquirers on the basis of fictitious or fraudulent 'receipts', and they disappear before the charge-backs arise.
- Making purchases by mail order or telephone, using genuine card numbers to get goods delivered to the address other than that of the genuine card-holder (or even, as in one case where a time of delivery for a yacht was pre-arranged, waiting outside the 'true' address and loading it onto a vehicle there).

The most common method is the use in retail outlets of genuine cards that have been lost or stolen: in 1997, such frauds accounted for half of the total UK losses and over half the US and Asia-Pacific losses, though only over a third of losses occurring in Canada or in Latin America. The proportion of counterfeiting, for example, varies over time and place, and has been (with Card Not Present frauds, especially those using numbers obtained over the Internet), the fastest growing area of card fraud in the UK.

APPLICATIONS FRAUDS

In the folklore of banking and law enforcement, applications fraud is commonly associated with organised crime, especially Nigerian (or, in Francophone countries, Congo) groups. The precise nature of these groups is less convincingly displayed: they are as likely to be loose, kinship/tribal networks as tight, hierarchical ones. There are Nigerian-produced manuals in the possession of police that illustrate how to commit such frauds, suggesting some strong communications structure internationally. Whether voluntarily or under pressure, and whether as 'subversives' from the start or merely part-time criminals, cleaners or others with access to personal data in unsupervised conditions generate sufficient data to support fraudulent applications for credit, both cards and other types such as car and home loans. 'Empty house' address data can be obtained from friends who work in municipal housing departments, and can be used to develop 'non-suspicious' applications for cards. These can be sent to a 'mail drop' and will show up as a genuine address on private sector computer systems that check for such things. If they are risk-averse, some applications fraudsters have a number of names and addresses that they use only once or twice, to reduce the chance that they will be spotted by the industry's sophisticated database systems, which search out for any discrepancies in personal circumstances on different credit applications, as well as for frauds associated with the same name and address. However, this cautious strategy also reduces the total yield from any one address, and the availability of 'mail drops' is normally quite limited. Applications may have to be supported by employment data, so unless the applicant is merely 'borrowing' the identity and creditworthiness of a real person, they may need 'front' companies or conspirators with genuine businesses to supply them with their *bona fides*. One couple posed to real estate agents as potential house buyers, pretending to negotiate for homes to which they obtained the keys. They then applied for cards using false names at the empty address, placing 'mail redirect' requests in those names to forward their mail to a 'drop' that they had rented. In effect, they used gaps in the diversified multi-agency control process to defraud hundreds of thousands of pounds.

A further aspect of the interaction between control measures and the organisation of credit card fraud lies in the documentation requirements which, as a 'private' issue, are determined generally by commercial considerations (except when the use of credit accounts for laundering is considered serious enough for the State to intervene). In the UK, photographic driving licences have just been introduced in mid-1998 for new drivers, and there is to be a standardised European driving licence. Stolen driving licences or those obtained in false names, plus stolen or computer-generated fictitious electricity and gas bills can be used to open accounts, particularly favouring 'instant credit' places where credit controllers may have to make decisions within at most five minutes. (Though in the long run, the introduction of photographic driving licences should make this difficult without expensive counterfeiting.) To allay suspicions, offenders might claim that they had only just moved to where they were now, and therefore were not on the electoral register yet. (Presence on the register is one method used by credit reference agencies to check the genuineness of the applicant for credit.)

Note that fraudulent applications give the longest lead time before discard, even though average losses per account are lower than counterfeit and card not received: this does not by itself illuminate 'runs of losses'from multiple applicants (nor, for that matter, from serial users of multiple stolen cards). Arrests and publicity signal to offenders that tolerance has reached its limit. Large databases -both 'not for profit' and commercially run- in which most British credit grantors pool all new applications for multiples and include not only credit cards and store cards but also consumer credit loans have had an enormous impact, but in societies where data-sharing has not happened, one can expect fraudulent applications to be much higher.

MANUFACTURE OF COUNTERFEIT CARDS

Except for France, and in the UK from 1999, most cards operate on the basis of data encoded on the magnetic stripe, with holograms and signature panels that discolour when tampered with for visual cues. (Until recently, signatures could be taken off by careful application of brake fluid: not a technique that required much sophistication or membership of a crime syndicate!) Syndicates with hi-tech abilities and financial backing manufacture cards with plastic, holograms and embossing of variable quality. They are usually Chinese-origin gangs based in the Far East, including Malaysia and China, where covert plants are established (Newton, 1994). They then distribute the cards through gang members in their global network, including Canada (Mativat and Tremblay, 1997) as well as Europe (Newton, 1994; my interviews). The gangs obtain the card numbers which are required to 'pass' the system checks either (a) from genuine cards that they 'clone' after obtaining details from collusive retail outlets, or (b) from number generators present in freely available software placed on the Internet which, when down-loaded, produces logically possible numbers in the 'bin ranges' that card issuers use, which do *not* correspond to real numbers in issue. (The numbers are ones that could be used at some stage in the future by the card issuers, but have not yet been so, and therefore they are not recognised as invalid by the communications software.) These programs have grown in sophistication since the period examined by Mativat and Tremblay (1997), and illustrate the criminogenic nature of the Internet, given human motivation and modest competence (Mann and Sutton, 1998; Grabosky and Smith, 1998; Levi and Pithouse, forthcoming). However, such techniques do not require 'organised crime' as their setting or origin.

One of the capacities of organised crime, and indeed a defining characteristic on some analyses (Maltz, 1986), is obtaining information and exploiting it by threat. Either threatening or buying in expertise from corrupt electronic specialists enabled some adventurous criminals, who believed what the scare stories in the trade papers told them about computer crime, to attempt such things as tapping the line between Automated Teller Machine (ATM or 'hole in the wall machine' that gives cash) and bank. However, the transmitted data are encrypted and include a Message Authentication Code that changes every transaction. These efforts have not yet (to my knowledge) met with success, though they have produced lengthy terms of imprisonment. Without doubt, 'organised' criminals will go 'where the money is' and will continue to attempt major counterfeit operations or infiltration and/or corruption of banking organisations, which is something of an 'open door'.

An alternative to careful counterfeit manufacture is to produce 'white plastic', i.e. cards embossed with genuine card-holder details, obtained by taking an extra copy of cardholders' details when they present their cards for payment at the store, or - for the more sophisticated or for those with 15 year-old children!- by loading electronic data from point-of-sale tills into a laptop. Retailer collusion is discouraged by the industry by charging back to the retailer transactions demonstrably fictitious and/or by the risk of being placed on a warning-list operated by Visa UK on behalf of the industry as a whole. Each nation has its own level of industry-wide agreement, and this is often seen as a commercial decision. Thus, various scams have occurred in which people pay by credit card for high-yielding investments in 'rare' (i.e. invisible!) Scotch whisky or wines: where fraud is proven, the card issuer in England must compensate the card-holder and, if the fraudsters have absconded, their merchant acquirer (which can be but is not necessarily the same bank as the issuer) must stand the losses. (The issue of 'who pays' depends on contract law which varies from country to country: it is partly a question of relative economic power, but also an attempt to locate legal responsibility where the opportunities for crime can best be controlled.)

THEFTS OF CARDS

The best cards to steal are those without signatures on them taken before the intended cardholder realises they are missing: hence the attractiveness to postal workers or sneak thieves of thefts in transit. In the UK, such frauds have been cut from £32.9 million in 1991 to £12.5 million in 1997. Since there is no 'natural criminal wastage' and the core activities of distribution remain the same, this reflects (a) increased monitoring of cards passing through the postal system, making repeated thefts much riskier[1]; and (b) delivery of cards by couriers to those who live in places where cards have not been received before. (The industry keeps on databases dynamic lists of risky places for opportunity reduction.)

Maximising the utilisation period leads the more professional walk-in thieves just steal one card, reasonably assuming that multi-card users will not notice or take immediate action, since they often assume that their card has been left at home: surely a common thief would steal their whole wallet?

---

[1] One postal worker used to come in with multiple self-addressed sticky labels on his shirt sleeves under his jacket and simply put the labels onto letters he believed contained cards, re-addressing them to his 'mail drop'.

OBTAINING GOODS OR FUNDS FROM CARDS AND DISPOSING OF THEM

My interviews and analysis of industry data suggest that about 1 in 12 cards lost or stolen is used fraudulently: cards stolen from cars, in burglaries and by pickpockets are most likely to be used by fraudsters. (As measured by the 1995 British Crime Survey, these crimes accounted for roughly half the cards stolen[2].) To date, there is no regional breakdown of ratios of fraud to lost and stolen cards in different parts of the UK: however, it seems plain that the majority of thieves and burglars either do not know how to make use of cards themselves (or are unwilling to do so, lest they be caught for the 'primary' crime) or have insufficient criminal contacts to buy the cards from them or exchange them for desired commodities such as drugs or sex. Credit cards are more likely than debit cards[3] to be used fraudulently, since offenders seldom know how much the victims have in their current accounts. As Sutton (1998) found, many heroin users nevertheless persist in using cards upfront, appreciating the risks which led to the conviction of several interviewees but being unable to resist the rewards: the more experienced sell the cards and check books on. Electronic 'hot card' files were developed during the 1990s to receive information from card issuers about lost and stolen cards and to transmitted these data immediately to retailers' point-of-sale terminals, where they can 'pick up' cards that are wanted after they have been 'swiped' through for purchases. These place a greater premium on quick purchases than was the case earlier (except where burglars know that householders are on holiday), creating a modest amount of displacement to the few outlets (such as local shops selling liquor and tobacco) which do not have modern Electronic Point-of-Sale terminals.

To obtain money requires either upfront self-presentation in a bank or knowledge of the PIN[4] at an ATM (automated teller machine). Without the PIN, the cardholder normally must have some plausible claim to be the *legitimate* cardholder. One way of negotiating environmental risk is to have friends in retail outlets who can tell you about those control measures of which they have knowledge, and/or to use stores where employee awareness is low. Others have covertly trained a surveillance camera on an ATM to record PINs and then have other gang members steal the card from users, enabling them to get cash. One interviewee used to pretend to be the banker from the credit card issuer in order to 'con' the victim of a walk-in theft into giving 'the bank' his PIN. An even more subtle trick is to ask the person who has lost his card to come into the bank, say, at lunchtime the following day (or at his convenience thereafter), to ensure more time to use the card.

---

[2] I am grateful for Catriona Mirrlees-Black of the Home Office Research & Statistics Department for this information.

[3] Debit cards lead to money going straight out of one's bank or other account, and are a substitute for cash, not a form of credit.

[4] Personal Identification Number, which requires carelessness by or collusion with cardholders.

WHO ARE THE FRAUDSTERS?

One difficulty in profiling credit card fraudsters is that the forensic difficulties and police disinterest means that there are few convicted ones to study. Even cheque fraudsters, where forensic analysis is easier because the banks and/or police have a better handwriting sample, are difficult to profile, but they are less unreliable, especially those who carry out large series of cheque frauds and may be caught eventually. A study of cheque squad files in one large metropolitan force, with substantial ethnic diversity, found that cheque fraudsters are predominantly white, under 30, uneducated past 16, long-term unemployed, and are equally male and female. These factors are accounted for partly by the legitimacy problems (or perceived legitimacy problems) that very young blacks (and whites) might have in obtaining credit (in the case of applications frauds) or in passing off as cardholders (in the case of lost and stolen cards). Though there are many 'student types' who commit fraud occasionally, few *persistent* offenders in my or in police samples are 'late onset' criminals. Most plastic criminals started in theft (such as shoplifting) before graduating to more sophisticated and profitable things.

Even those who are skilled at credit card fraud would see that (plus other credit frauds) as their limit in 'white-collar crime' aspirations. The majority interviewed were predominantly 'criminal opportunists' who drifted in and out of fraud. Those more heavily into an 'underworld' - and even some casuals who like to maintain awareness - are permanently on the lookout for gaps in security systems. Some scan all the commercial brochures put out by financial institutions to see if they can spot a criminal opportunity, including variations in practices between different banks and building societies; others pick things up from other prisoners and/or from watching television programs/reading newspaper articles about card fraud and prevention measures.

Some offenders steal (i.e. defraud) to order, but others use second-hand market opportunities (e.g. pubs) as redistribution mechanisms for goods they expect will have a ready sale. Prices are higher for these new, branded latest item goods than for the proceeds of most burglaries and thefts from cars. Some cards from a variety of sources, having been 'used up' by the risk-averse professionals, are passed on for small payments for use in buying groceries, for the people on the estate are always short of cash and this increases disposable income for other purposes. Industry data reveal that almost 1 in 11 of those card-backed *cheques* fraudulently used are used a year after the original reported theft, showing evidence of long-term storage by at least a few fraudsters. However, none of the fraudsters interviewed kept cards for as long as a month, and some appeared to have only a rudimentary understanding of the limits of 'hot card' files. Cheques are normally 3 a sheet, except at Xmas time when they rise to 10 a sheet because people need the goods: an interesting illustration of *criminal* supply and demand curves.

Avoiding conviction is normally easy, since the British police have only a modest interest and forensics such as fingerprinting are difficult in plastic fraud, since there are seldom any on the till-generated signature slip, which anyway becomes blurred in transmission. Fraudsters do run risks at the point of sale, though staff concerns about violence -especially where the offenders are perceived to be 'organised criminals' -may give fraudsters greater optimism, especially when the store itself is unlikely to lose money. Effective counter-measures, such as police operations involving surveillance and action against merchants who collude with fraudsters to pass genuine or counterfeit cards in large numbers, require substantial private sector assistance, provided in the UK by the industry in limited quantities.

CONCLUSIONS

In the UK, losses from plastic fraud totalled £122 million in 1997, the highest figure since 1992, though Levi and Handley (1998) estimate that without the fraud prevention measures introduced during the period 1991-96, the 1996 fraud costs would have been 350 per cent higher. As a percentage of *sales volume*, these plastic card *fraud* (as opposed to bad debt) losses constituted only 0.09 % of sales volume for all cards combined in 1996 and 1997: almost quarter of the proportionate loss of 0.34% in 1991.

Since around 1992, British card issuers have become increasingly worried about counterfeiting, which has risen from £4.6 million in 1991 to £20.3 million in 1997. They have funded a study by one police officer (Newton, 1994) into international counterfeiting rings. They have introduced an extra code printed on the genuine card (which cannot be copied electronically), to limit the capacity to defraud once the fraudster is suspected and asked for this number, unless the offender is disciplined enough to write down the unembossed number -which is not on the magnetic stripe - when the details are 'borrowed' and to keep it with the appropriate card number or credit card receipt. Bankers have refined the holograms and signature panels, making alteration and copying harder, though only a small proportion of cards normally can be changed over to any new system at any given moment in time: the rest are changed when they expire. Some UK banks such as Barclaycard -the most creative and research-oriented of the UK issuers - have developed sophisticated customer transaction modelling which searches pro-actively for 'out of character' transactions and then checks with the card-holder that the transaction is theirs. Such inconsistent transactions also show up as indicators of card 'cloning' discrepancies which are logically impossible, such as the purchase of items in more than one city or country at the same time on the same card. The industry has even banned in some regions such as Asia-Pacific the typing in of card details by retailers, to by-pass electronic controls on the cards, with dramatic fraud reduction benefits (though causing some irritation by customers and traders when the technology fails and there is no fall-back). Fuelled by the Canadian experience, where 'skimming' of cardholder details onto existing cards (without necessarily altering the embossed details) has gone on relatively unchecked, the British card industry has been motivated to spend up to £3 billion on rolling out 'chip cards' which would require code-breaking and reconstitution of the encrypted data on the card in order to use counterfeits. Counterfeiting constitutes only one fifth of the UK total plastic fraud costs, though this percentage has been rising. Nevertheless, it is feared that these costs are less controllable than other areas, since without checking the card numbers on the till print-outs against the number embossed on the card -a laborious operation on every card for busy and/or uninterested retail staff- the normal electronic technology cannot detect skimming.

Some types of fraud -e.g. those conducted through the Internet- may spread very rapidly once devised, escalating world-wide risks. However, at the low-tech end of the spectrum that includes some simple human co-operation, some form little teams in which one at a time is persuaded to 'lend' his/her card to one or more others until the end of the day, at which point s/he will report the card as stolen, modestly supplementing normal income, provided they are disciplined and do this very rarely. As with many other areas of crime, the motto seems to be 'small-scale is beautiful': people fall when they become addicted to risk-taking and believe themselves to be invulnerable.

Interviews both with fraudsters and with the police confirm the portrait of socially and culturally distinct fraudster networks in the Montreal research of Mativat and Tremblay (1997), though the smaller size and greater population density of England and Wales than Canada means that it is easier and quicker for British criminal groups to operate in different regions of the country, which some do but most do not. (This applies in a similar way to other European countries.) But none of the above indicate that plastic fraud is 'disorganised': what it means is that different forms of crime *require* different levels of organisation, and that there is no one optimal 'size of firm' for plastic fraud overall.

In the future, technology may generate enhanced *card-holder* verification by methods such as iris-scans, finger-scans, or most likely (as in France) having the customer tap in the PIN at point of sale against data encoded on the 'chip cards'. Via more developed crime networks (and international travellers such as truck drivers), this may displace some fraud internationally to those jurisdictions which do not have smart cards or which - despite an agreed interoperability world-wide standard- operate different systems: it might even boost the Canadian tourist trade! More analytical investment by mathematically inclined individuals and networks into breaking the encryption and re-encoding cards will continue. However, the *lumpenproletariat* of the underworld will remain able to commit frauds for some years yet, since smart cards are aimed at preventing 'skimming' other people's card numbers onto genuine cards and other forms of counterfeiting: they have no immediate impact on the opportunities to obtain goods on lost and stolen cards, which are easy for 'ordinary' criminals to do. The growth of remote Internet sales will enable new fake businesses to be created which pretend to be authorised to accept credit card payments but actually exist only to capture card data. But card companies will monitor the Net to try to close them down quickly.

In conclusion, although many fraudsters are embedded in wider criminal networks - how else would they get their cards and re-distribute the goods that they buy? -one can be an organised plastic fraudster without being part of 'organised crime' as commonly represented in the media. (For a particularly sharp analysis of the stereotypes of organised crime, see van Duyne, 1997). To be well organised in this context means to make efficient use of information, purchasing and resale of goods: the *method* of organisation depends on what resources and skills one has at one's disposal, and those resources can include networks or even -in some countries at some times- a hierarchical management system, though they can also exist outside it. But usually, especially in Britain but by no means exclusively so, it is only by conforming to the public stereotype of 'organised criminal' that one is likely to be of interest to the public police, rather than merely the private police.

LITERATURE

Duyne, P.C. van, (1996), The Phantom and Threat of Organised Crime, *Crime, Law and Social Change*, 1996, *nr. 24*, 341-377

Ericson, R. and K. Haggerty, *Policing the Risk Society*, Oxford: Oxford U.P., 1997

Freiberg, A., Regulating markets for stolen property, *Australian and New Zealand Journal of Criminology*, 1997, *30*, 237-258.

Grabosky, P. and R. Smith, *Crime in the Digital Age,* Brunswick, Transaction, 1998

Hagan, J., *Structural Criminology*, Oxford, Polity Press, 1988

Levi, M., *The Phantom Capitalists*, London, Heinemann, 1981

Levi, M., Organising plastic fraud: Enterprise criminals and the side-stepping of fraud prevention, *The Howard Journal of Criminal Justice*, 1998, 37, (*4*), 423-438.

Levi, M., P. Bissell, and T. Richardson, *The Prevention of Cheque Credit Card Fraud, Crime Prevention,* Paper 26, London, Home Office, 1991

Levi, M. and J. Handley, *The Prevention of Plastic and Cheque Fraud Revisited*, Home Office Research Study 182, London, Home Office

Levi, M. and A. Pithouse, (forthcoming) *White-Collar Crime and its Victims: the Media and Social Construction of Business Fraud*, Oxford, Clarendon Press.

Maltz, M.D., On Defining Organised Crime: The Development of a Definition and a Typology, *Crime and Delinquency*, 1976, *nr. 22*, 338-346.

Mann, D. and M. Sutton, Net Crime: more change in the organisation of thieving, *British Journal of Criminology*, 1998, *nr. 38*, 201-229.

Mativat, F. and P. Tremblay, Counterfeiting credit cards, *British Journal of Criminology*, 1997, *nr. 37*, 165-183.

Newton, J., *Organised Plastic Counterfeiting*, Police Research Group, London, Home Office, 1994

Shover, N. *The Great Pretenders*, Boulder: Westview, 1996

Sutton, M. Supply by theft, *British Journal of Criminology*, 1995, *nr 35*, 400-416. Sutton, M. *Handling Stolen Goods and Theft: a Market Reduction Approach*, Home Office Research Study 178, London, Home Office, 1998

Tremblay, P. (1986) Designing crime, *British Journal of Criminology*, 1986, *nr. 26*, 234-53.

Chapter 10

FRAUD AGAINST EUROPEAN PUBLIC FUNDS[1]

Brendan Quirke

Senior Lecturer in Accounting & Finance in the
Business School of Liverpool John Moores University

INTRODUCTION

The European Community budget attracts both the organised fraudster who may be an intrinsic part of, or closely connected to, organised criminality, or entrepreneurs who resort to fraud as a means of supporting a failing enterprise or helping a company or organisation in financial difficulties. The 1997 General Community Budget is approximately, 82 billion ECU. Of this, 46% is represented by EAGGF Guarantee and Export Refunds: the cornerstone of the Common Agricultural Policy, where the drive to spend the funds has far outstripped the means of accountability and control. As the National Audit Office recognises, in its background paper,' Combating Fraud and Irregularity in the European Community Budget', (1997), fraud and irregularity affects all sectors of European Community revenue and expenditure.

An important point to note at the outset, is that in the area of expenditure, member states carry out 80% of the budget outlay, both in the CAP and Structural Funds. This puts an enormous amount of onus on member states to expend the same amount of effort on countering fraud against the community's financial interests as they would against their own financial interests. They are required to do this under Article 209a of the Maastricht Treaty. The treaty also requires Member States to co-ordinate their action aimed at protecting the financial interests of the Community against fraud and to organise with the help of the European Commission, close and regular co-operation between the competent departments of their administrations. As organised criminal gangs are said to be increasingly behind many of the frauds perpetrated against the budget, the question

---

[1] The research was conducted during 1997-98. It involved desk reviews of published material and interviews with both EU, and UK national agencies dealing with fraud in relation to EU funds.

that must be posed therefore is: can national structures combine to fight transnational crime or are the efforts too little, too late and too fragmented to do so effectively?

This paper considers types of fraud conducted against two specific areas of the budget, namely EAGGF expenditure (Common Agricultural Policy) and Structural Funds expenditure as well as the links between business fraud and organised crime and the attempts of organised crime to defraud the European Union budget. The paper then goes on to consider the role of the European Commissions' anti-fraud unit (UCLAF) and how it seeks to support the efforts of Member States by gathering intelligence, ensuring co-ordination and maintaining databases of information concerning fraud and irregularities. The paper focusses on one member state namely, Britain, to consider the efforts it is taking to combat fraud against the Common Agricultural Policy and also to examine the efforts of Britain to fight fraud against the Structural Funds. Proposals to construct a common European legal space to deal with crimes against the European Union budget: the Corpus Juris are examined: these would seek to prevent criminals hiding behind legal frontiers. The paper then seeks to draw some conclusions as to how effective national organisations are in fighting transnational crime.

Research Methodology

Research for this paper is based on interviews conducted with officials of UCLAF in Brussels as well as Court of Auditors officials based in Luxembourg. Interviews were also conducted with officials of the UK Intervention Board as well as H.M. Customs and Excise. Reviews were undertaken of desk material but it was not possible to analyse information contained in the various databases of UCLAF or the national agencies.

THE COMMON AGRICULTURAL POLICY

'The setting up of a common market in the 1950s by the six founding Member States of the European Community meant the replacement of individual marketing structures with individual agricultural products, by a Community marketing structure. This led to the establishment of the CAP and a common system of prices for which the Community took financial responsibility. The objectives of CAP were laid down by the Treaty of Rome and were to raise agricultural productivity, to ensure a fair standard of living to the agricultural community, to stabilise markets, to assure availability of supplies and to ensure that supplies reach consumers at reasonable prices' (White 1995). The CAP has proved to be a very controversial policy, described as a welfare policy for inefficient farmers and also 'has been a permanent thorn in the side of some of the wealthier member States' (White 1995) .

The usual types of CAP fraud are integral to the functioning of the CAP system and essentially are concerned with the manipulation of purpose or procedure, including: false declaration of destination (to obtain higher export subsidy); false declaration of quality or nature of goods (e.g. frozen skimmed milk); swindling the milk quota; overdeclaration of livestock (suckler cow premium); cashing in set aside premium whilst producing on the soil.

Thus 'fraudulent activity in the export field works on the principle that most agricultural goods are subsidised under the Common Agricultural Policy. Goods when they are exported from the single market have their prices subsidised, by funds provided by the guarantee section of the EAGGF so as to make them competitive in the global market place' (Sieber 1997). The duty level usually depends upon the quantity, type and quality of the goods - and where - refund rates vary according to the country for which the goods are destined - then this information also is of importance for determining the level of subsidy. These variables therefore determine the main points of manipulation for the perpetrators of fraud.

Another offence is the illegal attainment of grants or intervention measures. In the area of the Common Agricultural Policy, the EU intervenes not only by means of import duties and export subsidies, but also with the help of a complex grant system. The system's many features include non-marketing premiums, compensation for storage costs, production grants and grants relating to agricultural area size. The grant system which now exists has been constructed by means of numerous basic Council Regulations, European Commission implementation Regulations and national implementation provisions: 'the system is so complex however, that even those people who possess expert knowledge relating to its constituent parts face difficulties when attempting to assess the overall functions'(Sieber 1997).

The various assistance schemes correspond to an equal number of fraud techniques. In relation to some agricultural production schemes the fraudulent exploitation of subsidies can be relatively easily detected. On the other hand, where legally complex intervention measures are involved, for example with the milk quota, the level of complexity of the fraud is reflected in this. Such instances of fraud are rarely discovered, and when they are it is only through the extensive analysis of financial accounts and computer data.

FRAUD AGAINST THE STRUCTURAL FUNDS

Structural funds are as vulnerable to fraudulent exploitation as those of the Common Agricultural Policy. The targets are EAGGF guidance section, the European Regional Development Fund (ERDF), the European Social Fund (ESF) and the Fisheries Guidance Instrument (FGI). Regional development plans, development concepts and the various programmes form the basis for the allocation of funds. These schemes are usually of a co-financing nature, where a member state has to provide 50% of the financing. Fifteen types of fraud have been noted by UCLAF: multiple financing or financing beyond the limit of the law; in the process of transferring funds: parasitic practices such as the siphoning off of interest; the selection of the beneficiaries of a programme; at programme start-up: expenditure incurred before the Commission receives the request for assistance; diversion of subsidies; public procurement: frauds committed at the award stage, either by firm themselves (collusion, cartels) or with the intervention of the awarding authority (corruption, favouritism, splitting-up of contracts); non-existent or duplicated studies, with funds being diverted for personal ends or for the financing of political parties; purchase of land, expropriation and property speculation; non-existence of the activity or operation being subsidised completion of works: inflation of prices by firms (over-invoicing); works known to be of no utility; completion of works: fraud in technical services; failure by contracting authority to impose penalties, damages or default interest on the firms involved; ineligibility of expenditure; ineligibility of beneficiaries; refusal to allow checks.

(UCLAF document SEC (97) 9445-en 'Non-exhaustive list of possible types of fraud in the field of Structural Policies)

EUROPEAN UNION: BUSINESS FRAUD AND ORGANISED CRIME

'Organised crime is not restricted to the traditional forms of crime like drug trafficking. Given the definition of organised crime, systematically planned commercial or tax fraud are to be considered manifestations of organised crime as well' (Van Duyne 1995). Firms perform legal functions and seek to maximise their profit margins by means of 'occupational crime'. In certain areas of business, competition is so intense that firms who work legally talk of an immense economic pressure to actually commit fraud with smaller firms that are more prone to indulge in fraudulent practices, because they have lower market profiles and perhaps are more vulnerable to manipulation by dominant personalities. Where the areas of concern here are in either the use of legitimate companies as fronts, or fake companies under the control of organised crime for fraudulent purposes. However, how large a part organised crime plays in defrauding the European Union depends on how organised the crime is. The UCLAF(the EU anti-fraud unit) view is that the organisation of personnel, a factory or warehouse, a fleet of lorries, denote some kind of organisation. From this perspective there is very little to differentiate organised crime from organised business crime although 'there is a need to distinguish businesses which turn to crime, as opposed to criminals who establish the means to commit fraud' (Van Duyne 1995) . When one assesses cases it is clear that both types are well able to undertake the same types of fraud.

Tackling the complexities of business fraud, particularly cross-border, or across private sectors is problematic, particularly if the fraud is the consequence of circumstance or opportunity. Structural fund fraud committed by the same groups is a clearer more consistent target. Certainly UCLAF perceive that organised hierarchical crime groups such as the Sicilian, Calabrian and Neapolitan Mafia are certainly interested in trying to defraud the European Union (Interview with author December 1997). They look for opportunities wherever they can find them, whether from frauds involving beef, olive oil or aspects of public works schemes funded from structural funds, on the basis of quick benefits with lower risk. They have excellent legal and financial support and, particularly in Southern Europe, their motives are not merely financial but seeking opportunities to increase their power and influence.

Van Duyne (1995) as part of his empirical investigations into business crime enterprises has considered organised fraud against EU regulations such as the import and export of meat and other agricultural products. The organised meat frauds could be characterised as Europe-wide cooperative crime enteprises. Van Duyne describes one such fraud where: 'In Poland the fraudsters bought cattle which would be exported on paper to North Africa from Spanish ports. In reality the export documents had been falsely stamped in Spain, while the cattle had been sold in Germany, the Netherlands, Belgium, France and Spain...The Polish cattle first had to be changed into EU cattle so that import duties could be avoided. This meant new false health certificates, new earmarks and invoices to show that the animals had been bought on the European innermarket. Subsequently the cattle had to be brought to the places of destination which implies a meticulously detailed organisation: the animals have to be fed, have to drink etc. Parallel to this the export documents have to be arranged...Though a Mr Big was never found, this organised crime trade could hardly be carried out without a coordination and monitoring at a higher level...' (Van Duyne 1995). This type of fraud is referred to by Van Duyne as the 'price- wedge market' where there is organised fraud with cost-price changing regulations; this usually has a cross-border dimension as can be seen from the example quoted above. Outwardly legitimate firms were involved in the fraud outlined above, one of which was 'nothing more than an integrated crime enterprise' (Van Duyne 1995).

There do appear to be a substantial amount of interactions between organised crime and legitimate business. This assertion can be justified by reference to the work of Van Duyne quoted above as well as work undertaken by researchers like Passas and Nelken (1993).

COMBATING FRAUD IN THE EUROPEAN UNION: UCLAF

UCLAF is currently the EU agency taking lead responsibility in the fight against fraud. UCLAF ('Unite de Co-ordination de la Lutte Anti-Fraude',) was created in 1988 following the recommendations of a Commission report concerning means by which the fight against frauds on the Community budget could be intensified. UCLAF is part of the Secretariat-General of the European Commission. It has a staff of 130, of which 60 are permanent. Its budget for the financial year 1996 was 12.4 million ECU.

UCLAF is organised into six units: F1-F6. F1 and F2 are horizontal units that support the four operational units. F1 deals with co-ordination and legal matters; F2 deals with intelligence, data capture and analysis; F3 covers structural funds; F4 and F5 cover agriculture: F4 deals with import and export issues; F5 deals with the activities of market organisations; F6 investigates and co-ordinates activities in the area of own resources. These units are also supplemented by the activities of special taskforces which have been established to cover particularly vulnerable areas; such as tobacco, and olive oil to combat large-scale sophisticated fraud under the Community transit arrangements more effectively: 'the aim is to strengthen the official system, prevent major losses of customs duty and national excise revenue and smash the criminal organisations responsible for fraud' (The Fight Against Fraud Annual Report 1994) The taskforces consist of experts from Member States and the European Commission: 'their role is to share information common to a number of fraud files' (The Fight Against Fraud Annual Report 1995). The taskforces centralise the information gathered, through the Commission, so that the operational departments of the Member States can gain access to it and co-ordinate their activities more closely.

UCLAF and Inter-Country Activity

UCLAF states that 'the primary duty for the fight against fraud remains the responsibility of the individual Member States who are responsible for the front line enforcement and verification work which is essential in deterring, discovering and stopping fraud. Every Member State is obliged under the terms of Article 209a (future Article 280 of the Amsterdam Treaty) to take the same measures to counter frauds on the Community budget as they do to protect their own financial interests' (European Commission UCLAF Background Document (D97) October 1997). Although its purpose is to co-ordinate and support the activities of Member states with each other and the relevant offices of the Commission, UCLAF has also moved into investigation in its own right, looking at suspected fraud cases with the aim of establishing the sums at risk to be recovered and preparing a case suitable for submission to public prosecutors in the Member States. While UCLAF has the power to request that investigations be carried out by the competent services of the Member States involved, it may also instigate an investigation on economic operators where there are reasons to think that irregularities may have been committed. This power is given to it under the so-called 'spot check' Regulation 2185/96. These checks have to be notified in advance to Member States, although how far in advance is a matter of some debate (an Irish official revealed that a fax was received at 6pm on a Friday evening to say that UCLAF officials were arriving at 9am on the following Monday) (Interview with author, Dublin, September 1997).

The Court of Auditors special report 8/98 on the Commission's services involved in the fight against fraud noted that UCLAF has to cope with a huge variety of different systems and procedures. It is faced with 15 legislative systems of the Member States while 'within each Member State different enforcement and investigative bodies exist...Each of these can have different sets of rules which must be respected. Any further enlargement of the EU can only complicate this situation...' (Official Journal C230/12). The Court observes in its report that UCLAF is trying to address this problem by the preparation of instructions for the carrying out of enquiries under the new Regulation: 'however, it is not yet in possession of a complete set of national laws, rules and procedures requested from the Member States and there will inevitably be a considerable delay before complete instructions can be compiled...' (Official Journal C230/12). Experience has shown that the actions of UCLAF officials have come under close scrutiny of legal representatives of the organisations visited and by July 1998 only five missions had been carried out under the new Regulation.

The Court has also commented on the fact that in relation to co-operation between the Commission and Member States 'it is of particular importance that the European and the national authorities deal in a constructive way with the requests presented by their partners'. The report makes the point that when Member States seek the co-operation of the Commission in the course of an investigation the Commission has to apply the Protocol on the privileges and immunities of the European Communities in a way that allows the Member States to carry out the required actions. The Protocol is designed to avoid any interference with the functioning and independence of the Commission; 'therefore if no danger of interference exists, the Commission is obliged to waive the immunity of the inviolability of its premises in order to allow a search by competent national authorities (Article 1)' (Official Journal C230/12).

Although officials are immune from legal proceedings in respect of acts performed by them in their official capacity, the Commission is required to waive the immunity when the interests of the Communities are not at stake, according to Article 18 of the Protocol. Despite these provisions, the Court has identified problems with respect to actual cases: 'in three of the cases examined by the Court the Member States did not start the procedures requested by UCLAF although evidence was produced. Also, in another case the Commission only lifted the immunity of three officials some twenty months after a request from the competent national authority' (Official Journal C230/12). The Commission's view is: 'that the cases in question are still in the hands of the appropriate judicial authorities, one of which has led to substantial recovery action by the Member State. In the case involving the lifting of immunity for three Commission officials, there were difficulties with the initial request which resulted in a prolonged exchange of correspondence before the matter was eventually concluded' (Official Journal C230/39).

UCLAF also has to seek co-operation from member states for operational as much as for political reasons. UCLAF are unlikely to act on their own for a number of reasons - for example, lack of detailed knowledge of a particular country - but, more importantly, because of the legal implications. Interviews of UK citizens must be made under the requirements of the Police and Criminal Evidence Act. Failure to be advised of their rights would result in any evidence being ruled inadmissible in any subsequent legal proceedings in the UK. Furthermore, UCLAF has no independent criminal investigative powers i.e. the power to arrest and question suspects, or to search premises and seize documents. These powers remain with the responsible agencies of member states. UCLAF is thus a hybrid organisation whose move into transnational work has been curtailed by issues of national sovereignty.

Computers, Committees and Co-operation

Member States are obliged under the terms of the Maastricht Treaty (Article 209a, paragraph 2) to establish close liaison in order to protect the financial interests of the EU between the competent departments of their administrations with the assistance of

UCLAF. Meetings between UCLAF investigators and representatives of the investigative services to decide and co-ordinate anti-fraud operations take place nearly every week. The Advisory Committee on the Fight against Fraud (COCOLAF), a committee of senior officials from services of Member States (mainly from Customs, Finance and Agriculture) meets regularly to discuss relevant matters.

This committee was established in 1994 and its function is to advise the Commission on the broad lines of its policy for protecting the Community's financial interests and organising action to combat fraud (The Fight Against Fraud Annual Report 1994). The view of the Commission is that they have been able to set out and develop the main features of its anti-fraud strategy, ensuring that initiatives and respective powers complement each other. This view of the effectiveness of COCOLAF contrasts with the views of certain officials, who characterise it as being little more than 'a talking shop' (Interview with Author January 1998).

There is also an Irregularities meeting two or three times a year in Brussels, hosted by UCLAF. Representatives on the committee receive statistics prepared by UCLAF which show the number of irregularities and degree of recovery of sums at risk to indicate how effective Member States have been in this area. This information can be used as one element of risk analysis. When Member States are reluctant to disclose certain information, this can be discussed in the Irregularities/Mutual Assistance meeting as a means of encouraging them to be more co-operative.

To facilitate liaison with Member States in relation to CAP there are two nominated liaison officers for each country - one dealing with the internal market, and one dealing with the external market. There are specific bodies in the UK for example, like the Intervention Board and Customs and Excise with which UCLAF has regular contacts but over 50 different police forces in the United Kingdom, a central intelligence service (NCIS) linked to the National Crime Squad, as well as two prosecuting authorities, and the Serious fraud Office, make relations with police and prosecuting authorities problematical.

UCLAF consider that there is no agreement as to how effective the co-ordination of UK fraud investigations is, and no guarantee of co-operation between forces and agencies. There is no evidence that the Home Office recognises its important role with regard to liaison matters. While Interpol could help to facilitate co-operation, and a co-operation agreement has been discussed, UCLAF considers that Interpol gives a lower priority to fraud after drugs and terrorism.

UCLAF assists Member States in focusing their verification and control efforts on high risk sectors and areas of activity based on past experience of frauds in these areas, and ongoing information gathering efforts. This information can be transmitted by informal contacts or more formally in training seminars in Member States in co-operation with Directorates-General with specific interest in the budget area under discussion but it has limited resources to deploy on anti-fraud work. The 1994 Fight against Fraud Report sought to address this by focussing on 'on areas of activity or categories of firms that present a high risk potential, while at the same time ensuring that most trade flows are able to cross frontiers relatively easily' (The Fight Against Fraud Annual Report 1994).

To collect and analyse information to be used in developing risk analysis techniques, UCLAF maintains a database of information regarding suspected frauds under enquiry by the Commission (pre-IRENE) as well as a database of investigation cases reported to the Commission by the Member States (IRENE) which holds over 20,000 cases, largely reported to UCLAF over the last few years. In the area of Customs co-operation, the SCENT network facilitates exchange of information between Customs services and is one of the carriers to the CIS database which will contain information exchanged between Member States. Member States cannot access these databases directly, having to request information from UCLAF (with the risk that UCLAF and national bodies carry out enquiries on the same case without being aware that their efforts were being duplicated).

The Court of Auditors has noted that the methodical processing of different forms of intelligence provides a better understanding of various types of fraud and fraudster and should help to ensure that Community finances are protected on a cost efficient basis - 'the Commission has invested considerable resources to expand its databases and information networks and develop a rational and integrated approach' (The Fight Against Fraud Annual Report 1994) - but notes that this is not heavily used by Member States.

The Commission counter-argues that the present version of IRENE is a system that dates from the 1970s, and requires knowledge of a specialised and now outdated computer language to operate it, with its use restricted to a relatively small number of specially trained operators. The Commission is in the process of replacing the outdated computer systems when IRENE and pre-IRENE will be integrated in 1998.

UCLAF Staffing and Organisation

UCLAF officials are drawn from a variety of backgrounds, such as police, accountancy and judicial with no overall requirement for detailed specialised knowledge. In 1995, at the initiative of the European Parliament, 50 extra posts were provided which gave UCLAF a complement of 130 staff. Many of these posts are of a fixed term nature and staff have to submit themselves to the competition procedure at the end of their term in order to be considered for a further term. There is a possibility that they could be unsuccessful, and therefore they would have to leave the Commission. This means that this expertise built up over a four year period would be lost and new investigators would have to be trained. Furthermore, the expansion of member states will lead to priority being given to the nationals of the new entrants with the potential of being disruptive to UCLAF's work. The intention of the Commission is to convert a substantial number of these temporary posts into permanent posts when the temporary posts become vacant although it is not clear whether the present incumbents will obtain the permanent posts as the Commission does not state whether they will have to submit themselves to the whole competition process. It has been noted by the Commitee of Experts that there is a lack of audit/forensic accountancy skills within UCLAF which has not yet been addressed. Only approximately 10 agents have this kind of background. Obsession with achieving a balance of nationalities will not necessarily help alleviate this problem.

How Effective is UCLAF?

The UK view is that UCLAF performs a valuable role in co-ordinating the fight against fraud and acting as a catalyst to encourage Member States to get their act together (Interview with Author, February 1998). UCLAF believes that it has been given strong support at a political level by the European Parliament, who see it 'as one UCLAF official put it' as 'its baby'. Parliament did initiate the expansion of staffing in 1995 and takes a close interest in its activities. However, events in 1998 moved fairly rapidly, following embarrassing revelations of fraud and corruption in a number of programme areas, particularly in its humanitarian aid project, ECHO: 'where 600 million of aid could not be accounted for... and a number of instances of corruption: where nine cases involving Commission officials had been referred to the police, eight had been removed from their posts, six downgraded and twenty were under investigation' (Guardian October 7th 1998). Jacques Santer asked Members of the European Parliament to endorse his call for a Fraud Investigation Office (OLAF) with sweeping powers to investigate all EU institutions. The new body will still be part of the Commission but will have its independence safeguarded by a Supervisory Committee made up of five independent experts and the Office will report not only to the Commission but also to Parliament and to the Council of Ministers. This was in response to severe criticism of UCLAF by MEPs who felt it did not press hard enough in case involving EU officials because of fears of possible repercussions upon the career prospects of UCLAF officials. The problems faced by UCLAF and outlined above, will still be faced by OLAF despite the new organisational and reporting arrangements.

There is no effective way of judging UCLAF's performance. UCLAF claims not to use performance indicators although its annual report presents information in the form of irregularities communicated by the Member States as well as Irregularities detected by the Commission in co-operation with Member States, as a type of performance indicator. UCLAF argues that they cannot know how many frauds or irregularities are going to be reported, and so any meaningful performance indicators would be difficult to generate. Nevertheless its operational effectiveness is currently seen as problematical. The Court of Auditors acknowledges that the Commission has made a major effort in its fight against fraud and this has led to a better legal and administrative framework in this area but has expressed serious concerns regarding use of databases, relationships with Member States and the lack of standard methods of documentation and file management.

CONCLUSIONS

There are fifteen different legal systems operating within the European Union. They have differing criminal law provisions, yet the EU is seeking the protection of its financial interests across these legal frontiers. Following a request from the European Parliament, the European Commission commissioned a study by a group of legal experts under the direction of Mireille Delmas-Marty, a professor from the Sorbonne, to consider criminal law provisions for the protection of the Union's financial interests. The study concluded that this type of crime reveals an impressive level of organisation and remains largely hidden in so far as it is 'integrated into economic operations through particularly complex systems employing a whole series of intermediaries, some fictitious, some from traditional commercial structures' (Delmas-Marty et al 1997 p.12). Aspects of this type of crime are largely international and in the view of the legal experts, the more that borders of the single market are opened up, the more the persistence of legal frontiers provides immense difficulties to law enforcement, in terms of providing havens for the criminal. The study suggested that criminal justice in this area comes up against obstacles pertaining both to the lack of continuity in criminal procedure (criminal justice authorities being competent only within the confines of their respective national borders) and to the disparity of legal systems.

The study published in 1997 proposed a common legal space or Corpus Juris proposed to harmonise procedure on the basis of three common fundamental principles.

> 'Firstly, there must be a principle of European territoriality the implementation of which requires the creation of a European public prosecution service, which could be mainly decentralised but with identical powers in all the countries of the European Union. Secondly, a common meaning should be applied to the principle of judicial control so that judicial control is exercised by the competent legal authorities and the Court of Justice of the Communities in respect of any appeals. Thirdly, there is a need to bridge the gap between inquisitorial and accusatorial procedures in favour of a 'truly European procedure under which all sides are heard' (Delmas-Marty et al 1997).

Whether these proposals are carried forward or whether they become enmeshed in political stagnation remains to be seen. There is an inherent tension between an accusatorial and inquisitorial system. Article 29 of the proposals aims to clarify the rights of the accused including the right to remain silent, the right to a defence lawyer, the right to know the charges against him/her and so on. The study aims to synthesise the guiding principles applied by the majority of Member States as far as the three components of substantive criminal law are concerned. These are the offence; the offender; and the penalty. These guiding principles are: the legal basis of crimes and penalties, fault as the basis for criminal liability, and proportionality of the penalty to the seriousness of the offence. The objective of this study is to draw up a number of precise rules on the basis of the aforementioned guiding principles. The Corpus Juris proposals are not put forward by the legal experts as a criminal code or as a unified code of European criminal procedure but as a set of penal rules. Such proposals could well be seen by those opposed to further European integration as too big a step to take. Given that they make significant inroads into territorial legal integrity: national self-interest is likely to rear its head once more. It could also be argued that without establishing a European Legal System to deal with these types of offence, anomalies may well result. Will like offences be treated in the same way in different Member States? Will national authorities view offences against the European Union budget with the same amount of concern as offences against their own legal codes? Certainly their adoption will provide a test of the seriousness of Member States' intentions with regard to the fight against fraud because the supranational/national framework structurally militates against effective anti-fraud work. The role of UCLAF has been criticised both by the Court of Auditors and the European Parliament for not being seen as sufficiently independent of the Commission. The proposal by the former President, Jacques Santer to establish a body outside the Commission to lead the fight against fraud will still face the same problems as UCLAF in terms of dealing with different legal systems, even with a pivotal role as a means for ensuring co-ordination and gathering and processing of intelligence. OLAF will need to rethink its recruitment and selection procedures as there is the possibility of losing experienced investigators after only four years by virtue of the competition procedures if it decides as UCLAF did, to recruit temporary staff. It will need more powers and more staff .In any case the fight will continue to be hampered by the ability of criminals to find havens across legal frontiers without the introduction of the Corpus Juris proposals. Once the legal framework has been put into place, there will then be scope for turning OLAF into a European Fraud Squad, structured perhaps along the lines of the FBI with the powers of arrest and interrogation. Only then will the fight against fraud be properly resourced.

LITERATURE

Court of Auditors Special Report no1/94, OJC 75 12 March 1994

Court of Auditors Audit Manual June 1998

Delmas-Marty, M., et al, 'Corpus Juris', Economica, 1997

Doig, A., 'A fragmented organizational approach to fraud in a European context', *European Journal on Criminal Policy and Research*, 1996,*3-2*, 48-73,

Duyne, P.C. van, 'Workshop:'Corruption in Europe', In: M. Punch, E.Kolthoff, K. van der Vijver, B. van Vliet (eds.), 'Coping with Corruption in a Borderless World' Proceedings of the Fifth International Anti-Corruption Conference', Deventer, Kluwer Law and Taxation Publishers 1993

Duyne, P.C. van, The Pantom and threat of organised crime, *Crime, Law and Social Change*, 1995, *24*, 4, 341-377

H.M. Customs and Excise., 'Management Plan 1998-1999', Intervention Board., 'Annual Report and Accounts 1995-96

Laffan, B., & Shackleton, M., 'The Budget', In: H. Wallace & W. Wallace(ed) *Policy-making in the European Union.*,Oxford, 1996

Official Journal of the European Communities, C/230, 22.7.98

The European Commission., 'The Fight Against Fraud Annual Report 1994', Com (95) 98, 29 March

The European Commission., 'The Fight Against Fraud Annual Report 1995', Com 96 173 final, 8 May

The European Commission., 'The Fight Against Fraud Annual Report 1996' Com (97)1997

The National Audit Office., *The Intervention Board for Agricultural Produce: Preventing, Detecting, and Acting on Irregularities*, December 1995

The National Audit Office., *Combating Fraud and Irregularity in the European Community Budget*, October 1997

Sieber, U.,'EUROFRAUD - Organised Fraud Against the European Communities', Paper delivered at *Judicial and Administrative Co-operation and Mutual Assistance Common European Legal Space' Conference*,Helsinki, June 1997

Usher, N., 'The European Court of Auditors - The Fight Against Fraud', *UCLAF Seminar,* Brussels, December 1997

Vliet, B. van, 'Workshop:'Corruption in Europe', In: M.Punch, E. Kolthoff, K.van der Vijver, B. van Vliet (eds.), *Proceedings of the Fifth International Anti-Corruption Conference*, Deventer, Kluwer Law and Taxation Publishers 1993

White, S., Fraud against the European Community budget: the context of Community enforcement, *London School of Economics*, Draft Conference Paper 1995

Chapter 11

FINANCIAL INVESTIGATIONS AND CRIME-MONEY

M. Pheijffer

Registered Accountant at the Dutch Fiscal Intelligence
and Investigation Service and Lecturer at Leyden University

INTRODUCTION

Organised and major criminal organisations all over the world have grown to a level where law enforcement agencies have to use sophisticated means to detect, investigate and control criminal activities. Traditional reactive law enforcement methods are no longer sufficient to tackle the sophistication of modern criminal organisations, nor are a single agency or a single discipline able to succeed by operating by in 'splendid isolation'. Instead of the traditional single-agency approach 'multi-disciplinarity' should be considered the key to success.

Long term results can only be achieved using a combination of investigative, legal, financial, technical and intelligence expertise in a multidisciplinary environment, where information-sharing between agencies, when possible both public and private, is the key to a criminal policy. A modern, sophisticated approach to criminal intelligence activities will provide society with meaningful protection from the growing problem of (organised) crime.

This chapter will concentrate on some aspects of financial investigations. Definitions of 'financial investigations' and its objectives will be discussed. Three examples of financial investigations will make clear that it can be a successful tool in the fight against organised and corporate crime. The first example, the so called Kolibri-case, is an example of a *tactical* financial investigation. The second one is about an *abstract strategic* financial investigation (cash generating businesses). The last one, operation Clickfund, is an example of a more *concrete strategic* financial investigation. Furthermore I will pay some attention to the multidisciplinary approach.

FINANCIAL INVESTIGATIONS

Introduction

The definitions of financial investigation that prevail in the literature may be criticized for their restriction to organised crime and criminal entrepreneurs and for the fact that they are based on a penal law approach. It would be more accurate to broaden its meaning such that it will encompass all *'inquiries on behalf of law enforcement'*. Accepting this broader radius as a basis for financial investigations implies that this approach is not limited to organised crime, criminal entrepreneurs or a strictly penal law approach, but applies to all forms of transgressions and all sorts of perpetrators. This also corresponds with the perspective of the Dutch government, which is devoted to an comprehensive approach of the crime problem, combining repressive penal law action with a preventive regulatory 'administrative' handling of violations. Concerning financial investigation the Attorney General Steenhuis expressed this approach in 1996 as follows:'Within three years, financial investigations must have developed into an integrated part of the *law enforcement chain'*. This chain of law enforcement does not necessarily start with a criminal investigation. Environmental or fiscal control actions may equally be the first link of this chain.

Another objection against the definitions mentioned in some papers concerns the exclusive focus on information directly relating to money or flows of money. I am of the opinion that this perspective is too narrow. In order to effectively apply the method of financial investigations *all kinds of information* must be included. For example, the financial investigator must also take notice of the observation and surveillance reports of the lifestyle and social relationships of suspects drawn up on behalf of common criminal investigations. Such reports could show that suspect A and person B have been in contact with each other at a certain moment, which may be an indication that person B is involved in the criminal organisation which is presumably led by suspect A. Such relationships always have a financial connotation and the non-financial information may contribute to the collection of evidence or -at least- provide the financial investigator with a more complete picture of the potential financial interests of the investigated criminal organisation.

From this elaboration one can deduce that the financial investigator operates with *information*. Using his *financial expertise*, the financial investigator must *gather, check, refine, process* and *analyse* all sorts of information. The financial investigator seeks to construct a picture as complete as possible of the relevant information and checks it for correctness and reliability.

A Simple Definition

On the basis of the previous section I propose the following definition of financial investigation:

* *investigations in which -on behalf of law enforcement- financial expertise is used in order to gather, check, refine, process and analyse (financial) information.*

In the introduction I hinted already at a tactical and a strategic form of financial investigation. A *tactical* financial investigation is directed at specific targets, whether it concerns (an) *object(s)* (for instance a stolen car or a plastic bag found unattended, containing a certain amount of money) or (a) specific *subject(s)* (an offender or group of offenders). A *strategic* financial investigation is aimed at a certain *subject matter* (for instance the opportunities for money laundering, tax evasion, or the commission of fraud through the stock exchange). This may also be considered a *thematic* approach.

The Objectives

Financial investigations are aimed at the realisation of the following objectives:

1. generating tactical information for investigations. In the most ideal form, this information is evidence. However, the information can also be the key to obtain evidence;
2. determining the volume of the unlawfully obtained assets;
3. tracing assets of criminals and/or criminal organisations;
4. confiscating the unlawfully obtained assets.

In a *tactical* financial investigation in the initial phases the emphasis is on the generation of evidence (as described in the first objective), more specific: evidence regarding *specifically described objects and/or subjects* related to offences. If this evidence has been collected, the attention will shift to the three other objectives, which are -in essence- directed at the finishing touch: the forfeiture of ill-gotten profits. If the gathering of evidence as well as the forfeiture procedure are successful, offenders can properly dealt with.

In a *strategic* financial investigation emphasis is also on generating tactical information for investigations, but by means of an analysis of the information of a certain *subject matter* or *theme*. The craft of strategic information consists of the craft of generalising from micro data to broader conclusions and -the other way round- to deduce specific statements to be transferred into concrete actions. The information for this inductive and deductive process may concern trade branch data or statistics, but may also be derived from day to day police information or court files. The objective of ferreting tactical information may further be differentiated along the following lines:

- generating tactical information for investigations includes -among other things- the gathering of evidence regarding a specific offence (for instance: money laundering), a specific branch of industry (for instance: the stock exchange), certain objects (for instance: real estate) or certain subjects (for instance: sellers of front companies). This goal for gathering the information is to set up and expand *knowledge files of specific law enforcement field*;
- generating tactical information for investigations is also aimed at gathering *risk signals* regarding certain offences, branches of industry, objects and subjects. These risk signals contain important information needed to set up a certain investigatigative strategy;
- generating tactical information for investigations also includes the supply of *management information* on behalf of *prioritisation*. In order enable the management to employ people and resources effectively and efficiently, it is important to make rational choices on the basis of the valid information. The prioritisation also includes a choice of the most adequate instruments that should be applied to reach law enforcement targets;
- generating tactical information for investigations further includes the gathering, checking, refining, processing and analysing of information from *tactical* investigations or old cases. After all, if it appears from a tactical investigation that suspect X applied a certain laundering method, this method should be analysed in order to find out which data flows are necessary to detect other subjects that may have used the same laundering method. Brief: *learning from the past*;
- generating tactical information for investigations must also include the refinement of information in such a way that well-founded choices can be made concerning *changes in rules and legislation*. By generating case material regarding the violation of rules and legislation and by making proposals for the amendment of the applicable rules and legislation, so that violation is made more difficult (or better: prevented), strategic financial investigations can contribute to *policy making*.

As can be deduced from these brief descriptions of strategic financial investigation, it is not an 'olympic' endeavour, but directed to a concrete support for detective work and policy making alike.

AN EXAMPLE OF A TACTICAL FINANCIAL INVESTIGATION: KOLIBRI

In the beginning 1990s the Dutch fiscal police (FIOD) started with a small team, nicknamed for its small size the 'Kolibri team', after the small tropical bird, to investigate various obscure financial traces. The resulting widening investigation is a good example of how financial investigations can be a successful approach in cases of organised crime and money laundering. The Kolibri-investigation is based on two important pillars: the results of the investigation into the downfall of the Dutch 'Femis bank' and the results of various investigations relating to the hash trafficking. The Femis bank was -- according to the regulations of the Dutch National Bank Institution -- not a real bank but a financial institution that provided 'anonymously' banking services. When opening a 'bank' account the new account holder would receive a banker's card and a code. The account would not be registered in anyone's name. It may be clear that this way of banking was very suitable for safely hiding 'black' or crime money.

After seizure of the business records of the Femis bank in 1991, FIOD-investigators succeeded in 'decoding' a large number of codes, as a result of which the account holders could be identified.

During the nineties, the FIOD also conducted several investigations into the smuggling of hashish. At a certain moment, a further analysis of the Femis bank accounts showed that there were connections between the Femis investigation and the investigations into the hash trafficking. For example, it was determined that a money transfer relating to the purchase of a boat had taken place through a Femis bank account. It also appeared that this vessel had transported 118,000 kilos of hashish. The analyses spurred the investigators to follow the flows of money via the Femis bank. By means of rogatory commissions investigations were carried out at banks, trust companies and other (financial) institutions in most European jurisdictions, including those with high bank secrecy regulations, Pakistan, Singapore, the United Arab Emirates, Canada, the United States of America, the British Virgin Islands and the Dutch Antilles. There was only one reason for these investigations: to trace the suspect money flows.

These investigations produced sufficient evidence to identify the suspected owners of these foreign bank accounts with the Dutch Femis bank. Subsequently evidence could be produced concerning the owners' connection with drugs trafficking. A large number of suspects at a lower level in the hierarchy of the criminal organisation could successfully be prosecuted. In their closing speech to the court the Public Prosecutors indicated that the evidence gathered by means of financial investigations in addition to the traditional investigative methods were insufficient to produce conclusive evidence against the main suspects. For that reason the Public Prosecutor's Office requested the admission of the evidence of 'crown witnesses', one of whom has been discovered by following the flows of money. If these investigations had been conducted only by means of traditional methods without financial approach, the ringleaders of the criminal organisation would probably not have been traced and prosecuted. Furthermore, the reliability of the crown witnesses was mainly assessed on the basis of the results of the financial investigations.

In this case financial detective work produced specific tactical information for further investigations (objective 1 of financial investigations). As far as the forfeiture of the illegally obtained profits is concerned (objectives 2 to 4) success has been modest. According to the closing speech of the Public Prosecutors this is caused 'among other things' by shortcomings in the field of international co-operation and forfeiture of profits, which hamper the swift and expedient confiscation of the assets of the crime entrepreneurs.

Two Examples of a Strategic Financial Investigation

Organised Hash Trafficking

As described above, the Kolibri tactical financial investigation started with concrete information from the demise of a crooked 'bank' and the hash trafficking. In a strategic financial investigation the starting point does not consist of this kind of concrete information about crimes or certain suspects. It is rather the other way round. One has to formulate hypothesis to develop a path of investigation. For example: it is often said that it is easy to launder money in cash generating businesses like car parking lots, saunas or car laundries. In that kind of business it should be easy to launder money by generating a false (inflated) turnover. This method has one negative consequence for the launderer: he has to pay taxes on the extra profits.

Working as a financial investigator and picking up the signal about the alleged money laundering in cash generating businesses, one can transform this allegation into a hypothesis for further investigation, like:'Car laundries are used for money laundering'. That raises the question how to conduct a proper strategic financial investigation to test this hypothesis. The first step is to gather general information about car washes, for example by using open sources. How do car wash shops operate? What is their servicing process? Where are they based? What are the average turnover and profit margins? etc.. This investigative step is intended to learn more about the branch of business, providing insight into its usual business practices. The second investigative step is intended to obtain an overview of relevant legislation, regulations and supervising agencies related to the targeted branch. The staff of the agencies may be interviewed. In the third phase an analysis of the acquired information has to be made, of course from the angle of the working hypothesis. The analysis may not yet *prove* any wrongdoing, but may show the vulnerabilities as well as the strong point of the branch of trade and industry. For example its relative impenetrability for 'tainted' money. As a matter of fact, this would just be an adequate risk analysis.

Until the fourth phase the analysis has nothing to do with concrete persons or objects. This changes in the fourth phase in which a list will be made of all car laundries and connected persons. The fifth step is to check different kinds of databases to find out whether the car laundries and/or the people connected to them are suspected of any unnlawful activities. If that proves to be the case, it may be an indication for further investigation. To select more laundries and people for potential investigations, one may have to go through the advertisements in newspapers, for example to find out whether there are requests for the purchase of car laundries? If so, is a regular market price offered? If any car laundry has been taken over a (spectacular) rise of the turnover may be observed. If that happens to be the case corresponding changes in the firms should be observed, for example an extension of the staff. In case of deviation of the expected business developments, there may be reason for further queries: are the purchasers of the car laundries known by the tax authorities and or the police? etc.. The sixth step is to select potential suspects when unwanted persons happen to have penetrated or when too many questions remain unanswered, followed by a prioritization of cases.

The preceding section shows that much preparatory work is required before starting a criminal financial investigation. Starting with formulating hypothesis it takes time before one enters the more concrete phase of investigation. Why all these efforte? The answer is already given: to set up and expand knowledge files, to gather risk signals and information for prioritisation, to improve the results of tactical investigations and to learn about necessary changes in legislation and regulations. In the Dutch law enforcement situation this strategic or thematic approach will increasingly be adopted. It has proved its worth in cases of organised VAT- and excise fraud and in the combat against stock market fraud.

Fraud and the Stock Market

Introduction

In 1996 the FIOD started a strategic financial investigation with the stock market as field of attention. The objective was to investigate whether this section of the financial market was vulnerable to criminality. I will not elaborate the technical aspects of this example of strategic financial investigation. What matters in this context is that our inventory related to the field of interest and the risk analysis informed us about a potential connection between the above mentioned 'Kolibri' case and the risks we recognized in the stock market. The Kolibri case was based on the decoding bank accounts of clients known only by code names. Reading newspapers we detected that some stock brokers used a system of coded accounts too. Through our Kolibri-experience this was enough reason for heightened attention, which warranyted further investigation.

At this time of writing investigators of the FIOD are still in progress of decoding bank accounts of clients known only by code names. Although there are some similarities between the organised crime example and this case, the kind of criminals are totally different. In the Kolibri-case we had to do with stereotype underworld figure. In the current case it seems that we have to do with a 'white collar' type of criminals. These criminals are suspected to belong to a criminal organisation involved in insider trading, money laundering, bribery, fraud, counterfeiting and tax violations in relation to incidents dating back to 1985. In total at least 80 million (dutch guilders) black or otherwise criminal money is at risk.

Some Examples of Vulnerabilities

Tax fraud

The main reason to use a coded account is to hide money for the fiscal authorities. One can have such accounts opened by Swiss investment consultants. Some of them offer the possibility to invest the money on such a Swiss account in Dutch stocks. The only required technical aid is a Dutch intermediary. By choosing this system of funnelling back money the Dutch tax evader can kill two birds with one stone. Besides the return on investments of the black money (which can be profitable compared to the low interest rate on Swiss or Luxembourg bank accounts) one can make investments in one' own home stock market. By no means the Dutch tax authorities can retrieve the beneficiary owner of the property. To disclose the beneficiaries' identity the assistance of Switzerland is required. As is well known, the Swiss authorities do not provide mutual assistance in fiscal matters. In this case the fiscal authorities were lucky: as a result of a house search by the Dutch intermediary the coded accounts have been detected and some names of the beneficiaries could be identified.

Fraudulent bankruptcy
A coded account can also be used to withdraw money from (potential) creditors. In this investigated case a suspect, a Belgian physician practising in the Netherlands, transferred money to such an account, because he was afraid to be sued for the epidemic, which broke out in his practice. In case of a lost lawsuit the assets of his firm would not be sufficient to cover the claims, still he would not be broke, because of the money in his coded and secret account!

Bribes
If large pension funds or investment funds invest through a stock market agency, the agency will pay a commission which range range from 0.1 to 0.5 % of the transaction. These pension funds invest large sums annually. So they are highly valued clients for the stock market agencies. If the latter pays a bribe to the fund manager it is likely that the fund manager will choose the paying agency. The fund manager has some extra personal profit (which can be paid in cash or on a coded account) and the stock market agency a big customer. This form of commercial corruption could be discovered in the process of this financial investigation.

Money laundering
The stock exchange can be used for mixing undeclared (black or criminal) and licit moneys, such that the black funds flow with a legitimate justification into the licit funds. For example $ 500,000 crime-money and $ 300,000 legitimate money, deposited in a normal bank account are brought together by a bribed asset manger. He makes fictitious transactions with the $ 300,000 licit money, creating a paper trail. This paper trail represents a profit of $ 500,000 (covering the hidden sum) which will be added to your legitimate account.
Another possibility is to use a coded account as a security for a back-to-back loan. The money on the account can also be used to invest in the stock market. Again you can kill two birds with one key: (1) the use of black money by getting a loan and (2) make profits with the black money by investing on the stock market.

Insider dealing
Insider dealing and front running is the last category of fraudulent transactions to be discussed in this section. Price sensitive information is valuable, because big money can

be made with it. It needs no further explanation that stock brokers can easily use that kind of information if they have a coded account.

Results of the Investigation

The results of this fiscal financial investigation are diverse. The fiscal authorities settled many cases out of court, penalising the suspect 'administratively', which means a taxation with a 100 % fine of taxes due.[1] At the time of writing the first offenders have been convicted. The main suspects will be brought to trial in 2000. These convictions are important, but more important are other results of this strategic financial investigation:

- we learned much about the financial markets and we succeeded to create useful a 'knowledge data base' of this financial sector';
- the risk analysis provided insight into the strenghts and vulnerabilities ☐from a financial investigators point of view☐ of the financial markets;
- the detection of new money laundering techniques;
- increased attention for the negative aspects of coded bank accounts. Although they are not formally forbidden, most financial institutions no longer use them to prevent negative publicity;
- increased attention for issues like business ethics and integrity;
- self-regulation has been questioned as inefficient and stronger supervision by the financial regulators and new, better and stronger regulation have been proposed;
- a growing awareness that cooperation between agencies which form the chain of law enforcement is a key to success.

The last item may be the most important. The knowledge and experience gained from this investigation has been brought together in a newly established Financial Expertise Centre. The players in the Financial Expertise Centre are: the Fiscal Intelligence and Investigation Service (FIOD), the Economic Control Service (ECD), the Amsterdam Police, the Public Prosecution Office in Amsterdam and the financial regulators (most important: the Central Bank and the Securities Board of the Netherlands). The aim of the Financial Expertise Centre is to promote the integrity of the financial sector. All the players have an interest in this. The strengthening of mutual cooperation contributes to efficient and effective enforcement of suitable legislation and rules and, through a easier and wider exchange of information, enables the regulators, investigative and prosecution services to focus their ever scarce resources to areas where they are really needed. Signals that are known to one agency can usually throw a new light on a matter, when

---

[1] For the suspects as well as the Inland Revenue Service the administrative settling out of may be preferred for various reasons. The 'respectable' suspects have an interest in court out of sethlement, avoiding the publicity surrounding a trial, while the Inland Revenue Service has a primary interest in cashing the tax plus fine, realising that some courts have a lenient attitude to 'white collar crime', acquitting the defendant or meting out a lenient sentence.

scutinised in relation with signals known to another agency; unlawful practices or punishable offences that are not (fully) recognised by individual organisations can be revealed soomer than before. Furthermore, this will lead to a greater exchange of general information on methods of investigation, fraud profiles, trends and market developments. Financial and fiscal knowledge will be automatically collected and can be used in future investigations.

The Multidisciplinary Approach

Introduction

Multidisciplinary teams are more and more necessary, because the traditional policeteams using their own traditional investigative resources (like: surveillance, wire tapping and interrogating) are no longer sufficient to handle the complexity of the specialist disciplines necessary to combat modern crimes. It has become readily apparent that the traditional methods of investigating crime requires the assistance of other disciplines like lawyers or sollicitors, accountants (or other financial specialists) and information technology experts. To make the multidisciplinary approach succesful, it is necessary to bring people each with a different background together in one organisational structure, although each participant has his own tasks and responsibilities.

Co-operation

Multi-disciplinarity also implies the establishment of a team, if possible, with staff from different agencies. This provides a natural opportunity to share intelligence. A fragmented, inefficient or incomplete intelligence gathering network may be considered a 'reassurance' to organised criminals. It means that the essential connections will be missed and only an incomplete and distorted picture will be created of their activities. This stresses the need for co-operation between agencies. The above mentioned Financial Expertise Centre is a good example of co-operation between various agencies.

Co-operation should 'wherever possible' involve the sharing of information, resources, powers and skills, whether this applies information collection and crime analysis expertise, specific investigative powers, (inter)national contacts, surveillance or technical expertise and equipment. Because of legal restraints special agencies have only investigative powers for special cases, which requires some creativity to and adaptability. Employing liason officers in other agencies could provide a good opportunity for getting acquainted and develop cooperation. Special agreements or covenants between agencies may form another way of developing more interaction.

The particular advantages of a co-operative or multi-agency approach include:

- overcoming the geographical extension of such investigations. Criminal activities take often place in more than one geographical area (province, state or country);
- sharing of information which would not otherwise have been accessible for the purpose of a concerted investigation against significant targets;
- ensuring the availability of the various skills necessary for an effective investigation, not all of which are likely to be available to one investigative agency;
- making available the necessary range of powers to facilitate the investigation.

PUBLIC AND PRIVATE SECTOR CO-OPERATION

The required financial skills may also be found in the private sector. This is particularly the case when specialised commercial expertise is required for understanding the subject matter of the investigation. An corporate 'insider' will be better equipped with experience and knowledge about the industry than law enforcement officers. He knows 'usual business practices', which encompass the technical commercial, financial as well as the social aspects: the implicit rules and customs. A good example of public/private co-operation can be found in the banking sector. The Dutch Bankers' Association works closely with the law enforcement authorities to establish an practical list of indicators and signals regarding the reporting of unusual and suspected financial transactions. In addition, some banking staff is attached to law enforcement agencies. Several specialists within the banking community are available on a voluntary basis to inform law enforcement authorities about financial products and procedures and to give advice.

Not only law enforcement agencies should make use of the services of private sector experts to facilitate the investigation of criminal activities, but they also should, if legally allowed, exchange information. This would be a two way flow of information, which is likely to involve rather general aspect than specific subject related information. This will at least alert the private sector and law enforcement agencies to particular areas of concern, for example scams that are victimizing the private sector. This way of operating jointly must facilitate proactive actions by law enforcement agency and preventive action by the private sector entities.

CONCLUSION

The usefulness of financial investigations in the fight against money laundering and related organised crime has been illustrated by the description of the Kolibri-investigation. But it can also be a successful weapon in the fight against organised business crime. It is important to recognise that the financial investigation approach has a broad appliccability. It is broader than just busting an organisation, making arrests and recovering crime money.

On the other hand, one must make sure that financial investigations are not considered a universal remedy for every problem: it is just *a* method and not *the* method that can be used within the scope of law enforcement. For example: in this age of technology it is also necessary to invest and educate people to become more knowledgeable about digital crimes. This can be a crime committed through the use of internet, including digital money laundering. The combat of these kinds of crimes will also be a main topic for the Ministry of Finance in the Netherlands generally and the FIOD in particular. Not alone but 'preferrable' on a multidisciplinary and international basis.

LITERATURE

Dijk, E.J. van, *operation Clickfund*, lecture on Europol conference 1998, not published

Duyne, P.C. van, *de aard van financieel onderzoek*, Het Tijdschrift voor de politie, nr. 6, 1996, 11-16

Duyne, P.C. van, M. Pheijffer, J.G. Kuijl, A.Th.H. van Dijke and G.J.C.M. Bakker, *Financial investigation. Theory and practice of an international approach*, Vermande, 2001.

Irwin, M.P., *Co-operation, the key to success in major investigations*, Criminal Justice Commission, Queensland, Australia, 1992

Kolthoff, E.W. en A.L. Speijers, *Eindrapport project financieel rechercheren*, Project Financieel rechercheren, 1997

McCallum, P.B., *Multidisciplinary teams: accountants as fellow investigators*, Criminal Justice Commission, Queensland, Australia, 1992

Paumen, R., *Operation Clickfund*, lecture on Europol conference 1998, not published

Pheijffer, M., *Financial investigations and criminal money*, lecture on Europol conference 1998, not published

Pheijffer, M. en G.J.C.M. Bakker, *Multidisciplinair optreden: noodzaak of dwangbuis?*, in: Doelder, H. de en A.B. Hoogenboom, *Financieel rechercheren; verbetering van samenwerking door integratie van disciplines*, Gouda Quint, 1998

Pheijffer, M. en G.J.C.M. Bakker, *Rechtshandhaving verschuift van 'autonoom repressief' naar 'integraal preventief'*, in: Wielenga, A., Fraudebestrijdingsjaarboek 1999, Samom, 1999

Pheijffer, M., Kuijl, J.G., Dijk, A.Th.H. van en G.J.C.M. Bakker, *Financieel rechercheren; theorie en praktijk*, Kluwer, 1997

Swagerman, B., *The Financial expertise centre*, lecture on Europol conference 1998, not published

Chapter 12

FACTS AND MYTHS ABOUT THE SO-CALLED UNDERGROUND BANKING

Nikos Passas

Professor of Criminal Justice at
Temple University, Philadelphia US.

INTRODUCTION

Since the late 1980s and especially during the 1990s, official concern has grown about what is commonly called 'underground banking' and its use by serious offenders. Articles in the media and on the internet as well as government agency reports and memoranda have increasingly made reference to the threat posed by unregulated and informal networks that allow the transfer of value without leaving any tracks for investigators. Even some works by academic writers have echoed this concern and contributed to a conventional wisdom about what these 'underground banks' are, how they operate and what risks they represent at the domestic and international levels (Williams, 1997; Savona, 1997).

Unfortunately, much of what is accepted as fact and taken for granted is inaccurate or erroneous, similarly to other areas generally discussed under the loosely defined category of 'transnational crime' (Passas, 1998). Yet, this false conventional wisdom penetrates the policy-making field, as it becomes accepted by government and international bodies, such as the United Nations. It is, therefore, imperative to establish the facts and separate them from the myths and exaggerations, which can produce unnecessary and counter-productive measures and policies. This article is based on extensive interviews with scholars, regulators and law enforcers from all continents, a critical review of legal and scholarly literature, media and government reports, and a number of cases from around the world. This research was conducted on behalf of the Dutch Ministry of Justice and continued thanks to a sabbatical leave from Temple University. The paper aims at offering a more precise definition of the practices and issues involved in what is indiscriminately called underground banking, briefly looks at the origin of the practices in question, discusses the prevalent modi operandi, examines the factors contributing to their continued popularity and concludes with policy implications.

DEFINING THE ISSUE

The first task is to sort out the different practices and phenomena examined in the literature under the same rather misleading heading of 'underground banking'. Many authors discuss under this term informal or unregulated banks operating for the most part in Asian and African countries. These are small or large scale operations offering banking services, such as credit, deposit-taking, lending and other facilities. Since they are not supervised or authorized by regulatory agencies and violate laws currently in force, these institutions may be called 'underground banks'. Their services, incidentally, are not necessarily criminal or unethical in nature. Indeed, in many instances, they represent the only or most efficient option available to local populations in need of banking services.

On the other hand, a lot of ink (virtual and real) has been used to describe as 'underground banking' certain practices which are anything but underground and have little or nothing to do with what commonly defines a bank. Reports in the media, by government agencies as well as academics have been concerned with groups and individuals facilitating the transfer of money from place to place without resort to conventional institutions. One of the more reasonable accounts describes 'underground banking' as 'a commercial activity involving the transfer of money across national borders through a non-bank institution or organisation' (Schaap and Mul, 1995). These activities have been worrying law enforcement agencies in recent years, because they provide a potential route money launderers may use to avoid the increasingly regulated banking system. In many countries, however, these practices violate no law and are conducted openly in street markets. So, there is little or nothing 'underground about them.

The specific terms employed for such practices vary according to country and ethnic origin. They include hawala, hundi and fei ch'ien among many others. The bulk of the academic and journalistic literature on 'underground banking' refers to such practices. Occasionally, the existence of multiple systems and networks is acknowledged, but then hawala is used as a generic descriptive term (Commonwealth Secretariat, 1998). This usage may be convenient, especially in the light of many similarities in methods. However, it is important not to lose sight of substantial differences in the various practices (Carroll, 1999, Passas, 1999). Indeed, a good deal of the confusion and inconsistent use of various terms originates from the objective of those writing about such practices. Overwhelmingly, this objective is to find out how criminals launder dirty money. Once some vehicles for money laundering are identified, they are all placed in the same basket of 'underground banks' (e.g., see some contributions in Savona, 1997).

Yet, even the above definition has limitations. Firstly, there may be no commercial activity underlying the transaction (i.e. money sent to a relative who is studying or touring abroad). Secondly, sometimes it is not money, but commodities or other items that are transferred, such as gold, diamonds, electric appliances or computer equipment. Thirdly, the transactions are not always international; they can also be domestic. Finally, sometimes, the transfer takes place through no organisation or institution. It can be as simple as two individuals, a family or a small network of people.

If the practices worrying officials do not have much to do with banking and are not underground, the question is what term should apply to them. The central issue here is essentially with methods of money movements outside the institutional channels, which are supervised and monitored by government authorities. One author uses the concept of 'alternative banking' to refer to a 'system which is subject to no external auditing, control or supervision, whereby money or value can be transferred from one country to another' (Carroll, 1995: 3). However, some of these systems predate the conventional banking systems and in many parts of the world these 'alternatives' are actually the rule - the formal banking system is the exception, the 'alternative' system (Choucri, 1986).

Consequently, the term 'informal value transfer systems' (IVTS) has been adopted here. This will refer to any system or network of people facilitating, on a full-time or part-time basis, the transfer of value domestically or internationally outside the conventional, regulated financial institutional systems. IVTS originated and are still found most prominently among Asian ethnic groups. They have spread to the other continents as a result of immigration and social mobility. They are characterised by trust, a relative absence of written records, and a reliance on contacts around the world. In most instances, value/money is transferred without the movement of money.

THE ORIGINS OF IVTS

Most contemporary IVTS are derived from two main methods of value transfers, both of which originated in Asia centuries ago. Hundi/hawala emerged in South Asia (India and Pakistan), while fei ch'ien was practiced in China. A long list of common misunderstandings about IVTS begins with their origins. The overwhelming majority of writings erroneously assert that IVTS emerged for illegal purposes, such as the evasion of currency restrictions and the by-passing of various laws or in the context of political instability and distrust of banks (Bosworth-Davis and Saltmarsh, 1995; National Crime Authority, 1991; O'Hara and The Wild Palms Foundation, 1997; South, no date). The truth is that these networks were essentially benign and were established to serve perfectly legitimate needs (Akse, 1996). They served people well before the development of modern banking institutions. They facilitated legitimate trade or other transactions, while protecting against robbery and theft in highways. As has been pointed out, one function of 'hundis' was to enable people to get advances; hundis were either pure finance bills or trade bills (Jain, 1929). Fei ch'ien, on the other hand, emerged as a method of settling accounts between traders and local government authorities keen to minimise the risks of robbery and to avoid the inconvenience of physically transporting large amounts of money or goods from place to place. Indeed, some of the modern banks were developed out of former IVTS (Cassidy, 1994).

Both of these principal models of IVTS became so widely accepted that they became integral elements of the culture in Asian countries and communities of immigrants. More recently, a third important variety of IVTS appeared in the Americas commonly known as 'la vuelta' or 'stash house', which revolves around the Colombian black market for pesos and dollars. This market does currently facilitate the laundering of dirty money, but it also originated for less murky purposes. It started as a mechanism providing strong currency to Colombian importers, who needed to settle their accounts overseas, but faced currency restrictions at home. It now serves drug traffickers, who wish to repatriate part of their profits and the traders, who need hard currency in the USA or Europe (due to space constraints, this model will not be analysed here; for more information, see Passas, 1999).

THE MECHANICS OF IVTS

The most basic method is when a client wishes to send money to a friend, relative or business partner in another country. The client approaches an IVTS operator to request the transfer of a certain value to country X. The operator will call or fax the details to his counterpart in that country and payment will be made within hours. Oftentimes, a code will be given to the client for reference to the 'broker' in the country where the pick-up is to take place. This code will be communicated in the meantime by fax or telephone to the operator responsible for the payment. In this simple example, no money will actually cross borders. The client will hand over to the local broker the amount he wishes to transfer either in advance or, in some cases, when assurance is given that the money has been received on the other end. In some cases, the client may wish to pick up the money himself in the other country. Several features or modi operandi of IVTS are remarkably similar to the early banking practices in Europe, when Italian institutions issued drafts to facilitate business transactions in different countries. The services they offer today are slightly different from Thomas Cook, American Express, Western Union, etc. (Akse, 1996).

IVTS operators ('hawaladars', in the Indian subcontinent) balance their accounts with transfers in the opposite direction. When the overall transfers are of unequal value, from time to time the IVTS agents may wire transfer the difference. Alternatively, they may send a check, a postal order or may even smuggle the currency. A more complicated way of balancing the books involves invoice manipulation. This entails the occasional or systematic participation of traders in legal goods. The legitimate trades may be conducted either by hawaladars or associates, who may occasionally be part of an extended family. For instance, let us assume that less money has been transferred out of India than came into the country from the Netherlands, causing an imbalance of Euro 80,000 between the IVTS operators concerned. The operator based in the Netherlands may purchase Euro 150,000 worth of goods, such as electric or computer equipment, and ship them to India with an official invoice for only Euro 70,000. The Indian operator can then sell the merchandise and make a legitimate profit, retrieving at the same time the Euro 80,000 owed to him from overseas. The same method is employed when the funds must move in the opposite direction. Instead of under-invoicing by Euro 80,000, the overseas operator will over-invoice by that amount. Hawala and mis-invoicing have been used extensively for the purpose of tax evasion and/or capital flight (Bhagwati, 1964; Zdanovicz et al., 1995).

A common variation of the basic example outlined above includes transactions in gold (much more rarely, in other commodities too). The IVTS operators make use of the cash deposited for transfer in order to purchase gold. The gold is then smuggled into countries where there is high demand for the precious metal, such as India. Given the high demand, the price at which the smuggled gold is sold is often substantially higher than world market prices. In such cases, the gold-related transactions and smuggling furnish the main profit of IVTS brokers. Otherwise, their profit usually comes from the manipulation of currency exchange rates. In other cases, they charge a commission ranging from 0.25-1.25% of the amount involved (personal interviews; Miller, 1999). When the broker (hawaladar) understands that the transaction involves criminal proceeds or transactions by the client, the charged commission may be as high as 15-20 percent (Carroll, 1999).

One important difference between the two chief IVTS models is that the import-export and invoice manipulation practices are more prevalent in the hawala networks than the Chinese. Also, contrary to many press reports, the evidence and my interviewees suggest that the 'proof of claim' (such as the chit) is used primarily in Chinese rather than in hawala/hundi transactions. Some South Asian cases involving proof of claim are reported by law enforcers in Britain, but all such cases are related to drug proceeds (personal interviews). It may be tentatively hypothesised that such proofs are used and perhaps are necessary, when the element of trust is either weak or lacking, and when it comes to dirty money, transactions among people who do not know each other well or at all and large amounts.

Another difference is that the Chinese IVTS is mostly a one-way traffic. Money goes essentially to China, whereas hawala/hundi is bi-directional. The question of how the money is transferred to China and how the balances are set off remains a bit of a mystery. Interviewees have suggested that transfers are handled by people with access to large amounts of money, but no specifics are available. Anecdotal evidence suggests that corporations and state agencies may be involved in this. In one case, cheap goods were purchased in the US and then dumped in China. Despite the loss, it was worth it, given that the money was laundered and became 'usable'. In other cases, Chinese use front companies to move money to China. In yet other cases, they use conventional banks and wire transfers. However, the evidence is thin and inconclusive.

Most people who use the IVTS's services, know about them by word of mouth. However, the money transfer services are advertised in the ethnic press in many countries. The advertisements can be cryptic, simply referring to 'great' or 'beautiful' rupee deals (or the 'best rate for guilders') among other services they offer, or clear advertisements for 'same day delivery. Rupees, New York to Bombay'.

The IVTS operators range from corner shop owners to operators of giro houses, bureaux de change, brokers, wire services, other conventional money transmitters, and money changers to the more stereotyped hawala banker. Some networks interface a great deal with conventional business, organisations and people, while others are capable of operating entirely on their own. IVTS may operate either entirely openly or out of legitimate businesses, such as travel agencies, import/export or shipping companies, grocery stores, gold and jewellery shops, textile or apparel shops etc. In many cases, the transfer of money is a tangential activity and is done to provide fuller services to the customers who need it, as a way or attracting clients, or as a service to the ethnic community. In other cases, the legitimate business may be a sheer front. In England, for example, there are travel agencies that provide no travel services and are equipped only with a telephone and fax machine. Yet, they have security devices at the door for protection against robbers (interview with Jackson). The informal value remitters range from quite simple, small, one-time operators to sophisticated, long-term businessmen with family tradition and extensive networks (Miller, 1999). They may also be members of well-known banking families with an established reputation (Carroll, 1999).

VIOLENCE, GANGS, USE OF HI-TECH AND 'FACTS BY REPETITION'

Other errors in conventional wisdom include the assumption that IVTS are surrounded by violence and corruption, and that high technology may be used in the near future for more secrecy and confidentiality. In fact, typical IVTS operations are smooth, consensual and require only low technology, such as a telephone or fax machine. False conventional wisdom is often produced through a process I have described as 'facts by repetition'. That is, wrong statements made in widely circulated articles are later reproduced in other press articles, government reports, academic publications. Given a certain number of repetitions, they are considered to be facts beyond doubt.

As one interviewee has suggested, some violence is used for example in connection with drug money moved around through hawala. Yet it is unclear whether such violence has to do with hawala (the transfer method and the related network) or with the drug traffickers (the clients). Even in those rare cases, it is impossible to say with certainty that the hawala brokers were involved in violent acts. There is evidence that IVTS operators may become victims of violent crime, given that they routinely handle a good deal of cash (e.g., two hawaladars who catered to the needs of London's Bangladeshi community were stabbed to death by robbers in their home; Elliott, 1991). All my sources with direct experience of hawala networks emphasised the paramount importance of trust. It is trust, rather than fear and violence, that makes this system work efficiently and reliably. Violation of this trust brings about shame, ostracism and dishonour within the family and the wider community.

Finally, neither hawala/hundi nor fei ch'ien networks fit the Western description of 'gangs'. In many instances, IVTS operators are providing a desperately needed service to immigrant groups who wish to send funds back home, but the absence of adequate infrastructure and banking facilities makes that impossible.

Nevertheless, sensational stories were picked up by the media, academics, government officials and people working in international organisations. Given sufficient repetitions, erroneous or out-of-context statements became 'facts' worthy of inclusion in United Nations documents. The following is an illustration of how false conventional wisdom is generated with everyone referring to the same misleading statement (often without even referring to the original source)'

- 'These parallel banking systems are based on family or gang alliances and reinforced with an unspoken covenant of retributive violence.' (Malhotra, 1995: 1).
- 'These parallel banking systems are based on family or gang alliances and reinforced with an unspoken covenant of retributive violence.' (O'Hara and The Wild Palms Foundation, 1997: 1) [no quotation marks].
- 'Parallel banking systems are based on family or gang alliances and reinforced with an unspoken covenant of retributive violence.' (Williams, 1997: 6; in quotation marks, but without reference to source).
- 'These parallel banking systems are based on family or gang alliances and reinforced with an unspoken covenant of retributive violence.' (UN General Assembly, Special Session on the World Drug Problem 8-10 June 1998; no quotation marks).

Similar 'facts by repetition' were created through the above publications with respect to the Chinese system, the role of bribery and corruption, or the mechanics of hawala. Williams (1997), for example writes:'One of the reasons that these schemes work so effectively is that they are protected through bribery and corruption'. These are hardly necessary elements of efficient hawala operations. When they combine with smuggling or other activities, of course official blind eyes are purchased. Bribery and corruption are not vital at all, however, for the day-to-day activities, which typify informal value transfer systems.

Another statement that is unsupported by empirical evidence regards the use of new technologies by IVTS. Some have speculated that the arrival of the internet and cyber-payments will usher in a new era of high-tech 'underground banking', even more difficult to investigate because of the technology involved. As has been noted, the anticipated sophisticated methods 'have not yet been adopted by the Indian or Pakistani Underground bankers for the most part, but they are expected to make the transition to newer technology early in the 21st Century as a result of available technology and a rising generation which is more "tech friendly." As a practical matter, investigation of underground cyber banking is extremely difficult and requires expertise not only in the culture creating the system, but sophisticated techniques in computer investigation and cryptography. In order to secure its borders, all nations need to be aware of underground banking practices, not only as they existed in the past, and as they exist today, but where things are headed' (Lambert, 1996). This statement is sheer speculation and based on no known cases of such a transition. Indicating the lack of the necessary infrastructure in rural regions of developing countries, basic cultural understanding, most interviewees suggest that there is no need for IVTS to evolve in this particular way. The systems are so efficient, in part, precisely because they are so low-tech and cheap to operate.

CAUSES OF CONTINUING USE OF IVTS

Hawala and Chinese IVTS are still used quite extensively as remittance systems throughout the world. This raises the question of why they are so popular at a time of globalisation, unprecedented ease of travel, the introduction of new technologies, economic liberalisation and the growth of a multinational banking industry. The answer lies in the existence of the necessary infrastructure, the competitiveness of IVTS and a high demand for their services.

As Asian ethnic groups immigrated to the four corners of the earth, the networks which are vital for the operation of IVTS expanded. Close ties with the members of the family left behind and a culturally promoted practice of sending money back home to help out, enhance the business of IVTS operators.

In many places, especially in rural areas of the Third World, conventional banking facilities are non-existent or woefully inefficient, slow and expensive (Akse, 1996). The absence of banking channels between Kuwait and Pakistan, for instance, have forced non-resident Pakistanis to rely on the Hundi to remit money back into their homeland (Asia Pulse Staff Writer, 1998; see also Carroll, 1995 on Vietnam and African countries; Passas, 1999). The formal banking system often fails to deliver during financial, political and other crises. In Russia, barter trading has increased, although IVTS transactions are also taking place (personal interview). In Pakistan, in recent times, legitimate traders are left with no other option. Even when they go to conventional banks, officers there refer them to hawala operators, particularly for relatively high amounts (Miller, 1999). In China, the IVTS are used because the 'official currency exchange market does not have the capacity to meet the needs of the economy' (Jianping, 1998: 28). So, notwithstanding some adverse consequences, the economy of many countries relies extensively on IVTS. Also, a resurgence of hawala was noted in Southeast Asia during the Vietnam War, when a big black market developed in South Vietnam (O'Hara and The Wild Palms Foundation 1997).

IVTS are not merely more convenient than other methods. The presence of trust makes them cheaper and more pleasant to participate in because, in economic terms, it reduces transaction costs. As has been pointed out, transactions are 'made easier if the parties believe in each other's basic honesty: there is less need to spell things out in lengthy contracts; less need to hedge against unexpected contingencies; fewer disputes and less need to litigate if disputes arise. Indeed, in some high-trust relationships, parties do not even have to worry about maximising profits in the short run, because they know that a deficit in one period will be made good by the other party later' (Fukuyama, 1995: 151). This is precisely what happens between hawaladars, who may take a year or longer sometimes to balance their accounts. Another factor contributing to trust is the fact that many IVTS are managed by members of the same ethnic group or family.

Real or perceived discrimination against the Chinese, South Indians and Arabs has fuelled the continuing popularity of IVTS in the West (Fielding, 1993; South, no date). For example, in the aftermath of the Bank of Credit and Commerce International (BCCI) affair, British regulators closed down another two Asian-owned banks. With only one Asian bank left in the United Kingdom, it was expected that many would turn to hawala for their needs. Indeed, it was real discrimination against minorities in Britain and elsewhere that helped immigrant-friendly BCCI gain a meaningful share of business in the 1970s (Passas, 1995).

In some cases, the use of IVTS becomes so ingrained and part of a tradition or culture, that even when the reasons for their emergence and development eclipse or totally disappear, people still shun conventional financial institutions. This is highlighted by the example of baseball players from the Dominican Republic, who remit part of their legitimate income back home through alternative channels (US Embassy at the Dominican Republic, 1996).

An added advantage of IVTS is the lack of records and confidentiality. This makes them attractive for both legal and illegal transactions. For instance, illegal immigrants with legitimate jobs who wish to send money to their family back home, can do without identity or background checks with conventional banks and do not want to leave any paper trail of their remittances. Others wish to keep some of their assets hidden from authorities to avoid the risk of future nationalisation. Moreover, intelligence agencies make use of IVTS for payments to their operatives (Cassidy, 1994; Miller, 1999). In addition, when countries introduce currency controls and restrictions, the availability of IVTS comes in quite handy.

Finally, IVTS are used for downright criminal purposes. There is no denying the evidence of their use for the facilitation of capital flight, tax evasion, illegal covert operations by secret services, corruption, intellectual property violations, ransom collection, financial fraud, terrorism, smuggling of illegal immigrants, money laundering, as well as illegal trade in drugs, arms or commodities. On the other hand, it must be impressed that IVTS are far from infested or controlled by criminals. All that can be proven is that they represent nothing more than one of numerous alternatives available to individual offenders and criminal organisations. As a matter of fact, it appears that other options for money laundering or value transfers are preferred by criminal organisations, because IVTS cannot handle easily or at all the substantial amounts of money generated by illegal enterprises around the world. These alternatives include conventional banks, insurance companies, non-bank financial institutions (e.g., bureaux de change and money remitters), real estate and gold transactions, and currency smuggling (Passas, 1999).

EFFECTS OF IVTS

The informal transfer of substantial amounts of money has several consequences for the economies involved. The country from which the money flows is deprived of 'sometimes, desperately' needed revenue and investment funds. When commodities are used, as in the case of hundi/hawala and gold business, the smuggling operations violate customs laws and result into additional loss of revenue. The taxes that are often evaded directly or indirectly due to IVTS transactions reduce the resources of governments, especially those in the East and South. Trade gets distorted and government policies fail or are seriously undermined as a result of invoice manipulation and customs-related misconduct.

When money leaves developing countries with currency controls, it is not merely that some technical regulations and laws are broken. The economic effect of capital flight can be devastating to countries in political and economic transition or where the political and economic systems are comparatively unstable. Capital flight undercuts the efforts to stabilise the economy, improve services and infrastructure and bring about the conditions for growth and prosperity.

If money enters through IVTS into a developing country, that country misses the opportunity to acquire valuable foreign currency. At the same time, inflation goes up when large inflows of money enhance consumer spending. The conventional banking system is also affected negatively, because significant amounts of money never enter into it. Finally, the official normative order is weakened by the, frequently blatant, disregard of laws and government regulations.

On the other hand, the negative impact of IVTS should not be overstated. IVTS are neither necessary for, nor always linked to, invoice manipulation, capital flight, or other illegal value transfers. As pointed out earlier, they are but one of many alternatives open to criminals. Moreover, it must be emphasised that IVTS occasionally have stabilising effects on certain economies, given that they operate as a safety valve and provide liquidity in times of crisis (Grosse, 1994; Miller, 1999).

OFFICIAL CONCERNS AND RESPONSES

There is a lot of controversy on the extent and growth of IVTS business. With no reliable estimates and no hard evidence, a proper assessment is impossible at present. Many of the figures cited by reporters or government agencies either come out of thin air or are based on anecdotal evidence. While there is wide agreement that what is known constitutes only the tip of an iceberg, for some observers this iceberg is much bigger than for others. Interviewees of equal standing and integrity have argued in opposite directions. Nevertheless, it has been persuasively argued that IVTS do not have the capacity in most cases to transfer very high amounts of money. In addition, many criminals find that money laundering is not necessary, as it can be easily integrated in local economies. These facts, together with the availability to criminals of many other alternatives, suggest that the IVTS-related crime and other risks may have been exaggerated. Many IVTS practices are misunderstood and treated with suspicion even when nothing illegal or unethical is involved. A useful approach, when officials are worried about a potential problem in their jurisdiction, is to conduct studies into the existence and strength of conditions contributing to the use of IVTS.

Capital flight and tax evasion have worried officials in developing countries for a long time. The more recent official concerns in Western countries stem from the perception that IVTS are increasingly becoming a vehicle for money laundering and other crimes. So, as IVTS per se do not break any laws in the West, they had been left more or less alone in the past. The war on drugs and the anti-money laundering movement have changed this. Yet, the newly found (official) agreement that IVTS is an issue, is neither founded on solid evidence nor has it led to consistent policy approaches. The lack of a unified approach reflects the diverse interests of the West on the one hand and the South and the East on the other. The best illustration of the problem is, when Asian countries introduced bearer bond certificates with no questions asked about the origin of the money. This actually facilitated the laundering of dirty money, precisely the problem for which IVTS are now targeted in the West.

In broad terms, IVTS per se have been directly attacked only by countries concerned about currency controls, capital flight and the loss of business to their underdeveloped or inefficient banking system. The general trend among developing countries affected by capital flight and IVTS has been to liberalise their economies, allow the import of gold, reduce taxes on gold, float their currencies, and eliminate or reduce currency controls. Many countries have also sought to bring grey and black money into the mainstream banking sector by inviting non-resident citizens to purchase bearer bonds with tax privileges and no questions asked about the origin of the money. Although this may sound like an irresponsible policy which lures even dirty money and cleanses it into the conventional economy, it must be remembered that it is a measure introduced in the past by the USA and France (Naylor, 1995/96). Other countries, such as China, have taken measures against 'underground banks', which handle loans, stock deals, etc., but not specifically against IVTS.

Western countries, on the other hand, have not attempted to take IVTS out of business, but only to make them more transparent for the purposes of anti-money laundering controls. As part of anti-money laundering measures, many countries have introduced recording and reporting obligations applying to non-bank institutions. For instance, reporting cash transactions above a certain threshold is required not only by banks and financial institutions but also by 'casinos, securities dealers, automobile dealerships, currency exchange houses and other cash intensive businesses' (Bassiouni and Gualtieri, 1997: 140).

In short, the responses to IVTS have been inconsistent and function at cross-purposes. Developing countries have taken measures that might facilitate money laundering, whereas industrialised countries took or contemplate measures targeting only money laundering.

CONCLUSION

Although IVTS are undoubtedly used by criminals, IVTS do not seem to represent a cause for grave concern in most countries. Spectacular and publicised cases involving criminal abuses appear to be atypical and, thus, should not lead to hasty decisions and draconian measures. Such measures may be counterproductive or involve unnecessary invasion of innocent people's privacy. They may also give the impression that the cultural traditions underpinning IVTS are unfairly attacked. So, before implementing drastic measures, more solid evidence of negative consequences is required. The existing legislative arsenal in the West can adequately deal with criminal acts and abuses. After all, criminals are the main problem, not the way they move their money.

The extent and consequences of IVTS vary significantly from country to country. Therefore, the first step for each country should be to review carefully the facts, risk and interests involved before making policy decisions and implementing measures that might backfire. Country studies could employ archival/historical analysis along with participant observation methods and in-depth interviews. In addition, import and exports statistics can be analysed for the detection of invoice manipulation indicative of IVTS activity. Finally, where available, remittance patterns can be analysed in order to ferret out any transfer of value out of a given country that corresponds to amounts larger than the legitimate income of the senders. Misunderstandings and lack of policy co-ordination may be remedied through such studies. Increased awareness of the respective concerns, national interests and policy priorities can pave the way for improved collaboration among national and international control agencies.

Although one interviewee has asserted that 'there is underground banking in Russia today', I have not encountered any concrete evidence that IVTS are used for the transfer of illegal money or other misconduct in Eastern Europe or in the CIS. The absence of solid data on these practices makes policy planning harder. Yet, since a great deal of reported illegalities involve for the most part one-way movement of funds out of these countries, it may be suggested that these methods are not used in the same way in Eastern Europe and CIS, where barter transactions may present more intriguing policy challenges.

It is true that certain elements of IVTS modi operandi, such as invoice manipulation, can be found throughout Europe. This is, in fact, a locus where East and West, North and South meet. Traders from all sides have experience with invoice manipulation, albeit for different reasons. For some, it is a way of getting around currency controls or evading taxes; for others, it is a preferred method of making corrupt payments abroad or of engaging in capital flight. In all camps, invoice manipulation is part of abusing state interventions in the market, either in the form of subsidies (always in the arsenal of 'free trade countries', such as the USA, Japan or Member States of the European Union), tariffs, embargoes, price supports, and the privileged treatment of products with certain origin, quality, destination or final use (Passas, 1991; 1994; Tiedemann, 1974). These involve frauds and abuses that rightly concern officials and control agencies. However, simply because there are some methodological overlaps confused. Mis-invoicing can be dealt with without attacks on possibly innocently operated IVTS.

In the event it is established in a given country that IVTS are used by criminals for substantial amounts of money, a host of measures may be contemplated. These range from criminal law and public policy adjustments to administrative changes and training of law enforcement personnel. Criminal laws appear to be the least effective way of dealing with IVTS. US officials have recommended the extension of money laundering legislation (e.g., know your customer rules) to cover IVTS. Critics, however, point out that the operation of IVTS will be unaffected, while additional people (e.g., law-abiding clients) would be needlessly criminalised. It is essential to bear in mind that IVTS are often the only channel through which immigrants can send funds to assist their families in the homeland.

Another option may be to review existing rules to see whether they may be amended to cover the activities of IVTS under the rubric of 'unlicensed bankers' or 'unregistered money transmission service' (Interpol, 1991). Further, record-keeping requirements may be introduced, perhaps following consultation with representatives from the ethnic communities concerned. Also, given the frequent interface between IVTS with conventional financial institutions, the latter may be requested to assist the authorities by keeping an eye open for possible illegal financial transactions, such as the facilitation of tax evasion.

The most effective policies would be those going to the heart of the problem, the causes for the continuing popularity of IVTS: government over-regulation, discrimination, political and economic crises, inflexible bureaucracies, high taxes, unfriendly, inefficient, expensive or lacking banking services, lack of confidence in the economic system and banks. In developing economies, the most effective measures seem to be improvements in the formal banking sector, consistency in economic and other public policies, a higher degree of economic liberalisation (especially with respect to precious metals, interest and currency exchange rates) and fewer currency restrictions. Regardless of what measures and policies a government adopts, evaluation tools should be provided, in order to monitor the progress, successes and failures as objectively as possible.

Many of the above policies would have medium and long-term objectives. More immediate responses may include the training of police to be more sensitive to other cultures as well as to be able to identify IVTS patterns and irregular (possibly criminal) transactions. Finally, given that the issues are mostly international in nature, better collaboration and exchange of information among control agencies is essential. This can be achieved by avoiding unilateral and ethnocentric policies, while paying attention and respecting in practice the interests, priorities and policies of all countries concerned.

Literature

Akse, A. T., *Geldstromen Onder N.A.P.: Ondergrondsbankieren in Nederland*. FINPOL, KLPD\dCRI, 1996.

Asia Pulse Staff Writer, Lack of Banking Channel Hinders Kuwait/Pakistan Trade. *Asia Pulse*, 1998.

Bassiouni, M. C. and Gualtieri, D. S., International and National Responses to the Globalization of Money Laundering. In Savona, E. (ed.) *Responding to Money Laundering - International Perspectives*. Netherlands, Harwood Academic Publishers, 1997.

Bhagwati, J., On the Underinvoicing of Imports. *Bulletin for the Oxford University Institute of Economics and Statistics*, 1964, nr. 26, 389-397.

Bosworth-Davies, R. and Saltmarsh, G., Definition and Classification of Economic Crime. In Reuvid, J. (ed.) *The Regulation and Prevention of Economic Crime Internationally*. London, Kogan Page Ltd., 1995.

Carroll, L., Alternative Remittance Systems. *FOPAC Bulletin*, Interpol Secretariat, 1999.

Carroll, S., *Anti-Money Laundering Laws and the Quasi-Banker: A Report on Alternative Banking in Australia*. Sydney, AUSTRAC, 1995.

Cassidy, W. L., Fei-Chien or Flying Money: A Study of Chinese Underground Banking. Internet article (*http://users.deltanet.com/~wcassidy/wlrc/Flyingmoney.html*) (*http://users.deltanet.com/~wcassidy/wlrc/Flyingmoney.html*), 1994.

Choucri, N., The Hidden Economy: A New View of Remittances in the Arab World. *World Development*, 1986, nr. 14, 697-712.

Commonwealth Secreteriat, *Money Laundering: Special Problems of Parallel Economies*. London, Commonwealth Secreteriat, 1998.

Elliott, C., Banking on Faith and Dope. *The Sunday Telegraph*, 1991, *July 14*, 10.

Fielding, N., The Bank That Likes to Say No. *Mail on Sunday*, 1993, *Mar. 28*, 76.

Fukuyama, F., *Trust: The Social Virtues and the Creation of Prosperity*. New York, The Free Press, 1995.

Grosse, R., Jamaica's Foreign Exchange Black Market. *Journal of Developmental Studies*, 1994, nr. 31, 17-43.

Interpol, *System of Illegal International Financial Transactions: Underground or Parallel Banking*. Lyon, International Criminal Police Organization, FOPAC Working Group, 1991.

Jain, L. C., *Indigenous Banking in India*. London, Macmillan, 1929.

Jianping, D., China's Foreign Exchange Black Market and Exchange Flight Analysis of Exchange Rate Policy. *The Developing Economies*, 1998, nr. 36, 24-44.

Lambert, L. B., Underground Banking and National Security. *Sapra India Monthly Bulletin*, 1996, *February-March*.

Malhotra, A., India's Underground Bankers. *Asia Inc. Online*, 1995, Internet article, HYPERLINK http://www.asia-inc.com/archive/1995/0895bankers.html.

Miller, M., Underground Banking. *Institutional Investor*, 1999, nr. XXIV, 32-37.

National Crime Authority, *Taken to the Cleaners: Money Laundering in Australia*. National Crime Authority, 1991.

Naylor, R. T., From Underworld to Underground. *Crime, Law and Social Change*, 1995/96, *nr. 24*, 79-150.

O'Hara, K. and The Wild Palms Foundation, Underground Banking and Money Laundering. www.hackintosh.com/~ohara/ugbanking.html; it has also appeared in the Spring-Summer 1997 edition of *The Resister*, 1997, *nr. 1-4*.

Passas, N., *Frauds Affecting the Budget of the European Community. Report to the Commission of the European Communities*, Brussels, 1991.

Passas, N., European Integration, Protectionism and Criminogenesis: A Study on Farm Subsidy Frauds. *Mediterranean Quarterly*, 1994, *nr. 5*, 66-84.

Passas, N., The Mirror of Global Evils: A Review Essay on the BCCI Affair. *Justice Quarterly*, 1995, *nr. 12*, 801-829.

Passas, N., *Informal Value Transfer Systems and Criminal Organizations: A Study into So-Called Underground Banking Networks*. The Hague, Ministry of Justice (The Netherlands), 1999.

Passas, N., Transnational Crime: The Interface Between Legal and Illegal Actors. Presented at a *National Research Council* Workshop on Transnational Organized Crime. Washington, D.C., 1998.

Savona, E. (ed.), *Responding to Money Laundering - International Perspectives*. Netherlands, Harwood Academic Publishers, 1997.

Schaap, C.D., and Mul, V., Underground Banking. *Tijdschrift voor de Politie*, 1995.

South, N., On Cooling Hot Money: Transatlantic Trends in Drug-Related Money Laundering and its Facilitation. No date.

Tiedemann, K., Kriminologische und kriminalistische Aspekte der Subventions-erschleichung. In Schäfer, H. (ed.) *Wirtschaftskriminalität, Weissen-Kragen Kriminalität*. Hamburg, Steintor, 1974.

US Embassy at the Dominican Republic, *Money Transmitters, Remittances, Exchange Rates and Mechanisms for Money Laundering in the Dominican Republic*. Washington D.C., Dominican Republic's US Embassy - Economic Section, 1996.

Williams, P., Money Laundering. *The IASOC Magazine*, 1997, nr. 10, (also posted at www.worldcom.nl/tni/drugs/links/williams.htm), 1-16.

Zdanovicz, J. S., Welch, W. W. and Pak, S. J., Capital Flight from India to the United States Through Abnormal Pricing in International Trade. *Finance India*, 1995, *nr. IX*.

Chapter 13

Organised Crime and Money Laundering Trends and Countermeasures: A Comparison between Western and Eastern Europe

Dr. S. Adamoli

Senior Researcher at Transcrime, Trento University, Italy

Introduction

The scope of this contribution is to provide an overview of recent trends in organised crime and money laundering in the countries of Central and Eastern Europe and to underline the contrasting policies devised to prevent the infiltration of financial systems in these jurisdictions by organised crime groups. In order to achieve a better understanding of these phenomena and to make an evaluation of prevailing policies, it is necessary to adopt a wider perspective, which also comprises Western Europe. Some of the factors, in fact, which affect the development of cross-border crime and the countermeasures are particularly relevant in the European continent (Adamoli, 1998). The first is the globalisation of the economy, which in the European context means the extension of a single market, intensifying the contacts between its citizens and corporations. Related to this are the abolition of border controls between Schengen states and the commercial ties between Western and Eastern Europe after 1989 increasing the opportunities for illicit cross-borders transactions (Winer 1997). Moreover, particularly relevant when tackling the issue of money laundering are improved information and communication technology. Is explosively increasing application in business and banking and other parts of the financial sector allows the speedy use of wire transfers to shift enormous amounts of money around the world.

All these factors combine to make borders more and more permeable, furthering interdependence among businesses. Combined with the persisting national difference and segmentation of anti-money laundering legislation, they contributed to a rapid increase of cross-border crime. In fact, just as legal businesses are expanding internationally in response to the globalisation of markets, so are the crime enterprises seeking to develop both their structures and crime trade internationally in order to gain access to new markets, taking advantage of the discrepancies between the national legal systems

These 'environmental' changes, the changes in organised criminal structures and activities and the tightening of legislation and policies, also had an impact on the changes in money laundering operations. In fact criminals, balancing maximum profits against law enforcement risks, have been very quick to shift from one activity to the other and to enter new markets. In particular, the persisting discrepancies between anti-money laundering legislation in Eastern European countries coupled with, in some of them, its scarce and ineffective implementation, have to a certain extent created a 'displacement effect' on crime groups looking for 'friendly' commercial environments.

Describing organised crime activities, trends in money laundering operations and law enforcement policies in Central and Eastern Europe, the analysis has been divided into three main parts. First a brief outline will be provided of the most recent developments in the structure and activities in European by organised crime groups. Subsequently an analysis of some money laundering trends in eastern Europe will be provided. Finally the anti-money laundering legislation of Eastern Europe will be compared with European Union standards, highlighting at the same time the provisions in countries which have recently enacted domestic legislation (e.g Bulgaria, Estonia, Latvia and Romania).

ORGANISED CRIMINAL ACTIVITY IN EUROPE[1]

As already mentioned, there are a number of circumstances which favour the development of large-scale organised crime in Eastern Europe: for example the privatisation of state-owned property, the reduced size of the army (which results in a great number of surplus weapons), the new economic and political system and the new trade routes created after the restriction on travel (Aromaa 1998). As a consequence, the number and volume of criminal organisations operating internationally has rapidly grown.

In the international framework of organised crime, Central and Eastern European criminal organisations present an increasingly serious threat because of their rapid expansion and the large amount of illicit proceeds they produce. They are active at the European level in a variety of profitable illicit activities, such as trafficking in drugs, artefacts, stolen cars, arms and trafficking in women and children for the purpose of exploiting them in prostitution. In addition to these, other forms of organised crime linked to the transition to a market economy have rapidly developed: tax evasion, illicit activities in the privatisation process, infiltration of the legal economy by criminal elements, bribery, counterfeiting, extortion and, lastly, money laundering (Savona and Adamoli 1996).

Drug trafficking is still a very flourishing and lucrative traffic and it is a clear example of an illicit conduct traditionally carried out by organised crime groups world-

---

[1] This section draws from Adamoli, Di Nicola, Savona, Zoffi, 1999, pp. 37-57, and from Adamoli, 1999.

wide, and whose routes have always passed through Eastern European countries, all the more since the fall of the Soviet Union. In fact, over the years and particularly after the fall of the Soviet bloc, the number of trafficking routes has increased.[2] Europol reports reveal that this phenomenon is influenced not only by globalisation in general terms, but also by the migration of people, in particularly migration for economic and political reasons.[3] These report highlight the increased role-played by criminal groups of Eastern European origin in the production and distribution of drugs. For example the Albanian groups are carving out a significant role in the heroin traffic in some EU Member states, traditionally in the hands of Turkish groups. In Southern Europe, in fact, Albania has replaced the traditional transit route through the former Yugoslav republics for drug trafficking and 'to some extent' for smuggling aliens into Italy, a point of entry into Europe.

Money laundering or smuggling are frequently linked with drug trafficking. According to leaks in the foreign intelligence services of some CIS countries, money from Turkish drug turnover is still passing through Europe. The Balkan routes are preferred because the warring parties in the civil wars in the former Yugoslavia always need money. And this is true for the Kosovo Albanians, craving for money, and there is only one way to earn it: become a mediator for the Turkish underworld exporting drugs to Europe. Law enforcement agencies know how large consignments of heroin were disguised as humanitarian aid, easily crossed several European borders, and arrived in Russia (Ivanov 1999, 5).

Besides drug trafficking, however, in recent years a number of other crimes have gained importance and caused social alarm because of their diffusion. For instance, fraud in general 'and, in western Europe, fraud against the financial interests of the European Union' is an area in which organised crime groups work on a cross-border basis. Fraud, in fact, is increasingly committed not only by professionals in legitimate industry on the margin of their businesses, but also by extensive organised crime networks. The existence of a budget of the European Institutions, in fact, creates an atmosphere where a misuse of such funds represents a very favourable opportunity for criminals all over Europe, and it is a burgeoning source of illegal proceeds (European Commission 1998, 10). Organised European Union fraudsters operate more often than not on a cross-border basis. While the organisational kernel is small, they need a large and experienced network of co-operating fraudsters and legitimate entrepreneurs to carry out their fraud schemes.[4] It has recently become clear that eastern European entrepreneurs are no longer only 'receiving'

---

[2] One of the major routes recently used for heroin are the Balkan 'northern' route, which goes through Turkey, the Balkans, Hungary, and the eastern route through Uzbekistan, Azerbaijan and Tajikistan. In Tajikistan the drugs may take two routes. One goes through the CIS, in which case the cargo is sent through Slovakia and Poland to Germany, the Baltic states. A diversion of this route goes through Austria and the Czech Republic to Germany and Belgium, the Netherlands and Luxembourg. In the past heroin was sent to Austria and Germany via Albania, Bosnia, and Croatia, and to Poland through Bulgaria, Hungary, Slovakia and the Czech Republic (Ivanov 1999, 5). Austria, for example, has become a transit country for heroin from the central Asian regions and for cocaine, as far as it is arriving from central Europe and Russia.

[3] Interregionaal Rechercheteam Zuid-Nederland, Fenomeenonderzoek synthetische drugs, Eindhoven, 1996, as cited in Fijnaut (1998).

[4] For a more detailed analysis of fraud against the budget of the European Union see Savona, 1997.

documents and/or cheap goods, but are themselves exploring the fraud opportunities on the European market. At the end of the illegal chain, the laundering of the proceeds from fraud becomes a necessity for criminals for enjoying their illegal earnings.

The 'threat' of the progressive expansion of organised criminal groups from Eastern and Central Europe has been considered an element of Europe's modern criminal history. However, it may be more advisable to speak in terms of the 'threat' represented by the increased links between criminal groups in Western Europe and Eastern Europe. It should be noted that organised crime groups from Western Europe, for example, have not been slow in exploiting the many opportunities for profit created by the opening of the frontiers to Eastern European countries during their transition to a market-controlled economy.

It is noteworthy how local criminal groups in these countries have rapidly grown and even started crossing national borders. Russia is a clear example of this development. The role played by organised crime in the ongoing political and economic processes in Russia is extremely significant, since every sector of the economy seems to be at risk of criminal infiltration. According to some figures provided by the Russian Duma for 1998 (Fituni 1998, 360), organised crime controls over 40 per cent of private enterprises, 60 per cent of public enterprises and 85 per cent of commercial banks.[5] Similarly the civil service is affected by criminal infiltration and corruption is rampant at all levels of the bureaucracy, creating a favourable environment for the growth of organised crime, which often has ethnic links.[6]

This process of criminal infiltration has taken place in Russia, other CIS republics and is still taking place in the states of the former Yugoslav republics. It is important that it is closely watched, especially because of its future implications for the European 'geography' of organised crime. Talks with national law enforcement agencies in many European countries, in fact, confirm for example that groups of Russian, Polish, Czech, Romanian and former Yugoslav origin are active in most member states of the EU. Besides drug trafficking, their main activities are the export of stolen cars, alien smuggling and trafficking in human beings for sexual exploitation.

Many stolen cars exported to Central and Eastern European countries originate in the EU. It is necessary to note that these crimes, which are committed easily, can be perpetrated by single individuals, while in the data bases the category 'car theft' may also cover other illicit conducts, such as joyriding and insurance fraud. However, more often the trafficking in stolen cars is perpetrated by organised criminal groups. For example, according to local press sources, in recent years car theft has become a serious problem in Hungary, now sharing the fate of its western neighbours. About 16,000 cars were stolen in 1996, 3,000 more than in 1995, and car theft resulted in a loss of 16 billion forint to the

---

[5] RTR, Parlamentski Claș, 25 January 1998.

[6] The bounds created by ethnic ties is one of the most significant features of organised criminal groups of Russian origin. A number of ethnic groups are active both in Russia and in the other countries of the region. Among these, the role played by the Ukrainians, often perpetrators of violent crimes and, in some cases homicides, has recently increased. Moreover, the Georgian mafia is specialised in burglaries and the control of gambling. But the most significant threat comes from the Chechen organised criminal groups, who are

country. Since 1990, the number of stolen cars in the whole of Europe has doubled, but in Hungary it increased 20 times.[7] There has been a noticeable increase in the trafficking of stolen cars organised by, amongst others, Russian and Ukrainian criminal groups. In fact, Russia, the Baltic states and, to a lesser extent, Ukraine appear to be the most promising markets for stolen cars (Liukkonen 1997, 16).

In Bulgaria, organised criminal groups bribe customs officers and traffic police authorities, and 'legalise' cars stolen from western countries with forged documents.[8] Many car shops in Sofia have stickers in their windows announcing that they are protected by a security or insurance firm known to have underworld links. As a warning to rival gangs to keep clear, this practice seems the safest option for many Bulgarians (Savona 1998).

Alien smuggling, or trafficking in human beings -- whether adults, child prostitutes, or illegal aliens destined to 'forced labour' in workshops -- is a tragic phenomenon. It is a business that links immigration more and more closely to crime, and is characterised by the increasing involvement of organised criminal groups.[9] The break-up of the Soviet Union greatly increased the traffic in illegal immigrants, not only substantially increasing migration flows between Eastern and Western Europe, but also opening up numerous new routes for traffickers, mainly from East, South and central Asia.[10] Russia, together with the Baltic States and other eastern European countries, together with Finland, Sweden are becoming the new two-way-routes for illegal activities: drug trafficking and illegal alien smuggling from Southeast Asia to the West, and car theft from Germany, the UK and the Netherlands towards the eastern countries and Asia (IOM 1997). Two main migration routes pass through Poland. Another passes through the Balkans starting from Turkey and then through the Balkan States, usually with Germany as the final destination. Through this route the smuggled migrants either cross over to Romania and Hungary *en route* to Germany; or are transported through Macedonia and Albania and then head straight for Italy, from where they may continue to Germany or to other West European states. Another access way is not a route in the proper sense of the term: it comprises a number of countries on the borders of Western Europe with lenient legislation on entry permits and lax police border controls: Poland, the Czech Republic, Hungary and Romania are thus used as transit countries towards Europe.[11]

---

particularly active in frauds and money laundering, and in some cases motor vehicle theft and the collection of taxes from prospective buyers.

[7] Car theft serious in Hungary. In: Xinhua News Agency, April 17, 1997.

[8] Three main trafficking channels have been uncovered: the 'Vienna channel', where stolen cars are imported from Germany, Italy and Austria and sold wholesale to local car shops; the 'Russian or Moldovian channel' which exports stolen Bulgarian cars to the former Soviet Republics; and the 'Macedonian channel' which deals in stolen cars from Bulgaria and exports them to Macedonia and Albania.

[9] As for 1996, the International Organisation for Migration (IOM) has estimated the proceeds of this crime at the world level to be around 8 billion dollars. For more information on this topic see Paiva (1996, pp. 381 ss). See also Savona in co-operation with Di Nicola and Da Col (1996).

[10] There are for example the Baltic routes used mainly by people from central Asia. One route originates in the states of the former Soviet Union, from which Asians and Africans take trains reaching the Scandinavian countries after a final sea crossing from Estonia, Latvia or Lithuania.

[11] For a more detailed analysis see Savona (1998).

Moreover, smuggling of *nuclear material*, a relatively new criminal activity which is causing significant alarm in Western Europe, may also involve Eastern European organised criminal groups. For the time being, inspection of nuclear smuggling incidents between 1993 and 1996 allows no conclusions to be drawn as with regard to nuclear smuggling as an emerging activity connected more with organised crime[12] than with professionals. For the moment traffickers seem to be individual criminals, greedy freelancers, traders, adventurers or opportunists trying to make a profit[13] and looking for a demand in this market.

Analysing these illicit activities, some conclusions can be drawn regarding recent developments. Concerning their operational connections, as a matter of fact, criminals seem to use the same routes from Eastern Europe to Western Europe and vice versa. This suggests that there are well-established routes, such as the Balkan or Baltic ones, used by organised crime from Eastern to Western Europe to traffic, for instance, drugs, nuclear material and human 'cargo', and in the opposite direction for the illicit transport of drugs and motor vehicles (Savona 1998). Moreover, the number of transportation routes through Europe, being fairly limited for many years, have expanded radically with the disintegration of Yugoslavia and the Soviet Union.

Therefore, we can hypothesise the existence of established expertise in these crimes involving collusive agreements among the criminal groups in the countries along the trafficking routes, who co-operate in the illicit activity, or with customs authorities.

MONEY LAUNDERING DYNAMICS IN EASTERN EUROPE[14]

The above-mentioned crimes generate large amounts of illicit proceeds, which organised criminals need to disguise by integrating them into the financial system in order to use them freely. The global nature of the money laundering phenomenon, in fact, has rendered geographical borders increasingly irrelevant. Moreover, the introduction of stricter regulations against money laundering in most Western European countries, in response to the enactment of the European Directive 91/308[15] (hereinafter the Directive), has compelled money launderers to find new and 'more friendly' countries and sectors, with non-existent or weak anti-money laundering controls or strict bank secrecy, in which to invest their illicit proceeds (the so-called 'displacement effect'). In other words, launderers tend to move their activities where there are fewer risks for their transactions to be scrutinised and identified as suspicious. This may be one of the reasons why organised criminals are now directing their illicit proceeds towards countries belonging to

---

[12] German Senate Committee on Governmental Affairs, Permanent Subcommittee on Investigations, Chronology of Nuclear Smuggling Incidents. Worldwide Demand for Nuclear Weapons Materials, 20 March 1996.

[13] Atkinsons, R., Officials Say Contraband not a Threat. In: The Washington Post, 28 August 1998.

[14] This section draws from Adamoli, Di Nicola, Savona, Zoffi (1998, pp. 37-57), and from Adamoli (1999).

[15] Directive of the Council of European Communities on prevention of the use of the financial system for the purpose of money laundering, n. 91/308/EEC of 10 June 1991, in Official Journal of the European Communities n. L 166/77.

Central and Eastern Europe, to poorly regulated countries in Asia and Africa as well as placing them in international banking and other financial centres and offshore facilities with ineffective anti-money laundering regulations.

One of the reasons which has led them to the Eastern European countries may be the transition from a state-dominated to a market-controlled economy, which involves the liberalisation of markets and the abolition of state control in a variety of financial and economic sectors. These countries try to develop their economic systems by attracting foreign investments, but failing to introduce the relevant monetary and legal infrastructures, which would enable them to control the origin of the money which is invested, they are at risk of exposing their economies to 'free flowing' illicit wealth (Ali 1997).

This trend has been confirmed by many international organisations active in the fight against money laundering. According to the latest FATF (1999, 16-17) report on money laundering typologies, the countries in the region remain a significant money laundering concern. The transition to a market economy has provided criminals with ample opportunities to invest their illicit proceeds, while the opening of frontiers to Western Europe and the privatisation process act as strong incentives for the investment of dirty money.

Some considerations regard the sectors of financial system that can be misused for money laundering purposes. The banking sector, the financial non-bank institutions, privatised enterprises or the real estate market are all potential targets for criminals.

Unlike in the European Union, where the Directive on money laundering contains specific provisions to protect the banking system, banks in Central and Eastern Europe are still widely used for money laundering because of loopholes and, in some cases, a lack of legislative provisions. Moreover for various reasons, among which lack of resources and training of employees, even in countries provided with anti-money laundering legislation depositing large amounts of cash into bank accounts for subsequent transfer is not likely to be reported to the law enforcement, such as the Czech Republic, Hungary or Bulgaria. This makes them an ideal choice for the initial placement of illicit funds and enables criminals to place vast quantities of black money into these new banking systems and then to move it to other jurisdictions, avoiding the risk of being identified.[16]

Because of the lack of an anti-money laundering legislation, Estonian banks have been routinely used as a conduit for illegal proceeds flowing to and from Russia and western countries: these funds are transferred from one bank to another through a variety of businesses, shell companies and off-shore centres such as the Channel Islands, Gibraltar and the Caribbean basin. Local organised criminal groups involved in the illegal

---

[16] This is, for instance, also the case in Poland, where activities related to money laundering take the external form of either legal financial transactions (e.g., banking operations) or legal transactions which violate particular administrative arrangements (e.g., safety standards in the banking system), or illegal operations forbidden by regulations and subject to economic and penal law sanctions. This also seems to be true for Lithuania where, soon after its independence, there is evidence that attempts were made to launder millions of rubles through the banking system using forged documents sent in some cases from Chechnya, and in others from Kazakhstan.

oil trade and other smuggling activities launder their proceeds by transferring them to commercial accounts of an apparently legitimate company registered in a western European country. Although Estonian law regulates traditional financial institutions such as banks, other financial institutions still remain unregulated and offer readily accessible means to launder money outside the banking system (INCSR 1999). This situation, however, should improve after the coming into force of the new law in July 1999. Like the other two Baltic countries, Latvian banks may be facilitating the laundering of capital coming from Russia, since Latvian legislation does not explicitly prohibit Russian businesses and citizens from opening accounts with Latvian commercial banks.[17] In Russia too the banking system is also widely used for laundering illicit proceeds. According to the latest information available (January 1998), about 1,450 of the 2,000 Russian commercial banks were controlled or influenced, to some extent, by criminal groups (Fituni 1998, 366).

Some serious cases of money laundering through the banking system have been recently discovered and investigated. In a case recently revealed by the Slovak Finance police, other countries were also involved, namely the Czech Republic, Hungary and Cyprus. A total sum of 1.4 billion Slovak crowns, gained through criminal activities in Ukraine and Slovakia, was transferred to bank accounts in the three countries.[18]

Banks are only one of the money-laundering mechanisms used. In Bulgaria, for example, as the country moves towards a market economy, not only the 'classic' laundering methods have been used, but huge amounts of money are also reported to have been laundered through participation in the privatised tourist industry, light industry and other profitable branches, and through investment in 'projects of exclusive necessity'.[19] In particular, the task of organised crime to launder their illicit proceeds has been facilitated by the privatisation programmes and voucher privatisation schemes. This applies for instance to Russia, where a certain degree of chaos in its legislation, transparent borders and high levels of corruption, provide a favourable environment for money laundering. The authorities' lack of control over joint ventures and other private enterprises in Russia, as it moves toward a market economy, hamper the control such activities. The privatisation program was carried out through vouchers (government securities called 'privatisation cheques') issued by the government to represent the share of national wealth to be divided. Organised criminals bought a significant amount of these vouchers, but the authorities made very little attempt to prevent their participation in privatisation. Moreover, the 'bearer' nature of vouchers allowed a safe method for laundering (Fituni 1998, 360 ss.).

The money laundering operations carried out by eastern European criminal organisations often acquire a cross-border dimension, involving countries in Western Europe, which to some extent explains the enormous size of capital flowing from some countries in Central and Eastern Europe. There is, in fact, evidence that very large amounts of capital have been illegally transferred to western banks over the recent years.

---

[17] Mukhina, T., Capital Flight via Latvian Banks. In: Moscow News, 3 July 1997.
[18] Slovakia: World's Finance Intelligence Units Meet in Slovakia. In: CTK News Agency, 27 May 1999.

Offshore centres (like Antigua, Aruba, Cyprus and Vanuatu), but also others not traditionally considered off-shore financial centres (like Latvia, Estonia, Moldova or Hungary) seem to be favourable money laundering centres. After being moved to offshore companies in one or more of these countries, the illicit proceeds undergo a complicated process of layering and are finally invested, quite frequently in Western European countries

ANTI-MONEY LAUNDERING LEGISLATION IN EASTERN EUROPE[20]

Since the demise of the Soviet bloc, countries in Central and Eastern Europe began to orientate to Western Europe and initiated a process of progressive harmonisation with European standards, regarding *inter alia* money laundering.

A useful element, which indicates the attitude of jurisdictions in Central and Eastern Europe towards money laundering, is represented by the level of implementation, in their legislative system, of the obligations contained in the existing international instruments. Ten of the countries in Central and Eastern Europe [21] have Association Agreements with the EU.[22] Therefore, the Directive 91/308 can be used as the basis for an evaluation of the general situation in the region concerning anti-money laundering efforts. In the various countries, however, this harmonisation process is not uniform. In some cases, today some countries still have not introduced comprehensive and complete anti-money laundering legislation, such as in Poland, while in others the bill is still in parliamentary procedure, like in Russia. For some countries, which have very recently introduced anti-money laundering legislation, it is yet too early to provide an evaluation of its effectiveness.[23] In order to provide a comparative analysis of the legislative situation of the countries in the area with relation to money laundering, the following elements will be highlighted: the existence of the offence of money laundering, the identification and reporting obligations for financial and credit institutions, the existence of a Financial Intelligence Unit to receive and analyse the reports.

Article 2 of the Directive provides that money laundering shall be prohibited. Like the 1988 UN Convention, it requires that measures be introduced to counter the laundering of proceeds of at least drug trafficking and related offences. In practice, however, nearly all Eastern European countries have extended the definition of money laundering to cover the laundering of the proceeds of many other serious crimes. Russia,

---

[19] Police Officials Interviewed on Banking Offences and Organised Crime. In: BBC Summary of World Broadcast, 10 February 1993.

[20] Some of the information provided in this section is drawn from Task Force on Organised Crime in the Baltic Sea Region, 1999.

[21] They are Bulgaria, Czech Republic, Estonia, Hungary, Latvia; Lithuania, Poland, Romania, Slovakia and Slovenia.

[22] These agreements, which are signed between the EU and third countries, systematically include a specific anti-money laundering clause providing for a framework of co-operation targeted at the harmonisation, among others, of anti-money laundering legislation comparable with European standards.

[23] Some of the countries which have adopted or updated such legislation very recently, for example Bulgaria, Estonia, Latvia and, in January 1999, Romania.

though still lacking specific anti-money laundering legislation, has enacted a new criminal code which qualifies such illicit conduct as a crime.[24] Poland revised its anti-money laundering measures in 1998, providing for the prohibition of such conduct in Article 299 of its Penal Code.[25] Also in Slovenia, a draft law is pending which aims at widening the definition of money laundering and the list of predicate offences contained in Article 252 of the Penal Code (Council of Europe 1997-98, 10-11).

In July 1998 the Bulgarian Parliament enacted a new anti-money laundering act[26] thus revoking the 1996 law on prevention of money laundering, which did not criminalise money laundering and addressed primarily record-keeping and reporting requirement, but only provided for administrative fines for violations of its articles. Under the new law, those engaging in money laundering risk an imprisonment of three to twelve years, a fine of up to 30 million leva and confiscation of part or all their properties.

Also in Estonia a wide definition of money laundering has been introduced. According to the new Money Laundering Prevention Act, which was enacted on the 1st July, 1999, money laundering means the transformation, transfer of, or the conduct of legal operations with assets received as the direct result of a criminally punishable action, with the objective of concealing the illegal origin of such assets or the beneficial owner. The penalty for such illicit conduct ranges from a fine to ten years of imprisonment.

Also under the new Romanian legislation adopted in January 1999, money laundering becomes a specific criminal offence, punishable by three to 12 years of imprisonment. The legislation covers the proceeds arising from a wide range of serious crimes including trafficking in drugs, armaments, human beings and protected animals; illegal trade in human tissue and organs, in addition to prostitution, fraud, kidnapping, illegal gambling, nuclear crime, the proceeds of organised crime, fraudulent bankruptcy and robbery.[27] The Directive applies to credit and financial institutions, as defined respectively by Community banking legislation[28] and by the Second Banking Directive[29], including any professional financial intermediary.

---

[24] Money laundering (or legalisation of illicit incomes or property) is in fact criminalised in Article 174 of the Russian Criminal Code. The punishment range is a fine of up to 100 times the amount of minimal labour wage or imprisonment for a term up to 4 years. If the crime is committed by a group or repeatedly, the penalty ranges from 4 to 8 years. If the crime is committed by an organised crime group, the penalty ranges from 7 to 10 years imprisonment. Besides that, money or some other property that has been the object of money laundering should be forfeited to the State.

[25] Article 299 of the Polish Penal Code defines money laundering as follows:'Someone who has means of payment, securities or another foreign currency, property rights, property movable or immovable originating from the profit connected with a crime committed by another person in particular relating to producing or trading in narcotic drugs, psychotropic substances, robbery, counterfeiting of money and securities, extortion or ransom or trade in weapons, ammunitions, explosive materials or radioactive substances, accepting them, moving, transferring or taking them out of the country, assisting in moving their ownership or possession or undertaking other activities, which may defeat or significantly difficult assertion, hide their criminal origin or place of putting, their detection, seizure or decision of forfeiture, is liable to imprisonment from 3 months to 5 years'.

[26] Law on the Measures against Money Laundering, published in the State Gazette, issue 85 of 24 July 1998.

[27] Romania Adopts Legislation to Combat Money Laundering. In: The East European Banker, 1 February 1999.

[28] Directive 77/780/EEC (OJ L 322 of 17.12.77).

[29] Directive 89/6467EEC (OJ L 386 of 30.12.89).

Member States of the EU provide for the application of its measures to professions and activities beyond the financial sector. With regard to countries in Central and Eastern Europe, on the contrary, the situation is not as homogeneous. In some countries, the definition of such institutions is stricter and a series of financial intermediaries still has no obligation to implement anti-money laundering measures. This is, for instance, the case in Poland, whose 1997 Act of Banking Law and 1998 Directive of the Commission of Banking Supervision provide for requirements to be applied only to the banking sector, thus failing to protect other sectors of the economy which could potentially be used for money laundering purposes. Recently, however, a trend is noticeable, especially in the newly enacted legislation towards the inclusion, as institutions subject themselves to the anti-money laundering legislation, of professions and other operators beyond the strict financial and credit institutions. In this regard, some of these countries seem to fall in line with the proposal of amendment of the Directive[30] which in article 2a mentions, among others, accountants, auditors, real estate agents, notaries and other independent legal professions.[31]

Furthermore, in the subsequent articles the Directive introduces a number of obligations for financial and credit institutions concerning the identification of customers and the reporting of unusual and suspicious operations.[32] Some of the countries in the region, like Hungary and Slovenia, had already introduced this obligation in previous years. Others have done it more recently.

In Romania the scope of the law is not limited to credit and financial institutions, but also applies to persons involved in gambling, auditors, notaries, lawyers and accountants. Institutions are now required to identify customers that have effected transactions exceeding a determined threshold or where there is a suspicion that money laundering may be involved.

These identification requirements are a necessary precondition for the obligation to report suspicious transactions. When conducting money laundering investigations, in fact, it is fundamental to be able to follow the 'paper trail' to identify the origin of the illicit proceeds, which is only possible if an accurate record of transactions is kept. The purpose of criminals, in fact, is to make it difficult for the law enforcement to follow the trace of the money by 'layering' a series of transactions often involving different institutions in different jurisdictions, with a particular preference for those which have strict bank secrecy and confidentiality rules and for those in which reporting of suspicious transactions is less likely. With regard to the legislative situation in Eastern Europe all the jurisdictions which had already introduced anti-money laundering legislation in previous

---

[30] Commission of the European Communities, Proposal for a European Parliament and Council Directive amending Council Directive 91/308/EEC of June 1991 on prevention of the use of the financial system for the purpose of money laundering, COM(1999) 352 final, 99/0152 (COD).

[31] In Lithuania, for instance, not only financial and credit institutions, but also notaries and persons entitled to perform notary acts, and insurance companies are required to abide by the identification and reporting requirements.

[32] This principle of 'know your customer' is of fundamental importance for the prevention of money laundering operations. The Directive requires that clients opening an account or making transactions over a certain amount be identified, and that the records regarding such identification be kept for at least five years after the relationship with the customer has terminated.

years respect the reporting requirements. The same kind of suspicious transactions reporting system has also been introduced in the other countries which, most recently, enacted anti-money laundering provisions.

Among these, the recent Romanian bill also institutes a system of mandatory reporting for any transaction which, by its nature, may be linked with money laundering. In the case of cash operations, reporting is mandatory for all amounts exceeding 10,000 Euro. A written report must be sent to the National Office for the Prevention and Combatting of Money Laundering.[33]

The Directive implies that an authority or authorities be designated, which should be responsible for receiving and analysing the reports of suspicious transactions. These bodies are sometimes referred to as Financial Intelligence Units. However, in some countries they take different forms: some are administrative/intermediary bodies, while others are police or judicial authorities, or even a mixture. In Central and Eastern Europe the situation regarding this issue is far from homogeneous. Some countries, such as Latvia and Lithuania, have created Financial Intelligence Units. Others, such as Estonia will have a central agency (the Money Laundering Information Bureau) responsible for the receiving and analysis of suspicious transactions. In other countries, finally, there is no central agency, and suspicious transactions have to be reported to the police. This is again the case in Poland, where several institutions are involved in the fight against money laundering.[34] At present the Polish Ministry of Finance is drafting a project for the creation of such a central unit, whose task would be that of processing and analysing information regarding financial crimes in general and money laundering in particular. It is clear that the effectiveness of an anti-money laundering legislation depends on the efficiency of these central agencies.

As already highlighted, Russia is one of the few countries which still has no anti-money laundering legislation. The State Duma of the Russian Federation has adopted the federal bill on countering the laundering of illegally acquired profits in its third reading (even though enactment is still uncertain). This law would provide for all the basic identification and reporting requirements. A first step in this direction was made in 1998, when a law 'on State control over the correspondence of large consumption expenditures to actual income received by physical persons' was enacted. Among the assets whose licit origin is to be controlled are: real estate, aircraft, sea and river vessels, stocks, shares and saving certificates, cultural valuables and gold bullion.[35] Given the recent scandals involving alleged money laundering operations in and through the country, it would be advisable that this legislation be enacted as soon as possible.

---

[33] Romania Adopts Legislation to Combat Money Laundering. In: The East European Banker, 1 February 1999.
[34] These agencies are: the Polish National Bank's General Inspectorate of Supervision, the Ministry of Finance's General Inspectorate of Treasury Control, the Public Prosecutor's Offices, the police and the State Security Office.

CONCLUSIONS

Some conclusions can be drawn from the analysis of both the trends in criminal phenomena and of legislative developments.

As regards the criminal activities perpetrated in the region by organised criminal groups, several factors can be seen as favouring the growing criminal exploitation of Eastern Europe. The region have undergone major political changes, which have also involved the reorganisation of economic systems into free markets. Both local and foreign criminal organisations have benefited from the situation, using the opportunities offered by economic systems to expand their traffics and to invest their illicit proceeds in the financial system by corrupting political figures and public officials. Since the fall of communism, at the state level in some countries local groups have acquired significant power over illicit activities in the big cities, but also started to extend their illicit activities by crossing the borders of their respective national markets. In doing so, these groups are either in competition or build strategic alliances with foreign-organised criminal groups, who have extended their activities to these countries.

Besides the emergence of new organised crime groups and the internationalisation of those already existing, these countries encounter a number of additional problems. Political instability and corruption, coupled with high inflation and unemployment rates, facilitate the emergence of unregulated markets. The privatisation programmes that allowed for the establishment of new banking and financial institutions have also created problems of infiltration by criminal groups in some countries. A friendly environment was consequently created for money launderers, who have begun investing large amounts of capital through money laundering operations.

Experience in the fight against money laundering shows that as one door closes, launderers find their way through the window with new methods and countries where to launder their ill-gotten gains, and this is particularly true for the countries under consideration. The introduction of strict and effective anti-money laundering legislation in the European Union Member States has caused what has been called the 'displacement effect', which means that launderers have had to resort to less effectively regulated jurisdictions where is was easier to conduct their illicit operations. This has led to the use of Eastern European and other countries in transition in Asia and Africa, in addition to financial centres and offshore facilities.

In the attempt to fight money laundering almost all eastern European countries have enacted measures to protect the transparency of their financial systems. Many countries in the region are still lacking effective implementation. Anti-money laundering legislation, well drafted 'in the books' but often still insufficiently implemented 'in practice', makes it in fact relatively easy for criminals to circumvent the fundamental identification and reporting obligations of banks and other financial institutions. Moreover, there are very little reliable data on reports of suspicious transactions, nor are

---

[35] Situation on Combating the Laundering of Funds derived from Criminal Activities and Money Laundering Legislation in Russia, presentation by the Russian Delegation at the Training Seminar on Money Laundering in the Baltic Sea Region, Vantaa, Finland, 22-26 February 1999.

money laundering cases effectively prosecuted. If we combine this situation with the opportunities for investment created in these countries by the transition period, the risk of these countries being exploited for money laundering purposes becomes evident.

In general terms, it is possible to identify the main problems created by money laundering in Central and Eastern Europe. First, the failure of prevention strategies makes it easier, for criminal organisations, to manage the profits of their illicit activities. Second, such failure allows criminal groups to invest those proceeds in further criminal activities. Third, the easy use of the financial system by launderers jeopardises both single financial institutions and the financial system as a whole. Finally, the accumulation of power and wealth by organised criminal groups, made possible by money laundering operations, can seriously place national economies and democratic systems at risk.

Therefore, a comprehensive strategy needs to be elaborated, which should focus on a series of different but integrated approaches. Gathering information on organised criminal groups and their activities is fundamental to devise contrast policies. This 'know your enemy' rule involves the introduction of measures such as the establishment of specialised law enforcement agencies, special means of investigation and witness protection programmes. Moreover, profits being the main goal of criminal organisations, effective legislation on seizure and confiscation of illicit proceeds will greatly increase their costs, thus making it less profitable to commit crimes.

Controlling organised crime and money laundering is by no means easy. Legislation is only a part of the package of measures, which are necessary to control and prevent money laundering. A number of other issues are very important: to begin with, an environment which facilitates the integrity of the financial system, in order to avoid that illicit proceeds infiltrate the economy through the non-regulated investment in privatisation programmes and other sectors. Secondly, an effective anti-corruption strategy, which can make it more difficult for criminals to take advantage of complaisant bank employees or public officials. Thirdly, a co-ordinated effort through an effective international co-operation on law enforcement matters, facilitated by bilateral agreements between countries tailored to the specific needs and problems, can speed up investigation on organised crime, often hampered by existing national borders.

All countries in Europe are aware of the existence of organised crime, money laundering and corruption. The threats posed by them differ from country to country, but a co-ordinated and joint action between western and eastern European countries is essential to ensure that the most recent trends in money laundering are effectively taken into consideration and contrasted.

LITERATURE

Adamoli, S., Global Trends in Money Laundering, paper presented at the *Training Seminar on Money Laundering in the Baltic Sea Region*, Vantaa, Finland, 22-26 February 1999.

Adamoli, S., Council of Europe Standards and Activities in the Fields of Organised Crime and Money Laundering, paper presented at the *Bilateral Seminar on 'The Police in a Society in Transition',* Yerevan, Armenia, 23-24 June 1998.

Adamoli, S., Di Nicola, A., Savona, E.U., Zoffi, P., *Organised Crime around the World, HEUNI Publication Series n. 31,* European Institute for Crime Prevention and Control, affiliated with the United Nations (HEUNI), Helsinki, 1998.

Ali, S.A., A Gateway for Money Laundering? Financial Liberalization in Developing and Transitional Economies, paper presented at *The Fifteenth International Symposium on Economic Crime,* Jesus College, Cambridge, 14-20 September, 1997.

Aromaa, K., Organised Crime and central/eastern Europe. In: *Organised Crime in Europe: Priorities for Future Study and Research,* Record of a European Union meeting of leading academics on organised crime in Europe, Brussels, 18-19 May 1998.

Council of Europe, Select Committee of Experts on the Evaluation of Anti-money Laundering Measures, *Annual Report 1997-1998,* PHARE.

European Commission, *Protection of the Financial Interests of the Communities -- Fight against Fraud. Annual Report 1997,* COM (98) 276 final, Bruxelles, 6 May 1998.

Financial Action Task Force, *1998-1999 Report on Money Laundering Typologies,* 10 February 1999.

Fijnaut, C., Drug trafficking: current views and priorities for future research. In: *Organised Crime in Europe: Priorities for Future Study and Research,* Record of a European Union meeting of leading academics on organised crime in Europe, Brussels, 18-19 May 1998.

Fituni, L.L., Russian Organised Crime and Money Laundering. *Journal of Money Laundering Control, vol. 1, n. 4,* April 1998.

International Narcotics Control Strategy, *Annual Report,* 1997.

IOM -- Migration Information Programme, *The Baltic Route: The trafficking of Immigrants Through Lithuania,* Budapest, January 1997.

Ivanov, D., Russia: Drug Routes Cross in Kosovo. *Russian Story Defense and Security,* 2 June 1999.

Liukkonen, M., *Motor Vehicle Theft in Europe, HEUNI Paper no. 9,* HEUNI, Helsinki, 1997.

Paiva, R.G (IOM), Multilateral Efforts to Combat Trafficking in Migrants: An International Agency Perspective. In: ISPAC, International Conference on *Migration and Crime. Proceedings of the International Conference on Migration and Crime. Global and Regional Problems and Responses,* Courmayeur, 5-8 October 1996, Milan, 1998.

Savona, E.U., Illicit Trafficking in Arms, Nuclear Materials, People and Motor Vehicles: The Most Important Lessons Learnt and the Priorities for Future Study and Research. In: *Organised Crime in Europe: Priorities for Future Study and Research,* Record of a European Union meeting of leading academics on organised crime in Europe, Brussels, 18-19 May 1998.

Savona, E.U., Recent Trends in Economic Crime in Europe, paper presented at the *Bank of Portugal Meeting on infracções fiscais e sistem financeiro* Lisbon, 1 July 1997.

Savona, E.U. and Adamoli, S., The impact of Organised Crime in central and eastern Europe, paper presented at the *Council of Europe 'Multilateral Seminar on Organised Crime'*, Minsk, Belarus, 16-18 September 1996.

Savona, E.U. in co-operation with Di Nicola, A. and Da Col, G., Dinamics of Migration and Crime in Europe: New Patterns of an Old Nexus, paper prepared for the *ISPAC, International Conference on "Migration and Crime: Global and Regional Problems and Responses"*, Courmayeur, 5-8 October 1996.

Task Force on Organised Crime in the Baltic Sea Region, *Manual on Combatting against Money Laundering and Asset Tracing*, prepared by the Finnish Delegation, Vantaa, Finland, April 1999.

Winer, J., International Crime in the New Geopolitics: A Core Threat to Democracy. In: W. F. McDonald (ed.), *Crime and Law Enforcement in the Global Village*. Highlands Heights, KY, and Cincinnati, OH: Academy of Criminal Justice Sciences and Anderson Publishing Co.

Chapter 14

INTERNATIONAL INSTRUMENTS FOR THE RECOVERY OF THE PROCEEDS OF CRIME

Claire A. Daams

Researcher at the Law Faculty of Basel University, Switzerland.

INTRODUCTION

During the past decade money laundering has become increasingly a 'hot item'. Since we all are familiar with what is meant with the term money laundering, there is no need to dwell on the meaning of the words. Over the past 10 years various counter measures and instruments to fight this phenomenon have been established by several international forums. Their aim in general is to deprive criminals from the ill-gotten proceeds of their criminal activities. In this paper I will focus 'in chronological order' on the most important of those instruments and highlight their main points. As starting point the United Nations Convention against Illicit Traffic in Narcotic Drugs and Psychotropic Substances of 1988 is taken. Since this convention was formulated, significant advances in understanding the phenomenon of money laundering and the threat it poses to our society have been achieved. Valuable experience has also been gained from the refinement and further development of countermeasures against money laundering in a variety of forums. The description of the United Nations convention is therefore followed by the Basle Statement of Principles, the Council of Europe's Convention, the 40 Recommendations of the FATF and the EC Directive. After this, a presentation of some of the trends and new techniques in money laundering is given. An answer to the question how the available international instruments relate to these and to what extent the presented instruments are suitable to fight these new trends and techniques can finally be found in the conclusions.

THE UN CONVENTION AGAINST DRUGS TRAFFICKING OF 1988[1]

The fact that traffic in illicit drugs threatens not only the sovereignty of States, but also disrupts economic, social and cultural structures of society created inter alia the need for this convention. Moreover traffic in illicit drugs generates and supports other serious forms of organised crime[2], like conspiracy, bribery, corruption, tax evasion, violation of banking laws and money laundering. Various expert groups met in 1982-1984 looking for possible measures to deprive drugs traffickers of their illegal proceeds. Law enforcement agencies needed tools in order to be able to undermine the financial power of criminal groups and networks. A set of proposals[3] was produced to include in an international instrument, elements or clauses that would supplement the sanctions concerning deprivation of liberty following conviction for serious drug-related offences that already existed in conventions in force.[4] During the 11th meeting of the Operational Heads of National Narcotic Law Enforcement Agencies Far East Region[5] in November 1984, the opinion was expressed that any new convention 'might very usefully address means of streamlining mutual judicial co-operation and other assistance in order to facilitate the tracing, freezing and forfeiture of the proceeds of drug crimes at the international level.'[6] This intention is expressed in the Preamble paragraphs 5 and 6, article 3 as it relates to money laundering[7] and article 5 on confiscation of the 1988 Vienna Convention.

Paragraphs 5 and 6 of the Preamble

Paragraph 5 of the Preamble contains an observation of a factual character. This observation forms the legal basis for the deprivation of persons engaged in illicit traffic in narcotic drugs and psychotropic substances and related offences from their illegal proceeds as is expressed in paragraph 6 of the Preamble. In turn this leads to the adopted measures to be found in article 5. Confiscation of the proceeds deriving from the offences established in accordance with article 3, paragraph 1 is also one of the sanctions envisaged in article 3, paragraph 4, subparagraph (a).

---

[1] Adopted at the plenipotentiary conference in Vienna, 20 December 1988. The Convention was open for signature from 20 December 1988 to 20 December 1989 and entered into force on 11 November 1990.

[2] United Nations Commentary on the 1988 Vienna Convention, New York, 1998.

[3] MNAR/1984/13.

[4] These were inter alia the '1961 Convention' for the Single Convention on Narcotic Drugs, 1961, done at New York on 30 March 1961, reproduced in United Nations, Treaty Series, vol. 520, No. 7515, p.204 and the '1971 Convention' for the Convention on Psychotropic Substances, done at Vienna on 21 February 1971, reproduced in United Nations, Treaty Series, vol. 1019, No. 14956, p. 175.

[5] In 1986 the name changed into Heads of National Drug Law Enforcement Agencies, Asia and the Pacific

[6] E/CN.7/1985/9.

[7] Although the term money laundering is not specifically used in the text of the 1988 Vienna Convention, from the commentary on art. 3, paragraph 1, subparagraph (b) it follows that this provision was designed to satisfy this need.

Article 3, Paragraph 1, Subparagraph (b)

The provisions of article 3, paragraph 1, subparagraph (b) deal with money laundering and make the creation of offences mandatory for all parties. In all cases covered by these provisions, the offence covers only conduct that is committed 'intentionally'.[8] The first part of subparagraph b deals specifically with acts of conversion or transfer of property. The second part is dealing in a more broader sense with steps taken to conceal or disguise the property and rights and interest in it.

A problem which arose afterwards in connection to the transfer or conversion of property is that the word 'transfer' can be applied to the person who committed the predicate offence. In some legislations however, up until today money laundering is an offence distinct from the predicate offence and therefor essentially committed by another person in aid of the predicate offence. The 1988 Vienna Convention does not give a binding view of this matter. Therefor it seems that all parties had to create the money laundering offence in the terms of subparagraph (b), whatever limitations may have existed within their own legal systems on the creation of offences of participation.

Article 3, Paragraph 4, Subparagraph (a)

In some legal systems an offender is under certain circumstances deprived of the benefit of the proceeds of crime by the imposition of a fine or other pecuniary penalty rather than by the confiscation of specific assets. These varying provisions are covered under the broad scope of this article.

Article 5 Confiscation

Not only different forms of confiscation are used throughout various national laws, also the concept of confiscation varies in national systems. Some treat it as a preventive measure, others as a sanction. Confiscation is expressly referred to in article 3, paragraph 4, subparagraph (a). In this context the commission of offences should be made liable to sanctions which take into account the serious nature of the relevant offences. Article 5 can not be considered without taking the state of legal development in 1988 into account. Only during the 1980s states began to develop comprehensive domestic legislation dealing with the confiscation of the proceeds of drug trafficking and other crimes and with related matters such as money laundering.

Action by the parties is mandatory; each party must do what is required within its national system for confiscation as dealt with in article 5, paragraph 1. Nevertheless each party has some discretion as to the nature of the measures that are necessary. Since the obligation to each party is to 'enable' confiscation, a party is not obliged to make confiscation mandatory in all or even specific cases. It seems that the intention of this

---

[8] Art. 3, paragraph 1, introductory paragraph.

provision is that each party must take the measures necessary to provide either for the confiscation of proceeds or for the confiscation of property of corresponding value. It is not required that a state adopts both forms of confiscation; but each party must be able to co-operate with other states, whether or not they adopt the same approach to confiscation.

The main purpose of article 5, paragraph 3 is to deprive offenders of the advantages offered by bank secrecy. Its scope is however wider. It covers also other financial records. A party must ensure that these records can be made available (for examination), if necessary through production orders, or seized on the order of a court or other competent authorities as defined in national law.

It is of significant importance for a state to be in a position to prosecute an individual for involvement in money laundering activities even when the underlying criminal activity that generated the proceeds took place elsewhere. The 1988 Vienna Convention addressed this issue of mutual legal assistance. For the first time even the controversial topic of bank secrecy was covered in a provision: Article 7 paragraph 5 (Pieth, 1999).

THE BASLE STATEMENT OF PRINCIPLES[9]

There has been a general acknowledgement of the importance of requiring financial institutions to take appropriate steps to identify their customers[10] and to keep records of both identity and specific categories of transactions for a set period of time, because banks and other financial institutions may (unwittingly) be used as intermediaries for the transfer or deposit of 'crime-money'.[11]

The 'know-your-customer' rule is also frequently associated with the identification of beneficial owners. It gives expression to the belief that the credit, financial or other institution is more capable then the law enforcement agencies to judge whether a customer or a specific transaction is bona fide (Westerweel and Hillen, 1995). Purpose of the know-your-customer is to ensure that an audit trail can be determined and to assist the authorities in tracing money-launderers and the movement of their crime-money with a view to their eventual confiscation.

Nevertheless, the various banking supervisory authorities represented on the Basle Committee on Banking Regulations and Supervisory Practices[12] considered on the one hand that they do not have the same role and responsibilities in relation to the suppression of money laundering as the authorities. The primary role of banking supervision is to maintain the overall financial stability and integrity of banks, rather than to ensure that individual transactions carried out by their customers are legitimate.

On the other hand they felt that supervisors could not be indifferent to the use made by criminals of banks, since this could undermine public confidence in banks. Therefore

---

[9] Basle Statement of Principles on prevention of criminal use of the banking system for the use of money-laundering, issued in December 1988 by the Basle Committee on Banking Regulations and Supervisory Practices.

[10] As is stated for example in art. 3 of the EU directive. This is also know as the 'know-your-customer rule'.

[11] From the preamble of the Basle Statement of Principles. Art. 4 EU directive.

[12] Hereinafter the Basle Committee. This Committee was established in 1974.

the members of the Basle Committee considered that banking supervisors have a general role to encourage ethical standards of professional conduct among banks and other financial institutions. A further point of attention is that it is necessary that the institutions concerned initiate and develop training programmes for their employees in order to make them aware of the legal requirements, to help them recognise transactions that may be related to money laundering and to instruct them how to proceed in such cases.

In order to enable prevention full co-operation between the institutions and law enforcement agencies concerned is required. In other words this is an area where there are clearly gaps between the theory and the praxis.

One way to achieve such ethical behaviour is to reach an international agreement. This has been done in the Statement of Principles mentioned above. Financial institutions are expected to adhere to these. The principles are: (1) banks should make reasonable efforts to determine the true identity of all customers, (2) business should be conducted in conformity with high ethical standards, laws and regulations pertaining to financial transactions should be adhered to, (3) banks should not set out to offer services or provide active assistance in transactions which they have good reason to suppose are associated with money laundering, (4) banks should fully co-operate with national law enforcement agencies, (5) when banks become aware of facts which leads to the reasonable presumption that money derives from criminal activity they should take appropriate measures, for example to deny assistance, sever relations with the customer and close or freeze accounts, (6) all banks should formally adopt policies consistent with these principles and ensure that all members of their staff concerned, receive training on how to act in such cases and that they are informed about the bank's policy in this regard.

THE COUNCIL OF EUROPE'S CONVENTION ON LAUNDERING

Believing that one of the methods needed in the fight against serious crime consisted in depriving criminals from the proceeds[13] from their illegal activities, the Council of Europe concluded the Convention on Laundering, Search, Seizure and Confiscation of the Proceeds from Crime.[14]

In this convention the criminal offence of money laundering goes beyond the narcotics predicate. In this Convention one finds besides a typification of money laundering, rules on seizure and confiscation (articles 13-16) and especially the granting of mutual legal assistance (articles 7-12) in matters of seizure and confiscation (Pieth, 199). As far as confiscation is concerned, each party is obliged to introduce in its domestic law measures which enable the confiscation of the proceeds of crime or the confiscation of the value that corresponds with such proceeds. These instruments may however, be limited to certain (categories) of offences.

---

[13] By proceeds is meant any economic advantage deriving from criminal offences. These may consist of any property, whether corporeal or incorporeal, movable or immovable and legal documents or instruments evidencing title to, or interest in such property, as is stated in art.1 of this Convention.

THE FATF 40 RECOMMENDATIONS

The Financial Action Task Force on Money Laundering (FATF) was set up as a multi-disciplinary and inter-governmental body, currently consisting of 26 countries and 3 international organisations. Its recommendations designed in 1990 have been revised in 1996 in order to reflect the changes in the money laundering offence. The recommendations are of universal application, although it is recognised that countries have diverse legal and financial systems. Therefore they might not all be able to take identical measures. FATF countries have committed themselves to accept the discipline of being subject to multilateral surveillance and peer review. In each of the member countries the implementation of the recommendations is monitored via annual self-assessment as well as a more detailed on-site mutual evaluation process.

According to Pieth (1996) the role of the FATF has changed during the last few years. Nowadays its main task is to co-ordinate the work of central units in Member States involved in screening of notifications of suspicious circumstances. The original purpose of the FATF was, however, to develop and promote policies against money laundering in order to prevent that the crime-money is used in future criminal activities. The recommendations start by encouraging each country to take immediate steps to ratify an fully implement the 1988 Vienna Convention. The offence of money laundering is not limited to drugs offences (recommendation 4) but extended (in 1996) to all serious offences.[15] An effective anti money laundering program needs also to include multilateral co-operation as well as mutual legal assistance. This is area where there are gaps between theory and praxis.

Enhancement of the role of the financial system in an attempt to create an inhospitable and hostile environment for money-launderers is also central to the programme elaborated by the FATF. Therefore recommendations 10-29[16] do not only apply to banks, but also to other financial institutions. Governments are required to ensure that these institutions are subject to the same anti-money laundering laws or regulations[17] as banks.

A topic on which the 1988 Vienna Convention as well as the Council of Europe's convention remain silent is whether criminal liability for money laundering should be created for corporations. The creation of corporate criminal liability would help to resolve a number of difficulties that can arise when money laundering is pursued through different legal persons. Complex management structures can render the identification of the person(s) responsible for the commission of the offence difficult or even impossible.

---

[14] ETS No. 141, Strasbourg, 8th November 1990. The Convention opened for signature on 8th November 1990 and entered into force on 1st September 1993.

[15] Although drug trafficking is not the only source for criminal proceeds, it continues to be the chief source, according to FATF-IX annual report (1997-1998) on money laundering typologies.

[16] Customer Identification and Record-keeping rules 10-13, Increased Diligence of Financial Institutions 14-19, Measures to cope with the problem of countries with no or insufficient anti money-laundering measures 20-21, other measures to avoid money-laundering 22-25 and implementation and role of regulatory and other administrative authorities 26-29.

[17] In this case one might think of 'bureaux de change'. Since it is very difficult to trace the origin of the money once it has been changed, this is a very important link in the money-laundering chain.

In such circumstances the imposition of liability on the legal person may be the only possibility to avoid that the activity remains unpunished. The FATF introduced the idea of criminal liability for corporations in recommendation No. 6.

THE EC DIRECTIVE

With this Directive[18] co-ordination at the European Union level in the field of money laundering was achieved for the first time. This was not only necessary for the protection of the financial systems; money laundering is usually carried out in an international setting so that measures exclusively adopted at a national level would have a foreseeable limited effect, but also to avoid measures that would be inconsistent with achieving a single market. Above this: if certain co-ordinating measures had not been adopted at Community level, launderers would have had increased opportunities to take advantage of the freedom of the movement of capital and financial services.[19]

Probably influenced by the 1988 Vienna Convention and the Convention of the Council of Europe, it was stated once again that money laundering has an evident influence on the rise of organised crime in general and drug trafficking in particular and that combatting money laundering is one of the most effective means of opposing this form of criminal activity. According to article 2 of the Directive this was an important reason to prohibit money laundering in all member countries. In most Member States this has been achieved by the creation of a specific money laundering offence.[20] By using the general words 'criminal activity' it is clear that combatting money laundering is not limited to drug offences. A majority of countries have also covered the laundering of proceeds of other crimes in their legislation.[21] The legislation's that have been adopted apply to the whole financial sector, including life insurance companies[22], investment firms, bureaux de change etc.

The definition of money laundering given in art.1 of the Directive, also provides that money laundering 'shall be regarded as such even when the activities which generated the property to be laundered were perpetrated in the territory of another member state or in that of a third country'.[23] Cases where the predicate offence took place in a foreign jurisdiction therefore are included under the Directive.

Furthermore something had to be done to combat the increasing number of cases of fraud against the Community's financial interests. Art.1 paragraph 2, obliges the Member States to make fraud either a specific or an express offence or at least bring it within the general definition of the offence of fraud (Savona, 1997).

---

[18] Council of the European Communities Directive on prevention of the use of the financial system for the purpose of money laundering, No. 91/308/EEC, adopted on 10 June 1991.

[19] Official Journal of the European Communities, No. L 166, 28/06/1991, p.0077-0082.

[20] In Denmark and in the Netherlands money laundering is dealt with under the wider scope of the offence of 'handling stolen goods'.

[21] For example referring to the proceeds from any crime or from any serious crime.

[22] The conditions under which they are obliged to require identification can be found in art 3, subparagraph 3.

[23] See also art. 6, paragraph 2, subparagraph (a), of the Council of Europe Convention on Laundering, Search, Seizure and Confiscation of the Proceeds from Crime.

However, one should not focus only on a penal approach because the financial system can fulfil a highly effective role as well. In this respect it was necessary to ensure that credit and financial institutions require identification of their customers (and beneficial owners).[24] Special attention ought to be paid to transactions involving third countries which do not apply comparable standards against money laundering. In addition it was stated that in some cases bank secrecy must be lifted and that a mandatory system of reporting suspicious transactions should be created.

From article 12 of the Directive follows that it is intended that the provisions of the Directive also apply to certain vulnerable professions, which engage in activities which are particularly likely to be used for money laundering purposes.[25] Here one can for instance think of advocates, notaries, other legal professions, but also financial consultants. The obligations they have vary, however, considerably throughout the various Member States.

TRENDS AND NEW MONEY LAUNDERING TECHNIQUES

Frequently the proceeds or property derived from crime take the form of (crime-)money, which may be converted either into another currency or into some other form of property, for example by deposit in a bank or the purchase of shares or bonds. In its new form it may electronically be transferred to another jurisdiction. Since criminals try to maximise opportunities while minimising the risk of being caught (Savona, 1995) the purpose is evidently to disguise the illicit origin of the property. But the larger the organisation is that is involved to launder the money, the greater the costs and higher the risk of detection (Rider, 1999).

New trends and techniques for the laundering of criminal proceeds are developing, as has been formulated in the IX and X annual reports[26] on money laundering typologies by the FATF. In this respect one can think about new methods of payment, but also about non-financial professional activities. Not all of these areas are legally covered yet, let alone that they are mastered. It seems obvious that this will cause problems, since criminal organisations are just as capable as anyone else to exploit the advantages of developments in (communications) technology (Rider, 1999).

Bureaux de Change

New developments have been observed as regards inter alia bureaux de change. Manual currency exchange operations, which formerly were used essentially at the

---

[24] This has been achieved in art. 3 which says that Member States shall ensure that credit and financial institutions require identification of their customers. This requirement shall also apply for any transaction involving a sum amounting ECU 15,000 or more.

[25] It is however discretionary left to Member States which non-financial professions should be made subject to the Directive. Only some of the Member States for instance introduced specific rules for notaries.

[26] FATF on money laundering 1997-1998 and 1998-1999, reports on money laundering typologies.

placement stage, are now being used also at the layering stage. Cash proceeds from drug trafficking and other criminal activities still often transit through this sector. Two main techniques are reported at present: the changing of large amounts of local currency crime-money into low bulk international currencies for physical smuggling out of the country, and electronic funds transfers to offshore centres.

Electronic transfers are very often characterised by layering operations. One of the most popular techniques is simply to transfer illicit funds through several different banks in order to blur the trail to the funds' source. Another method is to make transfers from a large number of bank accounts, into which deposits have been made by 'smurfing', to a principal collecting account which is often located abroad in an offshore financial centre. In this case the adequacy of the present anti laundering measures can be questioned: to obtain the relevant information concerning an international transfer made in one day, the investigating services have to wait an average of about two years for the results of an investigation by the rogatory commission. This can hardly be considered as effective.

Cyberpayment

New technology systems banks are using,[27] may facilitate money laundering, because of the rapidity of transaction performance, the numerous opportunities for anonymity that are offered and the risk of a break in the audit trail and withdrawal from the traditional banking system.

With the development of cyberpayment the dangers of money laundering seem to be evident since it leaves no paper trail. Here the international character of the Internet and the difficulty of locating a site, which may be different from the one where the illegal practices were identified are complicating factors.

Also banking by telephone and on the Internet makes laundering easier. The intensive use of the 24-hour banking services has created a significant obstacle to investigations of laundering. Direct banking implies the establishment of a distance between the banker and his client and lead to the lessening or even disappearance of the traditional client identification contact. These services clearly offer advantages for both banks and clients in terms of flexibility, but the question how to comply with the know-your-customer rule in these cases has not been answered yet. Until now the risks associated with the opportunities offered by the internet have remained relatively low.

---

[27] In this respect one might for instance think of accounts on internet, offering a 24 hours service, but also of electronic purses and smart cards.

The Gold Market

Laundering of criminal proceeds as such are not a new feature on this market. The scale of laundering using gold however constitutes a real threat according to the FATF. Gold has some characteristics that make it a very popular recourse for launderers.[28]

Money Laundering and Non-Financial Professions

In many countries anti-laundering legislation nowadays covers, the banking and regularly even other parts of the financial sector. Therefor criminals are trying to find other intermediaries. They might find these in vulnerable professions like accountants and other auditors, advocates, (real estate) agents and notaries.

The Euro Currency Unit

The primary period of potential risk are the six-months (1 January - 30 June 2002) during which the national physical currencies will be exchanged into the Euro. This is likely to increase exchange activities in those European countries outside the Euro zone, especially involving traditional strong currencies such as the US dollars, UK pounds and Swiss francs. The exchange requires that the national currency is physically presented at financial institutions. As such this increases the risk for money launderers to get caught. On the other hand the financial institutions personnel might be overwhelmed by the increased volume of transactions during this period, missing or disregarding indicators of money laundering. Thinking about such indicators one could mention cases where large amounts of national currency are converted into other currencies than its country of origin. Another example is the conversion of large amounts of national currency to euro's by individuals residing in other countries. The Euro used in wire or electronic transactions may already turn up in money laundering operations anywhere after 1st January 1999.

CONCLUSIONS

The above mentioned international instruments have to be regarded in their contemporary context. For example the money laundering provisions of the 1988 Vienna Convention focussed especially on laundering of drug money and were designed to secure improvements in national criminal law systems. Consequentially they have had

---

[28] Some of these are: it is a universally accepted medium of exchange, it is safe in times of uncertainty, prices are set daily, and thus the value is reasonable foreseeable, it is a material which is traded on world markets, it grants anonymity, its forms are easy to change, there is the possibility for dealers of layering transactions to blur the audit trail and there are possibilities of double invoicing, false shipments and other fraudulent practices.

benefits for the scope and effectiveness of international co-operation. They did not address at that time elements of a strategy designed to counter money laundering, embracing a preventive philosophy. This dimension is reflected in the Basle Statement of Principles and the 1991 European Communities Directive.

Notwithstanding a number of important differences in the scope and ambition of the various initiatives mentioned, some important common principles have emerged as well. The 1988 Vienna Convention, the Council of Europe's Convention as well as the EU Directive contain specific rules on confiscation of the proceeds of crime. It is however left to the discretion of the Member States to decide how to enable confiscation. In some cases it is inevitable to create some country by country varying tailor made solutions.

A shared belief has evolved that effective efforts to counter money laundering require at least co-ordination, mutual legal assistance and the collective will and commitment of both the public and the private sector, working together.

In recent years it has been noticed that the proceeds from drugs offences are no longer the only source for money laundering. Other sources are for instance trafficking in arms, car theft, smuggling of human beings (illegal immigration and for prostitution), tax evasion, different kinds of fraud etc (Savona and Adamoli, 1996).

A question remains whether the existing international legal instruments are well enough designed to counter the rapidly changing money laundering situation. As the techniques of money laundering are changing, so should the international instruments and ways of international co-operation to fight this phenomenon. The major topics in relation to money laundering have (at least in theory) been dealt with, in the large frameworks of the conventions. Nevertheless there are still some important topics deserving attention in the years to come, such as offshore companies to give only one example.

Thinking about the development of new methods and techniques of money laundering, such as cyberpayment methods, the necessary adaptation of controls to combat criminal activity has not kept pace with the industrialisation of transactions. An answer needs to be found how to comply with the know-your-customer rule in cases where banks are offering 24-hours services to their clients via Internet.

Although in many countries anti-laundering legislation regarding the banking and other parts of the financial sector has been adopted, this is not sufficient to solve the laundering problem. Criminals are trying to find other intermediaries to help them launder their crime-money and they are not unsuccessful. Therefor it is necessary that the vulnerable professions will be regulated in a co-ordinated way in this respect as well. Regulation alone will not be sufficient to solve the problem if people working in these professions do not receive training on how to recognise cases which are or could be related to money laundering and how to behave in such cases. The programs the banks have adopted following from the Basle Statement could in an adapted form be useful in this respect.

During the period in which the national currencies will be changed in to the Euro, the risk that money launderers get caught is high. On the other hand staff of financial institutions might be so overwhelmed by the number of transactions they have to deal with, that they might disregard the potential indicators for money laundering. This risk could be reduced if financial institutions are able to give their staff extra training on how to deal with this situation and the indicators concerned and take appropriate measures at an early stage.

In my opinion it would be to pessimistic to say that the battle against money laundering is lost. But as topics and techniques are changing, so should the international instruments. These last have drawn the public and juridical attention towards the topic, but that is not the end of the story: much more needs to be done. Having the international instruments available, more effective international co-operation is needed. A wide perspective approach should be adopted in this respect instead of looking at this international phenomenon only from the various national oriented approaches. Not doing so will only enlarge the gap between law in the books and law in praxis.

LITERATURE

FATF on money laundering 1997-1998 and 1998-1999, reports on money laundering typologies.

Gilmore, W., *Dirty Money: the Evolution of Money Laundering Countermeasures*, Strasbourg, Council of Europe Press, 1995.

Pieth, M., *Money Laundering Problems and Counter-Measures*, Paper presented at the Council of Europe Seminar on Organised Crime, Minsk, 16th-18th September 1996.

Pieth, M., The Harmonisation of Law against Economic Crime, *European Journal of Law Reform, Vol.1, No. 4.*

Rider, B., The Crusade Against Money Laundering -- Time to think, to be published in *European Journal of Law Reform, Vol.1, No. 4.*

Savona, E.U., *Harmonising Policies for Reducing the Transnational Organised Crime Risk*, Paper prepared for the international workshop on: 'discontinuous institutional change and the economic system: theory and evidence', Castel Ivano, July 8th-13th 1995.

Savona, E.U. and S. Adamoli, *The impact of Organised Crime in Central and Eastern Europe*, Paper presented at the Council of Europe Seminar on Organised Crime, Minsk, 16th-18th September 1996.

Savona, E.U., *Learning from Criminals to combat them: The interdependence among Fraud, Money Laundering and Corruption in Europe*, Paper prepared for the eighth international anti-corruption conference, Lima, Peru, 7th-11th September 1997.

United Nations Commentary on the 1988 Vienna Convention, New York, 1998.

J.C. Westerweel and J.L. Hillen, *Measures to Combat Money Laundering in the Netherlands*, The Hague, Ministry of Finance, 1995, p.4.

Chapter 15

EXTRA AND SNEAKY LEGAL EVIDENCE IN CROSS-BORDER INVESTIGATIONS

Dr. W.E.C.A. Valkenburg
Senior Lecturer Criminal Law at Tilburg University.

INTRODUCTION

At present most organised crime trade flows are characterized by cross-border transactions. For that reason it is important that countries have agreements with other jurisdictions to ensure the successful prosecution of internationally operating criminals. Evidence gathered in foreign jurisdictions is generally necessary for such a successful prosecution.

As a rule the success of a prosecution depends on the evidence collected in various jurisdictions.

To give an example. Information about foreign bank accounts can be very useful to investigating bodies. As far as the Netherlands are concerned it is said that f70 billion has been deposited in offshore banks (Römkens 1998, p. 51). Probably a huge amount is kept in Luxembourg in view of the number of Dutch banking offices with Dutch speaking employees. Of course the banking secrecy in Luxembourg is one of the reasons for this money flow. This secrecy is an important handicap for law enforcement agencies to obtain evidence. To overcome these legal obstacles, as we observe in a later section, investigating bodies sometimes resort to very 'creative' methods indeed to evade international laws and regulations. In other occasions prosecutors seem to be very fortunate because they receive incriminating information 'by accident'. The question what to do or how to use this information, arose recently when secret information was handed over by discontented employees of a bank in Luxemburg to the Belgium tax authorities.

Situations like these lead to questions about consequences of illegal or improper investigative acts for the usefulness of information, e.g. violation of the bank secrecy laws. More concretely: what are the consequences if the information has been obtained in violation of national or international rules or international accepted principles? Should such evidence be excluded or are other options open? The next paragraphs address these questions. Before this elaboration, it is useful to present a short overview of different forms of (il)legal exchange of information. Subsequently, it is interesting to see what can go wrong with this exchange. In the third place I want to present a survey of Dutch and European (case) law with respect to the illegal evidence topic as well as the suggested approach in the Corpus Juris, the supra national draft bill of the European Community. I will conclude with a proposal of a framework that may be useful and acceptable in these matters.

INTERNATIONAL COOPERATION, LEGAL BASES

As a rule there are two ways of cooperation: administrative assistance (supervision or control and compliance) and criminal assistance.

Administrative assistance is bounded by e.g tax treaties and, of course, practical opportunities of countries. In 1977 an important European Directive has been accepted (77/779) including four openings for the exchange of information. The first one is by requesting information on a specific taxpayer. The second option is spontaneous transfer of information by one member-state to the other one. The third option is to deliver automatically information about individual cases or groups of cases within fixed periods. The fourth is the possibility of making agreements on maintaining mutual supervision. It will be clear that according to these options a huge amount of information can be exchanged. However, until 1980 exchanges of information between the member states of the EU was rather unusual. If there was an exchange it was on a mutual basis following a specific request. Since the 1980s an enormous increase of information exchange can be observed (Römkens 1998, p. 53). In fiscal investigations spontaneous dissemination became even very popular. According to the annual report of 1997 of the Dutch Inland Revenue foreign authorities had been spontaneously provided with information in 68.059 cases. Only in 2.085 cases has information been provided on request. However, international information exchange is not allowed with the preconceived intention to use the requested information for criminal investigatory purposes, though the information can result in the conclusion that there is suspicion of crime. Here we have the first problem. There is a certain risk that countries will intentionally use administrative procedures (e.g.. because of lesser restrictions) for prosecutorial purposes. This situation can be considered as 'abuse of powers'. It is argued that in such a case the evidence has been illegally obtained (Daniels 1990, p. 128).

Of course, in practice it can be very difficult to prove that this so-called 'abuse of powers' really took place. It becomes even more difficult when we realise that foreign jurisdictions may use administrative information in criminal matters after clearance of the Dutch authorities. Those Dutch authorities have to take into account the question whether such assistance could originally have been given for criminal investigative purposes. In practice the situation is as follows (Mulder 1997, p. 243). According to Mulder administrative cooperation and criminal cooperation should be kept completely separated because they serve different interests. Normally, a request for administrative assistance will be considered to be a request for criminal evidence if it was made *after* prosecution has been started.[1] Of course this practice only refers to the situation that foreign countries request information from the Netherlands.

It is important to emphasize that information necessary for imposing administrative tax fines is considered as 'non-criminal'; so administrative assistance is possible, despite the judgment of the Dutch Supreme Court following the case law of the European Court on Human Rights (ECHR) that those fines must be seen as criminal in the framework of the European Convention on Human Rights. In the Netherlands especially practical considerations like reasons of policy and processing capacity may contribute to the decision whether a case will be handled by tax authorities imposing administrative fines or will be referred to the prosecution's office. One may wonder, whether policy and capacity reasons are valid arguments for a proper level of legal protection.

Criminal assistance is mainly based on treaties like the European Convention on Mutual Assistance in Criminal Matters, the Benelux Treaty on Extradition and Mutual Assistance in Criminal Matters, the Convention applying the Schengen Agreement and the Treaty of Wittem, all containing special provisions with respect to prosecution of tax offences. As a consequence of these treaties art. 552m Code of Criminal Procedure was introduced formulating also special rules with respect to tax and political crimes. For example authorisation of the Minister of Finance is needed concerning tax offeences.

The question of 'abuse of powers' as mentioned before can also arise in situations of criminal assistance. A good example is a current case concerning Switzerland. The status of this country is a difficult one and brings Dutch prosecutors to creative interpretations. In the so-called 'exchange fraud'-case much incriminating information is derived from Switzerland. The 'trick' is that the request for criminal assistance to Switzerland was (intentionally?) based on general crimes (like participation in a criminal organisation) to avoid juridical problems. This is understandable because in Switzerland the 'speciality-principle' plays a very important role. This principle implies that Switzerland does not provide information with respect to investigations on political, military or fiscal offences. According to statements of the main suspect some documents also containing information about number accounts of other persons were illegally shown to other suspects during their interrogation. The plan was to persuade them to confess their participation in *tax fraud*.[2] At this moment 'pending the decision of then judge' one may question the lawfulness of this conduct in order to get confessions.

---

[1] Compare also the answer of our Secretary of Finance to questions of the Parliament as mentioned in: Tweede Kamer 1995-1996, 24 452 (R1551), nr. 5, p. 7.

[2] According to Van den Brink, R., Hoofdverdachte in beursfraude, *Vrij Nederland 26 September 1998.*

WHAT CAN GO WRONG?

Apart from the situation of 'abuse of powers' 'in the meaning of using the 'wrong' procedure' as discussed in the previous section, other problems may arise. Generally speaking two additional situations can be distinguished. The first situation is that information itself has been illegally obtained by authorities in foreign jurisdictions. The other option is that private persons have infringed (inter)national rules or principles before they hand over the information to the authorities. The question whether illegally obtained criminal evidence may be used for imposing administrative fines or determining one's tax arrears, will be discussed later on.

Unlawful Activities of Investigating Bodies

Concerning the evidence obtained by authorities there is a famous example in Dutch case law.[3]

> There were charges of tax fraud. The accused had concealed profits of a family company. Those profits were kept in an untraceable fund. The money flowed via a Luxembourg bank account to a bank in San Diego. The defence in this case argued that the evidence obtained in foreign jurisdictions must be excluded as two officers of the Dutch Fiscal Intelligence and Investigation Office pretended to act as councillors of the accused person in order to get information of two employees of a bank in Luxembourg. These so-called councillors got the information they wanted. It was subsequently used as evidence in court.

The Dutch Supreme Court argued that this evidence has been illegally obtained and therefore had to be excluded.

In his commentary on this decision Knigge (1993, p. 3262) discerns two questions with respect to the (il)legality issue. The first question is whether the prosecution has violated the jurisdiction of foreign countries. The second question is whether rights of private persons, including the rights of the defendant, are violated. The first question, is as far as Dutch law concerns, not too difficult to answer. Art. 539a Code on Criminal Procedure (CCP) determines that investigating bodies may use their powers in foreign jurisdictions as far as public international law allows them to do so. Generally a treaty forms the legal base for such prosecutoral actions. A treaty is not always needed, however. It is also possible that foreign authorities agree with the actions of foreign investigating bodies. This consent can be seen as supplementary to legal provisions in treaties.[4] If there is no consent or no legal base for actions in foreign jurisdictions the evidence will be considered as illegal. At this point it is good to emphasize that the statement 'evidence is illegally obtained' does not say anything about the potential usefulness of that evidence or any other consequences.

---

[3] HR 25 May 1993, Nederlandse Jurisprudentie (NJ) 1993, 784.
[4] HR 16 April 1985, NJ 1986, 769.

The Dutch Supreme Court appears to value the international public law highly and has excluded any evidence obtained by its violation. In Hoge Raad 26 April 1988, NJ 1989, 186, such a violation resulted in exclusion of evidence. The so-called Schutznorm-theory (principle of norm protection), indicating that the accused must suffer from an infringement of a rule protecting his interest -- well known in Dutch case law -- was no argument in the decision of the Supreme Court. Knigge argues this approach of the Supreme Court is understandable, because respect for jurisdiction of other countries differs fundamentally from protecting the position of the accused person. The tacit idea behind this strict approach of the Supreme Court may be the importance of maintaining good relationships with other jurisdictions. If those relationships are jeopardized because of illegal investigative operations it is possible that regular requests for assistance will be taken less serious or will be refused. If citizens have to play by the rule, so does the prosecution.

This reasoning was recently affirmed by a judgment of the Court of Appeal in The Hague.[5] In this drugs case Dutch civil under-covers had been acting in Colombia without previous or later consent of the Colombian authorities. The Court considered this a glaring violation of international jurisdiction principles and found it illegal. Important is that the court also argued that the question whether this was an infringement on the accused's interest, protected by the broken standard (respect of jurisdiction of foreign countries), was of no importance, because of the fundamental nature of this standard. The evidence was excluded.

An exception to this strict case law can be found in an older decision of the Supreme Court in 1988.[6] German authorities *afterwards agreed* with a seizure of Dutch police officers, which had been committed without any legal basis.

The possibilities for Dutch police officers to act in foreign jurisdictions are rather limited. They can only interrogate persons/witnesses who *are willing* to cooperate. If those persons refuse cooperation a so-called *commission rogatoire* is needed to request foreign authorities to carry out the requested investigation. Of course, the national law of that particular country determines if, and under which rules and principles, certain activities can take place. This brings us to an interesting question. What will happen when foreign authorities violate their own national rules in order to obtain evidence on behalf of another jurisdiction? Does this affect the usefulness of the evidence in the requesting country? Knigge (1993) argues that there are good reasons to handle such evidence in the same way as 'normal' Dutch illegal evidence. According to Dutch case law this usually means that exclusion of evidence is only a necessary consequence if the accused is affected in an interest protected by the broken standard (Schutznorm-theory). The question whether such an exclusion of evidence is the only possible reaction to illegal evidence will be discussed in the next section.

Another situation that brings us to the second question is the issue that evidence was illegally gathered by Dutch or foreign police officers in the execution of their duty during a rogatory commission. In this situation one can also argue that the Dutch rules and

---

[5] Court of appeal of The Hague 3 March 1998, NJ 1998, 923.
[6] HR 7 July 1988, NJ 1988, 987.

reactions are applicable. This implies that the Schutznorm-theory applies. For example, the evidence obtained during a house search in a foreign country without the required approval of a court in a foreign country can be used in court if the residence was owned by *another* than the defendant. However, there is one exception. The actions may be so much 'irregular' that they cannot be covered by treaty or consent. At that moment the two transgressions merge (Knigge 1993, p. 3262).

In our 'Luxembourg-case' it is obvious that the activities of the two officers of the Dutch Fiscal Intelligence and Investgation Office were not based on the Benelux-treaty. We may also assume that the Luxembourg authorities did not approve their deceptive activities. So there seems to be a violation of the jurisdiction. But even if we do assume there was consent one can argue that the activities were illegal towards the accused: deceitful violation of the banking secrecy can be seen as a violation of a the interest of the accused (Knigge 1993, p 3262).

Illegal International Criminal Evidence for Other Purposes?

An interesting question is whether illegally obtained evidence may be used for other purposes like determination of one's tax arrear. According to Dutch case law such evidence may be used for the determination of one's tax due as well as tax fines, except when the way of collecting was so improperly that using it under all circumstances should be considered as inadmissible.[7] One may wonder whether there are any limitations. Granted there are not many, there are some nevertheless. For example, violation of the right to refuse to testify or to give evidence against relatives and counsellors is such a limitation.[8] And what about illegal pressure and deception by investigating authorities (Wisselink, p. 280)?

Applying this case law on international relations, one can argue that in most situations illegally obtained criminal evidence is usable for tax (fine) purposes. Is this acceptable? I do not think so. This approach is not a real stimulus for legal operations of investigating agencies. I will discuss another approach in the last section.

Unlawful Activities of Private Persons

The situations discussed so far deal with illegal activities of (foreign) investigating officers. As mentioned in the introduction it is also possible that evidence is obtained by illegal activities of private persons, like private investigators. Revenge is in many cases the argument to hand over incriminating information to the investigating bodies. In 1990 the Dutch Supreme Court argued that as a rule such evidence can be used in court.[9] Of course, if the investigating authorities have provoked private persons to such activities,

---

[7] HR 9 September 1992, BNB 366/367.
[8] HR 12 March 1997, BNB 146.
[9] HR 16 October 1990, NJ 1991, 175.

the normal rules on illegal evidence are applicable. On the other hand there are also situations in which the private illegal activity is so outrageous that using the information would be improper. For example a confession compelled by torture or other violation of constitutional rights (Corstens, 1995, p. 638). In Belgium we can observe more or less the same approach to this phenomenon (D'Hont, 1994 p. 190).

ILLEGAL EVIDENCE, NATIONAL AND INTERNATIONAL RULES

General Remarks

Why is it necessary to react on illegal evidence? As a matter of fact the answer seems to be quite obvious. One of the principles of a state of law must be that the state itself must respect the rule of law. If those rules are violated some reaction has to follow (Corstens 1995, p. 636). But is exclusion of evidence always an appropriate sanction? This is a very difficult question to answer. Corstens discerns three arguments to justify the exclusion consequence. The first argument is what he called the *reparation* perspective: Any unlawful act needs reparation, if possible. Transgressions by the state can be remediated by taking away the 'profit' of the prosecuting authorities. In the perspective of this argument the Schutznorm-theory can be considered: there is no need to 'repair' the damage to the defendant if the violation did not concern a rule which serves to protect his interests. The second argument he mentions is the *demonstrative action*, implying that only the exclusion of evidence really makes clear that authorities have to respect rules of law too (also Schalken 1981, p. 9). The last argument is *effectiveness* argument. If the state wants to prevent illegal activities in the future, the most effective way is to react with a straight sanction. Thus, the relation between the unlawful act of the state and the reaction is very obvious. Corstens is sceptic about this argument because emphasising this argument could result in the concealment of investigative methods by the police in the future. I share his reservation.

On the other hand there are arguments against the exclusion of evidence. A strong argument is the importance of finding the truth as one of the aims of criminal proceedings. This idea is extensively excepted in the English law system (Adrews and Hirst 1992, nr. 14.13). This important aim can be frustrated in case of exclusion of illegal evidence. A second point is that 'depending on the situation' the accused has to be acquitted if no sufficient evidence was left to support the charges. In this situation the reason for this acquittal is not that there is not enough *reliable* evidence but the illegal performance of the authorities. This is difficult to accept if the constitutional rights of the accused are not really at stake. Moreover, these kinds of acquittals will be very hard to explain to the ordinary citizen. On the other hand one can argue that if illegal activities do not result in sufficient evidence necessary to prove the charge, exclusion has no influence at all. In that case exclusion is only a warning to the authorities (Schalken and Rozemond 1997, p. 1367). A last argument against exclusion of evidence is that judges do take notice of the particular evidence before they have to give their judgment on the illegality-issue. So the information is likely to influence the judge, despite the fact that it cannot be used as 'real' evidence.

The European Convention on Human Rights

After this brief and rather abstract intermezzo about reactions it is interesting to find out, whether there are concrete rules explicating how to react on illegal evidence. It is obvious to start with the European Convention on Human Rights, implying provisions to ensure the defendant will have a fair trial. Reviewing briefly the rules, it is remarkable that no real provisions with respect to the way of obtaining evidence can be found. This conclusion was affirmed in the case law of the European Court (ECHR). In the Schenk-case the Court argued:

> 'While Art. 6 Convention guarantees the right to a fair trial, it does not lay down any rules on the admissibility of evidence as such, which is therefore primarily a matter for regulation under national law. The Court therefore cannot exclude as a matter of principle and in the abstract that unlawfully obtained evidence of the present kind may be admissible. It has only to ascertain whether Mr. Schenk's trial as a whole was fair.'

And indeed in this case the trial as a whole was fair according to the Court. The quoted consideration emphasizes that the Convention itself does not know rules about exclusion of evidence or other possible measures. The Court clearly argues that matters of evidence belong to the internal competence of the member States. A major point is that the accused has had a fair trial, considering this trial as a whole. But there are examples of cases in which problems with evidence led to the conclusion that the trial, as a whole, was not fair. For example, in the Saunders-case the Court argued that in this particular case the right not to incriminate oneself was violated and therefore the applicant was deprived of a fair hearing.[10] Unfortunately, this decision did not give us more information about concrete measures to be taken in cases of illegal evidence.

The Dutch Code of Criminal Procedure

November 1996 art. 359a Dutch Code of Criminal Procedure (CCP) was introduced. According to this article the judge has three options in case of illegal evidence: Sentence reduction; the evidence can be excluded or the public prosecutor can loose his right to prosecute. Choosing between these options the judge has to take into account the interest served by the broken rule, the seriousness of the infringement and the harm caused by the infringement. Besides this there is always the principle that the violated rule must serve to protect the interest of the defendant himself.

The loss of the prosecutorial right is only an appropriate reaction if the unlawful activities were extreme violations of unwritten principles of due process. Moreover the

---

[10] ECHR 17 December 1996, ECHR Reports 1996-VI, p. 2044.

activities of the authorities have to be intentional or a serious disregard of the defendants' rights to a fair trial. Obviously, this reaction is a rather exceptional. This means that two reactions are left: exclusion of evidence and -- a new one -- sentence reduction. Though the Act is a rather recent without clear consequences yet, in a recent case the Dutch Supreme Court seems to support the reaction of sentence reduction.[11]

Corpus Juris

A research project ordered by the European Parliament aims to formulate a new code containing international provisions to fight special forms of crime against the European Communion like fraud, corruption, money-laundering and handling of the profit of those crimes.[12] This so-called Corpus Juris has no legal state (yet) but it can inspire us on various subjects of criminal matters. This 'code' also implies special rules on evidence, particularly regarding the use of illegal evidence between the member states.

In the explanatory notes we can see that the illegal evidence subject is considered difficult without easy solutions. The notes gave three reasons for this:

- rules with respect to coercive measures differ widely from country to country;
- rules of admissibility of illegal evidence are very different in the member states;
- it is very difficult for judges to know the rules of evidence of all member states necessary to give a proper answer to the question whether evidence is illegally obtained.

Taking into account these problems the code finally gives the following provisions.

- In case of prosecution of crimes against the Communion as described in the code, evidence must be excluded if it has been obtained in violation of essential guarantees as mentioned in the European Convention on Human Rights, evidence rules of the Corpus Juris or national rules without justification in European provisions.
- Subsequently, the code says that the national law of the country in which the evidence was obtained determines the question whether the evidence is (il)legal. If the evidence is considered to be legal in that particular country, it is also useable in another country even if in the latter 'according to its own national law' it would be considered illegal.

Of course this provision is not without risks to the defendant. It is possible to start investigations in the member state with the least guarantees for a fair trial in an early or preparatory stage, and subsequently transfer the case for trial to the member state that has prosecutorial competence, which can be considered 'a defence lawyers nightmare and a prosecutor's dream' (Van Bavel, C.J. not published). The only exception is if that

---

[11] HR 22 September 1998, NJ 1999, 104.
[12] The crimes of art. 1-8 Corpus Juris.

evidence has been obtained with a violation of the provisions of the ECHR or rules of the Corpus Juris.

It is clear that the Corpus Juris contains only one reaction: the exclusionary rule. This approach is not sensational if we take into account that several systems of the European Community[13] do apply the exclusionary rule, although circumstances and factors which can result in an exclusion are rather diverse (Van den Wyngaert 1993). Because of the problems with the exclusionary rule as mentioned in section 4.1 it may be the right moment to reconsider the framework of reactions on illegal evidence.

NEW APPROACHES?

In an interesting contribution Schalken en Rozemond (1997, p. 1368) argue that exclusion of evidence is more obvious if an unlawful activity affects the *reliability* of evidence, for example, if a statement was given after threatening. Under these circumstances it is possible that the reliability of the statement it self has become questionable. But in other situations they reject the exclusionary-rule. Their major arguments are:

- The original Dutch CCP does not know this reaction;
- Different from the United States, in the Netherlands the exclusionary-rule has never been a reaction to intentional unlawful activities and serious disregard (violence) of police officers;
- An important ratio of the exclusionary-rule is 'policing the police' and since excessive violence of police-officers is rather unusual in the Netherlands exclusion of evidence does not seem be to only necessary reaction;
- Referring to the case law of the European Court they stress that even a declaration that a rule has been violated can be an appropriate reaction;[14]
- Disciplinary reactions or prosecution of the police-officers in question can be effective as well and is also accepted by the European Committee.[15]

In the introductory section of this paragraph we observed that 'demonstration', 'reparation' and 'effectiveness' are important arguments to react on illegally obtained evidence. Schalken and Rozemond emphasize these arguments. They argue that exclusion of evidence is not an appropriate reaction in the perspective of those arguments in cases of serious negligence or intentional disregard of the defendants' rights to a fair trial. In such cases they plea for the sanction of loss of the prosecutorial right. On the other hand they question to the validity of the Schutznorm-theory, arguing that from the demonstration and effectiveness point of view it is desirable to overrule this theory in

---

[13] For example Belgium, England and Wales, Germany, Ireland, Italy, Scotland and Spain all know the exclusionary rule.
[14] For example Kruslin and Huvig ECHR 24 April 1990, Series A, nrs. 176a and 176b.
[15] ECRM 6 April 1996, nr 24775/94.

cases of serious violations. After all, the integrity of the criminal law system is at stake here and by using the Schutznorm-theory serious violations of state can remain without consequences. From the reparation point of view they argue that other reactions like sentence reduction or compensation are better alternatives. Also De Hullu (commentary on HR 22 September 1999, NJ 1999, 104) considers sentence reduction is an attractive reaction because it can combine both the interest of the defendant and the society. In addition I would say: also the interests of victims because it prevents situations in which after exclusion of evidence there is not enough evidence left for a conviction.

Usefulness in International Problems

As we have observed in the previous paragraphs, violation of rules with respect to obtaining evidence can take place in many different ways. If we apply the pattern of reasoning of the previous section on international evidence problems, this would result in the following framework. The foundation for reacting is the importance of three principles: demonstration, reparation and effectiveness.

The *demonstration* argument is very much related to the question whether the authorities *intentionally* violated rules or principles. If national authorities operate in other jurisdictions without previous or later permission this means violation of the laws of foreign countries I am of the opinion that this transgression is so fundamental (and in my opinion always on purpose) that exclusion of evidence is too weak a reaction. The demonstration argument requires that under these circumstances the prosecution must loose its right to prosecute. This reaction also expresses the mutual respect countries must display for each others jurisdictions which I think is fundamental in international relations. Because of the seriousness of the violation I would think that the Schutznorm-theory does not apply. This implies that if authorities intentionally use an *administrative* procedure for *criminal* procedural purposes, this 'abuse of powers' also has to result in a loss of the right to prosecution, because of the demonstration argument. This approach underlines that the state has to obey international (prosecutorial) rules. Besides that, disciplinary sanctions can be imposed on persons who violated the international rules.

As a rule in case of less serious disregard or unintentional violation of criminal procedural rules or principles the *reparation* argument is more important. Therefore other reactions (like sentence reduction or compensation) are more appropriate. In such cases it concerns illegal actions of authorities on their own territory. The evidence can still be used in other countries: for example, if authorities are using investigating methods which are not strictly regulated by law, so that it is not clear in advance whether those methods are permitted (Schalken en Rozemond, p. 1370). Another example could be the situation that the investigating authorities were acting in good faith.

I would also like to plea for sentence reduction if evidence stolen (or otherwise illegally obtained) by private investigators is handed over to the authorities of another country, unless those authorities provoked the illegal act. The demonstration argument demands that some reaction should be given although one cannot say that the state itself intentionally committed or induced a crime.

I realise this framework is somewhat 'eccentric' in the light of the developments in several European countries which followed more or less the American tradition of the exclusionary rule. Although I think there are good reasons to give the 'sentence reduction rule' a serious thought. My main arguments are the following.

From a European point of view one may say that the European Court already accepted 'sentence reduction' as a reaction to a violation of the 'reasonable time' guarantee of art. 6 ECHR. Why not explore this reaction in case of other violations of rules or principles?

A second consideration is what I would call the scale of fine-tuning opportunities. More than the other reactions sentence reduction offers the opportunity to take into account all the important conflicting interests in criminal proceedings like: finding the truth, demonstration, reparation, retribution and interest of victims (Fokkens 1991, p. 227-234). Moreover, application of sentence reduction can also prevent that illegal acts will not be reacted upon, because there is enough other legal evidence left. It also allows a reaction in situations that an illegal act of the authorities did not result in useful evidence, but nevertheless 'a conviction being possible on other evidence' deserve sentence reduction.

My third argument is that it can be a way-out for the problems with respect to different applications of the exclusionary rule in the member states of the European Union as mentioned in the explanatory notes of the Corpus Juris. Sentence reduction offers a new opportunity: the court has to focus on the *sentence* and not on the evidence system with all sorts of differences with respect to the exclusionary rule.

If evidence is obtained in an irregular/illegal way in country X (according to the law of country X) it has to influence the sentence in country Y. The court has to motivate in which way the illegal evidence influenced the final sentence. In case of an acquittal compensation offers a solution.

LITERATURE

Adrews, J. and M. Hirst, *Criminal Evidence*, London, Sweet & Maxwell, 1992

Corstens, G.J.M., *Het Nederlands strafprocesrecht*, Arnhem, Gouda Quint, 1995

Daniels, A.H.M., Het Multilaterale Bijstandsverdrag van de Raad van Europa en de OESO, *Fiscale informatieuitwisseling over de grenzen, preadvies Nederlandse Orde van Belastingadviseurs*, 1990

Delmas-Marty, M., *Corpus Juris: houdende strafbepalingen ter bescherming van de financiële belangen van de Europese Unie,* Antwerpen, Intersentia, 1998

Fokkens, J.W., Enkele gedachten over de sanctie op onrechtmatige bewijsgaring. In: *Met hoofd en hart*, Zwolle, W.E.J. Tjeenk Willink, 1991

D'Hont, F, Commentary on Hof van Cassatie 4 January 1994, *Rechtskundig Weekblad* 1994-1995, *nr. 61*, 88-190

De Hullu, J., Commentary on the Supreme Court 22 September 1998, Nederlandse Jurisprudentie 1999, 104

Knigge, G. Commentary on the Supreme Court 25 mei 1993, Nederlandse Jurisprudentie 1993, 784.

Mulder, C. Cooperation in Tax Matters. In: B. Swart and A. Klip (e.d.) *International Criminal Law in the Netherlands,* Freiburg, Max Planck, 1997

Römkens, J.M.H., Controle van buitenlandse banktegoeden, *Belastingmagazine,* 1998, 51-53.

Schalken, T.M., *Zelfkant van de rechtshandhaving,* Gouda Quint, Arnhem 1981

Schalken, T.M. and K. Rozemond, Nieuwe opsporingsmethoden: dient elke onrechtmatigheid te worden gesanctioneerd?, *Nederlands Juristenblad,*1997, 1365-1371.

Wisselink, M.A., *Fiscale informatie-uitwisseling tussen Europese en andere landen,* Deventer, Kluwer 1996

Wyngaert, C. van den, *Criminal Procedure Systems in the European Community,* London, Butherworths, 1993

Chapter 16

AFTERWORD
TRANSNATIONAL CRIME AND
TRANSNATIONAL ECONOMIES

Vincenzo Ruggiero
Professor of Criminal Law

Before developing my argument and relating it to the stimulating chapters which form this collection, I would like to describe a recent criminal episode, or chain of episodes, which most commentators would have no difficulty defining as 'transnational'.

A group of cocaine wholesalers buys quantities of the illicit drug from Peruvian producers and sells consignments to a number of distributors based in Europe. *Los Cammellos*, this is the name of the wholesalers, have business contacts with partners residing in Germany, Spain, France, Switzerland and Italy. Payments for consignments take place courtesy of the mediatory role of Switz banks. In the Italian component of this business, *los cammellos* rely on importers who 'mix' the drugs with industrial machinery and frozen fish, the items they deal with in their official trade. The money is physically brought to Switzerland by couriers, and from there transferred on to accounts in Miami and New York. Later, parts of the proceeds return to Italy, precisely to Sardinia, where connected investors are active in up market tourist development through 'Smeralda 94', a company building luxurious villas on the beautiful Emerald Coast. Among the individuals charged with criminal offences are entrepreneurs, developers, financiers, members of traditional organised crime based in southern Italy, and local politicians associated with them (Pinna, 1999).

The choice of this case is, of course, prompted by its exemplary nature, as it incorporates a number of crucial elements that need to be carefully examined if a definition of cross-border criminality is to be attempted.

Surely, a standard definition such as the following does apply to the chain of activities just described: we are faced with 'offences whose inception, prevention and/or direct effect or indirect effects involve more than one country' (United Nations, 1995).

What these effects are and how they impact on society is not easy to grasp, though one is led to assume that they are particularly bad by definition.

There is, in other words, a high degree of concern behind the very terms 'transnational organised crime' or 'cross-border crime', the nature and origin of which are somewhat vaguely implied in the terms themselves. These terms are suggestive of a powerful and evasive menace, and the fact that this menace its lingering across countries adds to its destructive character. *Mobility*, a quality incorporated in these terms, reminds one of ancient fears, like those addressed to the urban *mobs* of industrial cities, with the difference that the current *mob* is not precisely located: it can even commit crime while being away from the crime scene. The disquiet that 'transnational' and 'cross-border crime' elicit is such that any attempt to precisely identify its victims is deemed superfluous.

In this Afterword I will perform such a 'superfluous' task, and try to discuss aspects of victimisation related to cross-border crime. In doing so, I will perform a simple exercise, namely I will try to determine, first, why concerns for transnational crime are growing among institutional agencies and official commentators and, second, why these concerns should be deconstructed and turned into alternative ones.

RE-INVENTING ALIEN CONSPIRACY

Official concerns about cross-border crime appear to be centred on the feeling of vulnerability that developed countries harbour towards criminal activity originating in other countries. This new version of 'alien conspiracy theory' manifests itself through fears that illicit goods, more dangerous than any of those produced by advanced countries, may destroy the citizens and institutions of the civilised world.

Such fears, for example, focus with particular vehemence on illicit drugs. However, many commentators from Western consuming countries fail to take into consideration their own preexisting pharmacological culture, which partly allowed a culture of illicit drug use to develop. They also overlook the demand side of the equation, focussed as they are on foreign, ruthless producers and pushers. By building bridges with their countries of origin, communities of migrants are therefore depicted as a form of threat to the national security of the host country.

Thus:

> 'One factor that has led Colombia to become the centre of the cocaine production industry is the strength of its ties to a large immigrant community in the United States, which was established well before the drug trade was significant' (Reuter and Petrie, 1998: 20).

Foreigners are also singled out for the detrimental effects they might produce on the national economy, due to their potential ability to manipulate funds for criminal purposes and to disrupt the legitimate creation and distribution of wealth. This concern is based on the assumption that proceeds generated by illicit drugs are only appropriated by foreign producers and large distributors. Again, this is a selective concern, as it omits to consider the considerable revenues generated by illicit drugs within the consuming countries themselves, and the significant aggregate income which is shared by indigenous users and local distributors.

Transnational organised crime, in the main, seems the result of the growing numbers and variety of individuals and groups reaching advanced countries. Because such individuals and groups arrive from places scattered around the world and often from countries in transition or in turmoil, they are perceived as being increasingly 'illegible', as problematic to control and impervious to integration. The new comers, for example, are said to bring with them their social and commercial networks, which make law enforcement difficult and, at the same time, facilitate 'conspiracy'. In this way, no attention is given to similar difficulties encountered by law enforcers prior to migrants' arrival, and to the commercial 'conspiracy' which already features in host countries long before they are 'flooded' by aliens. In other words, that migrants find in the host countries the social and institutional environment making their illicit enterprises possible is normally deemed unworthy of any analytical effort.

Definitions of transnational crime imply a notion of ethnic succession. According to this notion, specific national cultures and groups are expected to climb the crime ladder, either taking turns or together. Official classifications of organised crime, for example, have often been inspired by ethnic qualifications and categories:

'To the ranks of Italian organized crime, they have now added Nigerian, Vietnamese, Chinese, Japanese, Aboriginal and Russian . Biker gangs become an ethnic-equivalent categorisation based on the presumed rationalisation that bikers are so offensive a species as to rank as a separate ethno-cultural community!' (Beare and Naylor, 1999: 32).

Criminological analysis has long disputed this 'ethnicity trap' (Albanese, 1996), both because of the large number of ethnic groups involved in transnational organised crime and because of the interaction in which they engage in criminal business. Given the increasing social, geographical and inter-cultural mobility, ethnicity may be seen less as a causal, or facilitating factor, than mobility itself.

The chain of illegal activities described in the opening of this Afterword is an example of how such geographical, social and cultural mobility may facilitate criminal undertakings. It also shows how, criminal activity conducted by 'aliens' needs a receptive environment, along with a range of indigenous partners and agents, in the countries in which it operates. However, as we have seen, official concerns seem to be mainly addressed to migrant communities or groups of ethnic settlers and the more these are marginalised the more they are believed to facilitate the criminal enterprises run by their compatriots. For example, it has been argued that in the Netherlands marginalised communities of foreigners are likely to support their criminal country-fellowmen due to the lack of integration and the want of legitimate opportunities they experience in the host country (Fijnaut et al, 1998). In sum, the fact that ethnic groups are denied access to the legitimate economic arena becomes evidence that they entertain close network relationships with criminal compatriots.

This assumption also prevails in other countries, like for example the UK, where transnational crime groups are designated *tout-court* by the name of their country of origin: Jamaican, Nigerian, Russian, Turkish, and so on. Even in Italy, where politicians tried for collusion with the mafia are being acquitted, social alarm in relation to home-grown organised crime is temporarily subsiding and is now primarily targeting Albanian and Kosovar groups. However, as already mentioned, such social alarm obscures the circumstance that ethnic groups, in order to develop criminal entrepreneurship, need partners among the indigenous groups of the very host society marginalising them. Partnerships with legitimate entrepreneurs of the host country, moreover, may offer larger guarantees that, along with official commercial consortia, effective smuggling lines are also set up.

VICTIMISING THE 'FREE' MARKET

Investment of illegitimate proceeds in advanced countries is another area of official concern addressed to transnational organised crime. According to shared wisdom, criminal groups are slowly abandoning involvement in visible economic activity and diverting criminal profits towards the more secretive financial sector (Banca d'Italia, 1999). This diversion is said to make detection more difficult and assets confiscation problematic. The entry of cross-border criminal operators in the financial world is believed to herald potential disruption, distortion of rules, erosion of ethics, suppression of the competitive game and, ultimately, it is assumed to foster a 'purge' among entrepreneurs leading to the survival of those more 'criminally fit'. Let us see some arguments behind this belief.

Organised criminal groups are, more specifically, charged with upsetting the harmonious relationship between demand and supply. By making illicit goods available, for example, they are said to reduce the aggregate demand for licit goods in the market, and consequently to cause a limitation of the revenues destined for legitimate companies producing and distributing them. However, this argument implicitly rules out that criminal proceeds themselves may be translated into demand for licit goods, thus returning into the official economic cycle. There is no evidence, in fact, that members of organised crime are more restrained spenders than ordinary consumers (Van Duyne, 1997). And yet, there are objections to this point that can be summarized as follows.

First, it is argued that organized crime members possess a low propensity for consumption because their illicit income continues to circulate within criminal markets to finance subsequent illicit initiatives. Secondly, members of organised crime are assumed to be inclined to save money with a view to helping associates and their families in case of apprehension or 'retirement'. This is seen as a form of social welfare for criminals and includes pension and career break schemes. Thirdly, it is claimed that criminals tend to transfer abroad parts of their earnings, thus depriving of substantial funds the country in which they operate.

Now, these are hardly specific characteristics of organised crime. Legitimate entrepreneurs also accumulate inert wealth and fail to translate all their earnings into dynamic investment or consumption. As for the transfer of money abroad, official entrepreneurs and politicians are prime actors in this practice and despite the existence of permissive rules legally allowing them to move their capital across borders, they find ways of increasing the sums moved by resorting to illegal practices. It is worth pointing out, in this respect, that so-called 'hot money', which is commonly, and almost automatically associated with criminal proceeds being laundered, in fact, includes money earned, legitimately or otherwise, by official actors (Arlacchi, 1993). Think of tax evasion, bribes, flight capital, proceeds from illicit transactions in licit goods (such as arms transfers), illegal funding of political parties (the German CDU moving millions of Deutschmarks around), money given to developing countries furtively returning to the developed world which has given the loan, and so on. Credible estimates suggest that the proportion of money laundered by organised crime only constitutes around 10 per cent of the overall amount of 'hot money' (Walter, 1989; Hampton, 1996; Banca d'Italia, 1999). However, this may be considered another unfounded '10 % guess' (Van Duyne, 1994).

According to another formulation, when engaged in protection rackets, organised criminal groups 'hamper the productive and occupational engine which moves investments' (Centorrino et al, 1999: 42). This type of economic analysis posits that any investment initiative is triggered by expected revenues, is affected by interest rates, and the cost of labour and infrastructures. The combination of these variables determines the 'marginal efficiency of capital' (Layard and Walters, 1978). The entry of organised criminal groups and their finances in the official economic world is said to reduce such efficiency.

It is specifically on the demand-supply relationship that organised crime is said to cause a significant impact. It is argued, for instance, that there is a 'natural' dialogue between demand and supply which helps calibrate the quality and quantity of the goods produced. Moreover, competition is alleged to reduce prices, which ideally should reflect production costs. If a market deviates from this competitive model, drawing closer to a monopolistic model, the entire price system no longer reflects customers' choice and production costs. The productive system as a whole loses in efficiency and becomes unable to use resources adequately. Organised crime, it is contended, disrupts the demand-supply balance by imposing its goods and services with violent means and by lowering the work condition of its staff. Moreover, it causes an unnatural increase in production costs by imposing protection rackets on business. In doing so, it also encourages tax evasion, as victims of such rackets end up believing that the state, which is incapable of protecting them, is undeserving of the fiscal authority it exerts.

These arguments presuppose the existence of idyllic free markets where perfect competition reigns. They fail to take into account the variety of devices which render markets skewed and distorted well before organised crime gains access to them. The emphasis on the loss of profits caused by the activities of organised crime, moreover, implies the belief that larger revenues for entrepreneurs turn into better social and economic conditions for all. But, after more than twenty years of favourable conditions for entrepreneurs, this 'trickle down effect' never materialized.

Contrary to the previous arguments, it could be suggested that organised criminal groups both teach and learn from their legitimate counterparts in the economic arena. By investing illicit proceeds in the official economy, for example, they learn the techniques and the rationalisations adopted by white collar and corporate offenders, thus being, in a sense, corrupted by the economy rather than corrupting it. See how organised crime may learn criminal techniques from fraudulent white collars. (On frauds against European funds, see Quirke in this collection).

Descriptions of organised crime members as too visibly 'different' to become accepted in the business world, perhaps for being culturally and linguistically inadequate (Nelken, 1997), do not consider how acceptance in that world is mediated by go-between individuals and groups. Investment of criminal proceeds in the financial market, for example, forces organised crime to open up to, and establish connections with, mediators and agents, who make 'pecunia non olet' their favourite motto. The recent example of partnerships between members of Russian syndicates, politicians, and New York bankers, all contributing to money laundering operations, is a case in point. Finances loaned to the Russian government became intermingled with other furtive money, totalling about $7 billion. Without the participation of legitimate actors and their willingness to utilize the services and practices of illegitimate partners, the laundering operations would have been impossible (*La Repubblica*, 30 October 1999). In brief, the encounter between organised crime and the official economy is not the result of an unnatural relationship between an harmonious entity and a dysfunctional one. Rather, it amounts to a joint undertaking of two loosely regulated worlds, both deviating from the rules. See, for the example, how the rules of fair competition are often disregarded by those very legitimate entrepreneurs, who claim their universal validity and, similarly, how the rules of 'honour' are ignored by criminal entrepreneurs, who claim their unconditional faith in them (Ruggiero, 1996).

VICTIMISATION OF HUMANS

Among the illegal activities attributed to transnational organised crime those associated with the trafficking in human beings are paramount. Examples of such activity are provided by some of the contributors to this collection. However, even within the present book different analyses are put forward and controversial points come to the fore. Some authors (see Di Nicola in this collection) appear to assume that the trafficking in humans is conducted by structured enterprises engaged in specialistic, long-term activity. Related to this assumption is the implicit association of this type of activity with 'organised crime', therefore conveying the notion that those engaged are full-time criminal entrepreneurs who have developed expertise and accumulated resources in previous illegal activities. Are we faced with groups formed by 'full-time miscreants', namely individuals with a criminal CV who have gone through the different stages of criminal apprenticeship to finally engage in big-time crime? Other commentators, instead, suggest that many of those involved in trafficking in humans have no previous criminal record (see Scheinost in this collection). Cases that came to my attention suggest that the second proposition is closer to reality. Enterprises involved in trafficking, in fact, derive their skills and expertise from the licit arena of business in which they operate. Travel agencies are involved, along with transport companies, often in connection with informal employment agencies. Usually, none of the staff of such agencies and companies has a criminal record, let alone is stably and organically linked to members of organised crime. While committing offences that also organised criminal groups commit, such companies may become partners of the latter, without sharing their overall culture and strategies. To define such companies as 'organised crime' adds to the definitional chaos which already characterizes this type of crime.

According to other analyses, traffickers frequently maintain control of illegal migrants once they reach the destination country, and force those trafficked to commit crime, engage in prostitution or work for low wages (Shelley, 1998). It is also assumed that girls and women are recruited in their home country and are promised jobs abroad, but are later forced into prostitution. Finally, it is remarked that illegal migrants who use the services of traffickers experience debt bondage, that, in addition to transportation, smugglers charge exorbitant rents for substandard, abandoned, or even condemned housing, and that debts force immigrants to work in sweatshops (Reuter and Petrie, 1998).

It is extremely controversial to portray this illicit business as one exclusively characterized by a victimizer/victimized relationship. As Van Duyne warns in the introduction to this book, one should be aware that there are willing as well as unwilling victims in this business, and that the very concept of trafficking should be properly unravelled if other dynamics are to be brought to light. According to representatives of the International Migration Organisation, for example, many women illegally entering developed countries are fully aware of the type of job to which they are destined. According to delegates of the Nigerian embassy in Italy, women know that their work in the host country will be in the sex industry. Many choose to pay a fee to traffickers who, in this context, could be more appropriately described as 'illegal migration operators'. Some of the women plan to stay in Italy for a number of years and return home with sufficient money to start a business. Upon returning, these women, who in their towns and villages are also known as 'Italos', display their newly-acquired economic status, describe the easy ways in which money can be earned, talk about the tolerance of the Italian police and the enthusiasm of Italian punters. Sometimes, they end up encouraging other women to follow their example, therefore acting as facilitators or, indeed, as 'migration operators' themselves (Gramegna, 1999).

As for the conditions under which illegal migrants are forced to work, this seems hardly attributable to traffickers, as responsibility for such conditions lie with the very labour market in which migrants are mainly employed. In this respect, it should be noted that the increase in flexible and casual work in most Western countries has created a situation where workers who display low social an economic expectations are highly desirable (for an analysis of similar shadow economies in East European countries, see Osyka in this collection). Among these workers, employing illegal migrants seems to have a formidable advantage, because as soon as their expectations become higher employers may always report them to the police as illegal. In sum, trafficking in human beings should be analysed within a demand-supply framework, as illegal migrants employed in the hidden economy, including the sex industry, meet a specific demand in economically advanced countries. Invisibility characterizes the condition of these migrants, an invisibility informing both the way in which they migrate and the way in which they are required to work and live in the country of destination (Ruggiero, 1999). Strict immigration policies, in this context, do not limit the flow of people seeking relocation in rich countries, but only contribute to lowering the expectations and demands of those who migrate. Paying a fee to traffickers is part and parcel of this strategy, as migrants are taught that it is a privilege to enter an advanced country and once there they are there, they had better not blow such unique opportunity by demanding too much.

ALTERNATIVE CONCERNS

If official concerns about the threat posed by transnational organised crime raise many controversial issues, it is worth investigating whether looking at the phenomenon from another perspective may help identify alternative, in my view more genuine, concerns.

Among the circumstances that generate official anxiety is the fact that members of cross-border crime take advantage of differences in legislation, therefore moving across countries with a view to exploiting normative loopholes and inconsistencies. Therefore 'criminal groups spread into sectors where the risk of being arrested and heavily sentenced is relatively low, especially compared to the attractive economic return' (Adamoli et al, 1998: ix). Responses are called for which reduce such normative inconsistencies while reducing the mobility of transnational organised groups. The creation of intra-national pieces of legislation is among the most popular responses, accompanied by the establishment of joint working groups and cooperation between law enforcement agencies. For example:

> 'The development of transnational police cooperation is an increasing common response strategy to transnational organised crime. Cooperation is framed through high-level bilateral and multilateral assistance treaties with other nations. States may agree to exchange subject-matter experts and investigative expertise and to provide training for police. Treaties set out rules for the sharing of intelligence and other evidence and for determining jurisdiction in specific cases. They establish standards for investigative methods, the extradition of offenders, and the imposition of sanctions. Frequently, they involve the stationing of law enforcement personnel in embassies abroad or even the opening of a law enforcement headquarters or training facility in a foreign capital'
> (Reuter and Petrie, 1998: 29).

This type of response, which entails that police forces around the world coordinate their efforts, may contribute to the establishment of networks and practices, of technical and political alliances that escape democratic control of both national states and the international community. Fear of the powerful threat posed by transnational organised crime, in sum, may be exploited with a view to cutting normative corners and eroding civil rights (Sheptycki, 1996). An example is provided by intrastate agreements among law enforcers within Europol and the Trevi group, which took place without the active participation of the European Commission and with the total impotence of the European Parliament. The explosive mixture of terrorism, drugs trafficking, money laundering and illegal migration, which the very concept of transnational organised crime conveys, may legitimize the recourse to such uncontrollable alliances and secretive agreements. Globalization, the opening of borders and economic integration become therefore the motivation for the claim of more police resources and of more space for enforcement action outside democratic control.

Globalization also entails a hierarchy, whereby more powerful countries may increase their right to intervene in the internal affairs of their less powerful counterparts. In this respect, international politics being turned into international policing is a process that raises serious concern. See for example the attempt of the US government to obtain the extradition of people residents outside their jurisdiction, or to prosecute Colombian citizens for the effect their criminal activity produces in North American society (Delcas, 1999). Critical commentators of these developments warn that a massive intervention in Colombia is being planned under the pretext of fighting the 'narco-guerrilla' and remark that:

'What Washington fears most in South America is not drugs, but losing control of the critical north-east corner of the continent when the US military reluctantly withdraws from the Panama Canal at the end of the year' (The Guardian, 16 October 1999).

With economic globalization, in sum, it is not only commodities, people and criminals who become more mobile: norms also experience a similar mobility. Entrepreneurs and police forces moving across borders, for example, are accompanied by rules and norms that they create and impose in the contexts in which they intervene. See, in this respect, the penetration of Italian entrepreneurs in Albania, where they establish codes of conduct for local people, identify norms and inflict sanctions. They set up their own private police force that guarantees the smooth running of their business.

Another concern regards the fact that cross-border organised crime, traditionally, ends up creating demand for the smuggled goods it brings into markets. Smuggled cigarettes are a case in point, a business that started in Mediterranean countries as early as the 1950s and contributed to the unpredicted success of American cigarette brands and the decline of national products. The current smuggling of goods such as cars, clothes, computers and mobile phones in developing countries and countries in transition (see Joutsen in this collection) may have the same deleterious effect, making those countries totally dependent upon Western products and keen to adopt their life styles.

There is widespread agreement that transnational organised crime is the result of new criminal opportunities. However, the nature and features of these opportunities deserve brief examination. According to a distinction suggested by Albanese (1999), there are opportunities which provide 'easy access' to illicit earnings with relatively low risk, and there are opportunities 'created' by offenders. The former include provision of illicit goods and services that are in high demand, but also opportunities made available by social and technological change. Opportunities created by offenders often involve bribery or extortion. Examples, in this case, include protection rackets and frauds involving otherwise legitimate business enterprises. The criminal activities examined in this book make this distinction extremely blurred, if not redundant. Transnational organised crime seizes 'easy' opportunities and 'creates' new ones at the same time. Its *modus operandi* is such that criminal acts become increasingly interdependent and multifaceted (Adamoli et al, 1998). Skills acquired in one field are utilized in new markets, while partnerships are established with a variety of actors, be they legitimate or otherwise. This movement from one activity to the other, crucially, entails an intermittent shift from areas which traditionally pertain to organised crime to areas which are the traditional preserve of white collar or corporate crime. In brief, transnational organised crime possesses some of the features of transnational white collar crime, like in the case of legitimate corporations making bribery payments to foreign officials for facilitating the marketing of their goods in countries where those goods are banned (Passas, 1996). The notion of transnational crime encapsulates this mixture of criminal behaviour, which may be a reason for serious concern. Let us see why.

It is a widespread feeling that white collar and corporate crime are less stigmatised and penalised than conventional organised crime. The reasons for this are among the subjects of our academic lectures and seminars. With the interconnection of the two types of criminal behaviour, the relative tolerance normally accorded to white collar criminals may be extended to conventional organised crime members. In an exercise I often propose to my students I ask them to list the different types of social harm produced by Salvatore Riina and Bettino Craxi respectively. When the list is complete, and includes financial harm, damage caused to the productive system, harm inflicted on the state, and so on, the variable violence finally props up. Riina, a big-time mafia boss, is of course accused of having caused more harm because of the number of lives he has, directly or indirectly, taken. However, when the discussion continues, it suddenly becomes clear that also Craxi, a corrupt politician currently on the run, may be held responsible for a numbers of deaths. The way in which his party conducted business, for example, encouraged favouritism and promoted a supporting clientele among entrepreneurs. Loyal businessmen were awarded contracts for work to be undertaken for national or local agencies. This corrupt allocation of contracts and subcontracts brought on the scene unscrupulous firms and cowboy companies, which cut corners when it came to work safety in order to maximise profits. Among these firms loyal to Craxi, some were entrusted with the building and restructuring work in preparation of the 1990 football championship staged in Italy. Dozens of workers lost their lives because their employers did not abide by safety regulations. Bearing in mind that Craxi is less stigmatised and penalised than Riina, what might happen if the development of transnational organised crime led white collar and organised criminals to blur their distinctive traits? One may presume that both types of criminals, now become one, may be met with very mild social disapproval. In this respect, a celebrated Durkheimian formulation should be borne in mind. Riina, with his visible, horrifying deaths, elicits a powerful social reaction that reenforces feelings of belonging and cohesion among law abiding people. Craxi does not cause such social reaction. The blurring of the distinctive traits of the two, namely the coalescence of organised and white collar crime encouraged by transnationality, may make social reaction disappear.

Conclusion

I would suggest that transnational organised crime increases the frequency with which episodes such as the one I have described at the beginning occur. The mixture of white collar and conventional criminal practices may well be one of the features of transnational organised crime. Contrary to suggestions that this type of crime is more dangerous than other criminal activity because of the particular callousness of those involved are contradicted by available evidence. Transnational organised crime should not be mistaken for activity conducted by centralised, highly structured organisations and ruthless market operators. Dispersed participants and diverse social actors are involved in networks in which opportunistic chances are taken and short-term alliances are set up (Williams, 1998). I have argued that these types of alliances and networks may well be an important matter for concern, less because they foster the growth of organised crime internationally than because they encourage partnerships between organised and white collar criminals. I am aware that, after my attempt to deconstruct official concerns and to identify alternative, more genuine ones, this exercise is destined to remain an open undertaking.

Literature

Adamoli, S., A. Di Nicola, E.U. Savona, and P.Zoffi, *Organized Crime Around the World*, Helsinki: European Institute for Crime Prevention and Control. 1998

Albanese, J., *Organized Crime in America*. Cincinnati, Anderson, 1996

Albanese, J., *The Causes of Organized Crime, paper presented at the International Conference on Organized Crime*, University of Lausanne, 6-8 October, 1999

Arlacchi, P., Corruption, Organised Crime and Money Laundering World Wide, in: M. Punch (ed.), *Coping with Corruption in a Borderless World*. The Hague, Kluwer, 1993

Banca d'Italia, *Il riciclaggio nel contesto dei rapporti tra economia criminale ed economia legale*, Rome: Banca d'Italia/Ufficio Italiano Cambi/Osservatorio Antiriciclaggio, 1999

Beare, E. and R. Naylor, '*Major Issues Relating to Organized Crime: Within the Context of Economic Relationships*', paper prepared for the Law Commission of Canada, 14 April, 1999

Cetorrino, M., La Spina, A. and Signorino, G., *Il nodo gordiano. Criminalita' mafiosa e sviluppo nel Mezzogiorno*, Rome/Bari: Laterza, 1999

Delcas, M., 'Washington demande l'extradition des traffiquants colombiens', *Le Monde*, 15 October, 1999

Duyne, P.C. van, Money-laundering: estimates in fog. *Asset Protection and Financial Crime.* 1994, *nr. 1,* 58-76

Duyne, P.C. van, Organized crime, corruption and power. *Crime, Law and Social Change,* 1997, *nr. 26,* 201-238

Fijnaut, C., F. Bovenkerk, G. Bruinsma and H.G. van de Bunt, *Organised Crime in the Netherlands,* The Hague, Kluwer, 1998

Gramegna, M.,'Trafficking in Human Beings in Sub-Saharan Africa: The Case of Nigeria', paper presented at *'New Frontiers of Crime: Trafficking in Human Beings and New Forms of Slavery',* United Nations, Verona, 22-23 October, 1999

Hampton, M., *The Offshore Interface. Tax Haven in the Global Economy,* London, Macmillan, 1996 *La Repubblica,* 30 October 1999 ('Usa, 3 ordini d'arresto per il Russiagate').

Layard, P. and A. Walters, *Micro-Economic Theory,* New York, Mc Graw-Hill, 1974

Nelken, D., Globalizations of Crime and Justice, in: M. Freeman, (ed), *Law and Opinion at the End of the Twentieth Century,* Oxford, Oxford University Press, 1997

Passas, N., The Genesis of the BCCI Scandal, *Journal of Law and Society,* 1996, *23,* 57-72

Pinna, A., 'Quelle ville da sogno vendute con lo slogan: La barca sotto casa', *Il Corriere della Sera,* 14 October, 1999

Reuter, P. and C. Petrie, (eds.), *Transnational Organized Crime,* Washington, National Academy Press, 1999

Ruggiero, V., *Organized and Corporate Crime in Europe. Offers that Can't Be Refused.* Aldershot Dartmouth, 1996

Ruggiero, V., Trafficking, Immigration and Invisibility, paper presented at 'New Frontiers of Crime: Trafficking in Human Beings and New Forms of Slavery', United Nations, Verona, 22-23 October, 1999

Shelley, L., Transnational Crime in the United States: The Scope of the Problem, paper presented at the Workshop on Transnational Organised Crime, National Research Council, 17-18 June, Washington, DC, 1998

Sheptycki, J. (1996), Transnational Policing and the Makings of a Postmodern State, *British Journal of Criminology,* 1996, *34*: 613-635 *The Guardian,* 16 October 1999 ('Phoney War', by J. Pilger).

United Nations, *Fourth United Nations Survey of Crime Trends and Operations of Criminal Justice Systems,* Vienna, United Nations, 1995

Walter, I., *Secret Money,* London, George Allen & Unwin, 1989

Williams, P., *Organizing Transnational Crime: Networks, Markets and Hierarchies, Washington,* Ridgeway Centre, University of Pittsburgh, 1998

INDEX

D

E

F

Y